High Vibe
Crystal Healing

About the Author

Jolie DeMarco is a spiritual lifestyle expert, author, inspirational speaker, and grounded intuitive. She is also a crystal healer (a.k.a. a crystal junkie), a guru of meditation, and a soul-talkin' clairvoyant. Jolie is the president and founder of two enchanted spaces you can visit: My Flora Aura, a mindful meditation center and metaphysical retail store in Boca Raton, Florida; and Crystal Junkie, a high-vibe zone in Deerfield Beach created for retail, workshops, and crystals galore! Jolie always says, "I am just a pipeline through which positive energy flows. I am a scribe, a messenger, and a tunnel for healing vibes that come directly from a Universal Source. I am just the conduit."

In addition to her books, Jolie has published oracle decks, phone applications, and seven popular guided meditations.

Visit her online at www.CrystalJunkie.com and www.MyFloraAura.com.

"A fun, insightful, and empowering book."
—Jack Canfield, #1 *New York Times* bestselling author

JOLIE DeMARCO

High Vibe
Crystal Healing

Crystal Frequencies and Body Layouts
That Will *Rock Your World!*

Llewellyn Publications
Woodbury, Minnesota

FIRST EDITION
First Printing, 2019

Book design by Donna Burch-Brown and Samantha Penn
Cover design by Shannon McKuhen
Cover image by Media Bakery/BLD0013048-2542x3824/©Plush Studios/Blend
Editing by Samantha Lu Sherratt
Interior art by Mary Ann Zapalac

Llewellyn Publications is a registered trademark of Llewellyn Worldwide Ltd.

Library of Congress Cataloging-in-Publication Data
Names: DeMarco, Jolie, author.
Title: High-vibe crystal healing : crystal frequencies and body layouts that
   will rock your world / Jolie DeMarco.
Description: First edition. | Woodbury : Llewellyn Worldwide, 2019. |
   Includes index.
Identifiers: LCCN 2019001232 (print) | LCCN 2019011142 (ebook) | ISBN
   9780738760735 (ebook) | ISBN 9780738760698 (alk. paper)
Subjects: LCSH: Crystals—Therapeutic use. | Crystals—Health aspects.
Classification: LCC RZ415 (ebook) | LCC RZ415 .D46 2019 (print) | DDC
   615.8/52—dc23
LC record available at https://lccn.loc.gov/2019001232

Llewellyn Worldwide Ltd. does not participate in, endorse, or have any authority or responsibility concerning private business transactions between our authors and the public.

   All mail addressed to the author is forwarded but the publisher cannot, unless specifically instructed by the author, give out an address or phone number.

   Any internet references contained in this work are current at publication time, but the publisher cannot guarantee that a specific location will continue to be maintained. Please refer to the publisher's website for links to authors' websites and other sources.

Llewellyn Publications
A Division of Llewellyn Worldwide Ltd.
2143 Wooddale Drive
Woodbury, MN 55125-2989
www.llewellyn.com

Printed in the United States of America

Other Books by Jolie DeMarco

Soul Talking & Relationships

How to Meditate Easily

The Energy Exchange and How to Manifest with It

Parallel Minds

The 2nd Shift: Mandalas, Mudras & Crystals

10 Things You Should Know about Your Psychic Intuition

The Enchanted Boy

You, Me & Chouky

Forthcoming Books by Jolie DeMarco

Levels of Contentment: Soul-utions for Life

11 Pennies

Charmed: How to Perform Readings with Crystals, Charms & Tchotchkes

I am grateful to the universe for allowing me to experience and succeed in life. I am thankful for my parents, who always believe in me, and for my sister—I love you unconditionally. I am grateful for my grandfather, who I have a soul-star connection with, and for all of my wonderful clients! I give an extra-appreciative shout-out to Llewellyn and their superstar team: Angela Wix, Sami Sherratt, Donna Burch-Brown, and Andy Belmas. Thank you!

Contents

Disclaimer   xv

Introduction   1

Part 1: About Your Crystals

Chapter 1: The Basics of Crystal Healing and How Crystals Work   11

Why Are Your Instincts and Crystals Related?   12

The Benefits of Crystal Vibration   13

Human Harmonizing and Crystal Harmonizing   14

Chakras, Auras, and Crystal Healing   16

The Difference between Grids and Body Layouts   20

The Effect of Thought and Intention   21

Other Influences and Enhancers during Crystal Healing Sessions   22

What to Expect from a Crystal Body Layout Session   23

Chapter 2: How to Select and Care for Your Crystals
and Gemstones   25

Raw vs. Polished and "Vibe" Factors   26

Crystal Cheat Sheet   27

Crystal Collection—My Favorite Crystals   29

My Top 11 Crystals: Rockin' Remedies List for Use in Crystal Healings   31

Considering the Size of Your Crystals   34

Choosing Power Stones   34

Consider Your Sign   35

Crystal Wands   36

Cleansing and Clearing Your Gem Babies   37

Choosing Crystal Frequencies: Combating Negative Energy   42

Making Friends with Your Crystals   44

Chapter 3: 66 Crystals and Their Level of Frequency   47

Agate, Blue Lace   49

Agate, Moss   49

Agate, Thunder   50

Agate, Various Colors   51

Amazonite   52

Amber   52

Amethyst   53

Angelite   54

Apache Tears   54

Apatite   54

Apophyllite   55

Aquamarine   56

Aragonite   57

Auralite 23   57

Aventurine, Green   58

Azurite   59

Calcite, Yellow / Orange / Golden / Honey   59

Carnelian   60

Cavansite   60

Celestite   61

Chalcedony   61

Charoite   62

Chrysoprase   62

Citrine   63

Danburite   64

Dioptase   65

Emerald   65

Epidote   66

Fluorite   67

Garnet   67

Herkimer Diamond   68

Howlite, White   69

Jasper, Ocean   69

Jasper, Red   70

Kunzite   70

Kyanite, Blue   71

Lapis Lazuli   71

Lemurian Seeds   72

Lepidolite   73

Malachite   74

Moldavite   75

Moonstone   76

Nirvana / Ice Crystal   77

Obsidian, Black   78

Obsidian, Snowflake   78

Opal, Pink   79

Opalite   79

Pietersite   80

Pyrite   80

Quartz, Clear and Rainbow   81

Quartz, Rose / Pink   81

Quartz, Rutile   82

Quartz, Smoky   82

Rhodochrosite   83

Ruby Zoisite   83

Salt   84

Selenite   85

Shungite   86

Sodalite   87

Sunstone   87

Super 7   88

Tiger's Eye   88

Tourmaline, Black   89

Tourmaline, Green   90

Turquoise   90

Unakite   91

Part 2: Crystal Body Layouts

Chapter 4: Prepping for Your Crystal Body Layout Sessions   95

Make Your Assessment   95

Exercise: Your Chakra Assessment   100

How to Prepare for and Chart Your Crystal Body Layout Session   101

My Experiences vs. Yours   104

Time to Experience   106

Start Here   107

Chapter 5: Body Layouts for Healing and Wellness   109

Layout #1: Chakra Healing—Alignment and Balance   110

Layout #2: Polarity Balance—Sync Your Mind and Body   113

Layout #3: Relaxation and General Self-Activation of Healing   117

Layout #4: Calming ADHD   120

Chapter 6: Layouts for Achieving Your Goals   125

Layout #5: Find Your Purpose   126

Layout #6: Attract Like-Minded Love   129

Layout #7: Money, Luck, and Abundance   132

Layout #8: New Beginnings and Fertility   136

Layout #9: Rational Mind   139

Chapter 7: Layouts for Attending to Your Spirit Self   143

Layout #10: Spacey Fun Out-of-Body Experience   144

Layout #11: Astral Travel and Exploring Safe Portals   147

Layout #12: Past Life / Parallel Life / Alternate Life Journey   150

Layout #13: Self-Exorcisms / Entity Removal   153

Layout #14: Elemental Balance   156

Chapter 8: Layouts for Personal Transformation   161

Layout #15: Erase and Release Negative Patterns for
Positive Vibes: Soul Talking   162

Layout #16: Self-Realization Wilderness Journey with Nature Guides   168

Layout #17: Self-Love, Trust, and Connection to Higher Self   171

Layout #18: Mother Earth Grounding: Being Present with Gratitude   175

Layout #19: Body Rejuvenation   178

Layout #20: Achieving Levels of Contentment   181

Chapter 9: Layouts for Spiritual Enhancement   185

Layout #21: Ask for Spirit Visitors and Loved Ones
Who Have Passed Over   186

Layout #22: Angel Connections   189

Layout #23: Downloading Higher Knowledge from Other Realms   192

Layout #24: Advancement of the Human Soul Living on Earth   196

Layout #25: Star Energy: Bring More Light to Your Eternal Being   199

Layout #26: Insights of the Future   202

Conclusion   207

Appendix A: Reference to Crystal and Gemstone Use for
Specific Ailments or Issues   209

Appendix B: Crystals for the Home Grids and Other Uses   257

Crystals at Night   257

Water and Crystals   259

Manifesting with Crystals Outdoors   263

Tincture   263

Holiday Crystal Centerpieces   264

Grids for the Home   265

Appendix C: 22 Essential Oils to Enhance Your
Crystal Layout Session   269

Bergamot   270

Chamomile   270

Eucalyptus   270

Frankincense   270

Geranium   271

Grapefruit   271

Jasmine   271

Juniper Berry   271

Lavender   271

Lemon   271

Lemongrass   272

Myrrh   272

Patchouli   272

Peppermint   272

Pine   272

Rose   272

Rosemary   273

Sage   273

Sandalwood   273

Sweet Orange   273

Tangerine   273

Ylang-Ylang   273

Recommended Resources   275

Resource List   277

Index   279

Disclaimer

High-Vibe Crystal Healing is not meant to replace medical treatment. Please consult your doctor for any ailments or pains you experience. The information in this book should not replace the advice of medical professionals and does not intend to provide cures. Instead, this book will provide knowledge of how crystals and their frequencies work in harmony for wellness.

Introduction

Are you mesmerized by crystals and how beautiful they look? I am. Crystals are more than beautiful objects from the earth: they are chunks of energy. That is how I used to describe them to people when I was eight.

It all started with a bucket of rocks.

I grabbed my small bucket of tumbled stones I collected from a local mall "rock" show and dumped them on my carpet. I ran my fingers through the tumbled stones, picked each one up, and stared closely at it. Then, I lay on top of all of the tumbled stones and crystals, rolling over them back and forth. I was eight years old. Smiling and laughing. Was this my first invention? A crystal carpet or a crystal bed? At that time I was just loving the vibes, unknowingly getting a crystal boost as the sun shone through the windows of my upstairs bedroom in South Jersey.

Moving ahead 39 years, I can now explain how crystals work with your body's energy fields in detail. I wrote *High-Vibe Crystal Healing* for everyone to benefit from its knowledge, from novices to the advanced. My goal was to create a book of reliable and accurate information on how to use crystal body layouts as gem remedies in everyday life. I wanted to show people the basic science behind the crystal vibes. Crystals emit frequencies that are real. I'll teach you details about your energy body and list 66 incredible crystals and how to use them in your everyday life. The vibe meter will help you notice and sense what level of intensity you may feel from each crystal. I added some fun names to help you remember them. I love to make learning fun. There are 26 crystal body layouts, including self-healing improvements, attracting love and abundance, complete body and mind balancing, and experiencing astral travel.

I have you prep for your crystal sessions and decipher what type of body layout you want to administer. Step by step, I have everything you can think of covered: body layouts for healing and wellness, achieving your goals, expanding self-awareness and spirit, personal transformation, and releasing attachments. I spark it up a notch by adding 22 essential oils to enhance your body layout experiences. I even created an innovative crystal chart (see Appendix A) that you can easily use to look up an ailment and know what crystals can assist you. That's not all! You'll be all the rave to your family, friends, or clients by showing off your crystal skills as a home and space master gridder. You will enjoy making any space feel positive.

I'll make a crystal pro out of you. Self-pro to crystal healing facilitator—you'll rock!

By the way, I'm Jolie DeMarco. People call me the crystal junkie. I have been into metaphysics for many years, learning, teaching, writing, and sharing. I've been attracted to crystals and all things metaphysical my whole life. I am and have been a metaphysical teacher and master crystal healer for over 20 years. I love what I do, and I am blessed to share. My specialty is crystal healing. I was taught about crystal healing intuitively from beings of light since I was a child. You may have heard of them: Archangel Michael, St. Germain, Archangel Raphael, the Atlanteans, and Lemurians. It was interesting and insightful. Trust me, you don't have to connect with them directly to learn what I am going to teach you. I am their messenger. I am excited to instruct and enlighten on their behalf. I can teach you tons of knowledge to make you a master crystal healer and highly educated crystal gridder. Yeah, I have mad skills when it comes to all things metaphysical, but enough about me—let's make it all about you. I'm excited that you chose to read and experiment with this book's high vibes.

Our Natural Attraction to Crystals and Gemstones

Are you attracted to certain crystals or gemstones that make you have to buy them? This magnetism is because your body's chemistry needs the crystals' elements. Intuitively, your body senses this. You might be thinking to yourself, "I'm not a psychic or intuitive person." But guess what? We all are. It's our human nature for survival and well-being. Instincts are part of who we are. Our intuition is that inner knowing and part of our self-healing knowledge.

This book explains energy at a caliber that everyone can understand—like GPS directions on how to understand your body on a level that we don't physically see.

To our bodies, crystals and gemstones are similar to modern-day vitamins. After all, medicines and vitamins originally derived from elements and minerals. As with supplements, medicine, and herbs, certain combos can be bad, especially if we use too much of something or mix too many. When it comes to crystals, often you end up needing to experiment, but, lucky you, I've done that for you! The crystal and gemstone layouts you will find in this book offer the perfect blend for positive results.

You may not think about this often, but everything is energy. That means that everything—each person, animal, tree, and basically every item, including rocks and gemstones—has a frequency. Think of it this way: As a human, you have good days and bad days. On a good day, your frequency is higher, and you are happier emotionally. On a bad day, your frequency, your vibes, are lower. Our chemical makeup stays the same, but our emotions flux, causing frequencies that can affect not only ourselves and our well-being, but our surroundings. For example, place four angry people in a room of 30 other people. As they express their negativity, it grows; that low vibration of anger is now making the other 30 people talk about their bad experiences as well. Not everyone will accept this frequency; some may leave the space or decide to talk about positive occurrences or not at all.

My point is that frequency, or vibrations, can be heard or felt. We can accept, allow, absorb, neglect, or be neutral to them. Everyone is different. People have different upbringings and different locales, and all of this is a factor of what a person "is." Each one of us has a frequency, and it can always be adjusted. Adjustments can be made by our own frequencies of thoughts and our environments. How do crystals come into play? Well, because each crystal can hold and emit energy as well as us humans. The only difference is that a gemstone, crystal, or mineral, in most cases, has the same frequency throughout its existence once it is formed. Some varieties of crystal are grown and enhanced, but mostly the frequency is sedentary, whereas humans morph and change more often than a crystal. Using crystal frequencies to reach optimal wellness or goals means knowing which crystals work with your frequency at that particular time in your life. Assessing yourself is the first step in deciding what you want or need to adjust, whether it is physical, emotional, mental, or spiritual.

This is how crystals and gemstones can help transform anyone or any space. Note that throughout the book, *frequency*, *vibrations*, and *vibes* all are terms I will be referring to, all meaning the same thing.

Matching Crystals to Your Needs

It's important to be aware and mindful while using crystals. Loving crystals is great, but you need to understand how to use them to balance your energy versus confuse your energy. I have noticed that some people hold an abundance of crystals or wear multiple varieties of crystal jewelry at one time. I only mention this because most people don't think of crystals and gems as vitamins. Too many crystals can confuse the energy in your body. Your aura and chakras can become unbalanced. Too much of anything all the time can be not so good. If you don't need 50 vitamins per day, would you take 50 vitamins?

I really love crystals immensely and understand the desire to pile them on. After all, I own a crystal shop! But it's important to know how to be balanced. To those of you who do wear a lot of crystals at once, you do look super cool, but just make sure you're feeling balanced as well. If you notice that you are unsure of how you feel on any given day, first see how many crystals you are packin'. It could be that you are wearing crystals with conflicting energies; for example, one crystal might be for focusing while another is for helping you sleep. If you're absorbing both frequencies at once, your energy will get confused. See what I mean?

Day to day we may have different emotions due to occurrences in our lives. Picking a crystal that works for that day can balance you.

Notice how you feel. If, for example, you feel tired but need to focus for work, look in this book and read what crystal will help with how you are feeling that particular day. These stones would be Ruby Zoisite to motivate you and White Howlite to attain focus.

Another example: You're going on vacation and can't stop overthinking because you are all wound up, and you need to get your mind off work mode. You can look up what would relax or calm you and your mind. You'll find that Amethyst and Moldavite will do the trick.

I can go on forever about what we all need. By the time you finish reading this book, you will be able to rattle off rock remedies all day long! Each gem, crystal, or mineral has certain components that create their makeup. This is what creates the frequency that they hold and emit, and this is how the crystals can affect you. Let's dig deeper and learn about 66 of the best vibin' crystals Mother Earth created for us to utilize. Before I take you there, let's discuss the numerology behind the number of crystal and body layouts.

What's Up with the Numbers 26, 66, and 22?

I thought you might want to know why I chose 26 layouts, 66 specific crystals, and 22 essential oils for this book. I like numerology. The number 26 is a sacred number. Many people feel 26 represents prosperity and wealth and brings peace and love into your life. To me, 26 has done just that. Besides all of that goodness, if you add two and six, you get eight. Eight is a sure sign of abundance and looks very much like the infinity sign! Abundance and never ending? I'll accept that! Eight is my absolute favorite number in all the universes. I've loved it since I was a child. In my twenties, I got a mini tattoo of an eight on the side of my foot. I actually didn't know anything about the infinity sign at that time in my life. Intuitively I must have been drawn to it for more than one reason. The symbolism of numbers is wild as you learn about each and how we use their energy in our lives.

Number 22 feels strong and promises betterment or goodness of the heart and of all things that exist in life. If I could bottle the number and label it, it would be like Buddhism in a jar: loving all and everything. I'm an intuitive feeler, and 22 brings me an awakening of inner knowing and connection to source, or a higher power of existence. This high vibrational connection can be to your source, or your soul's energy, offering you knowledge and insights to make good choices in life. When you make a conscious effort to understand why you should make good choices, you are truly mindful. Being mindful helps us love our imperfections and create balance and betterment, which in turn creates a more loving society.

When 22 is divided by two, we get the number 11—a highly spiritual number that represents Angels being present to guide you. The number 11 is believed to be a master number because of its double numbers, one and one. Double numbers are said to have a high vibrational frequency, especially when they consist of two prime numbers. The double primes increase the power of the frequencies.

The number 22 is a double number as well: super powerful. Two plus two equals four, which means reconstruction. The 22 essential oils in the book are used to help you with many ailments and to adjust and align you. Specific oils can help reset your system for what you need. The number 22 brings power to you, allowing positivity and change for reaching your goals or dreams. I chose the top 22 oils to get your body there.

The number 66 is a powerful number as well. Double numbers again. I feel 66 brings unconditional love from your soul and your source energy. Number 66 also helps you trust in the universe to know you are constantly divinely guided and provided with what you need and desire in life.

If you add each digit in 22 and 66 together, you get number 16. If you add them traditionally, it's an 88. I interpret both 16 and 88 to mean self-determination of inner power that encourages one to heal, adjust, and balance for complete harmony and abundance.

These numbers represent the main purpose of this book: to bring each of you that unconditional love through an abundance of self-healing assisted by your source. Your source can be your God, Buddha, Jah, Goddesses, Angels, Mother Earth, and beyond; all are goodness and want you to be your best. These 66 marvelous crystals of Earth and positive energy used during the 26 layouts will connect your soul to your source.

How You Will Benefit from Learning the Crystal Healing Trade

If you are currently an energy practitioner, this book will help you learn new layouts and practical ways to help advance your clientele. I hope you additionally try the layouts yourself to feel what your clients will experience. As a master healer, I have shared both common and very uncommon crystal body layouts. I want to make sure that you become the best crystal healer, and knowing intricate details and really specific grids for all aspects of a person's life needs is just one part of becoming a master of the holistic healing modality.

If you are a beginner, I urge you to try these layouts in addition to learning more about your energy system. Crystal healing is known for stress release, pure relaxation, cord cutting, pattern removal, astral travel, and spirit world connection. Crystal healing is a holistic metaphysical healing technique that is potent for deep cleansing of the soul. These crystal layouts can be used to make your sessions epic.

Feelin' is believin'. Once you relax with the crystal energies, you will melt into *ahhh*!

Part 1

About Your Crystals

Chapter 1
The Basics of Crystal Healing and How Crystals Work

Crystal healing is vibrational healing; it is considered an alternative medicine technique using stones and crystals for their healing properties. All stones and crystals hold and emit a variety of unique frequencies. Each frequency has resonance that can be absorbed in a human electromagnetic field. All crystals and gems have properties, minerals, and vibrations compatible with our human aura. As we choose certain combinations of crystals that vibrate well together or harmonize, they can help a person release, balance, adjust, advance, or heal. If you place your stones correctly, you can even have an out-of-body experience. I'm being serious!

Many moons ago, back in BCE, humans used crystals and gemstones for healing. Ancient scriptures spoke highly of purity and the earth. At that time, planet Earth was a source of clean healing: herbal essences of flowers, along with rocks and minerals, were commonly used for their healing properties. Rocks and minerals contained elements that are healing to humans; some specimens of rock and sediment contained iron, manganese, lithium, calcium, silica, and so on. When we are in need of adaptation or healing, our bodies can connect with these properties within the crystals and gemstones.

This is how I choose a crystal for each particular day. I have a bowl with an assortment of crystals in my living room. I keep one four-inch piece of Selenite inside the bowl. It's important to have Selenite in the bowl because this formation cleanses all other crystals. I call it the "cleaner." Selenite is also a self-cleansing mineral. It never needs to be cleaned or cleared because of its amazing properties. Having Selenite sitting in my bowl keeps all of my little crystal buddies clean.

Every morning I get up, get prepared for work, and then look into my magical crystal bowl. I see what I am attracted to for that particular day. If it's two stones, I take those with me. If it's five, I put 'em in my pocket. If it's none, I leave them all at home! I do the same with my crystal jewelry. I have lots of amazing necklaces, bracelets, and crystal pendants. I give them a gander and see what "speaks" to me. I listen to my body and my crystal gem babies!

There was one particular time a crystal called out to me loudly. I was with my mother at a huge crystal warehouse, and I felt gigantic energy coming from these Nirvana Ice Crystals. My mom is sensitive, but she always said she didn't feel anything from crystals—until that moment when I placed that rippled crystal in the palm of her dainty hand!

My mom's eyes opened huge, and she said, "I'm feeling a surge of energy to my heart; I feel like this crystal is pulsing in my hand!"

We can make even more use of stones by combining them in our practices. In Part 2 of the book, I'll provide knowledge and diagrams for creating a therapeutic healing with crystals and gemstones placed on and around the human body. I also included other content that will rock your world; I have done research with clients and myself to bring you the ultimate crystal experience. There is something in here for everyone. Before you know it, you will be bringing this book to your family and friends and asking them to share positive high crystal vibes with you!

Why Are Your Instincts and Crystals Related?

In tests I have done over the years, I've noticed how crystals work and how people react to them. I noticed how gemstones and various crystals affected me and other people physically and intuitively. I also noticed how they mentally, emotionally, and spiritually worked to create harmonious energy and balance my total body. Crystals and gemstones can help humans release, adjust, balance, heal, and advance.

My research shows that crystals can help us self-heal. When crystals, minerals, and gemstones are used specifically and intentionally, they can affect us.

Their curative properties can enhance your emotional and physical levels. Your mindset can become more positive as well. When combinations of crystals work well together, they can change your energy from *blah* to *yahoo!* and make a huge difference in your whole energy package! Crystals help you feel great, ease pain, release addictive behaviors, clear depression, become happier, gain new perceptions of life, and so on. Our bodies talk to us. Those crystals you are holding, attracted to, or decide to purchase are speaking to you! You might hear them faintly say, "You need me; I can help you."

The Benefits of Crystal Vibration

Crystals and gemstones are used to enhance, renew, release, revive, balance, and/or heal us physically, mentally, and emotionally. Most importantly, they help us feel and sense, giving us a sensation that affects all the layers of our auras to balance what is needed on those energetic levels of the human body. This results in the mind-body connection, which helps us learn, experience, and share. This is why we are here on Earth; it's the human experience of life.

Did you know that the same endorphins our brains release during meditations with crystals and gemstones are the same endorphins that give us that euphoric feeling when we drink alcohol or do drugs—without the negative effects? No wonder monks can meditate all day!

I believe in feeling good, but why destroy brain cells over it? Crystal healing is a new, healthy way to discover yourself. It is especially good for healing, floating, letting go, or for feeling superb!

I really should rephrase that: crystals aren't new—they have been around for billions of years. The crystal Auralite 23 found in Canada was 1.2 billion years old. Then there is a Tektite—basically a crystal formation from beyond Earth—named Moldavite. Moldavite is a meteorite that smacked down in the Czech Republic and formed into a glass-like substance—the same mystical substance said to be the green stone in the Holy Grail. NASA has no clue where in space the meteorite came from, which I find super interesting. Egyptians buried their rulers in crystal and gemstone tombs. Indian medicine men and women used crystals for healing their tribes. That's just to name a few!

The reason why crystals, minerals, and gemstones can give you the feelings of a high or enlightened experience is because they can change your vibrations. The frequencies of a certain energy, such as stone or crystal vibrations, can affect your senses and brain waves. This means the crystal is energy. Basically everything in the universe holds, emits, or absorbs energy. When we humans hold an object or have it in close proximity, we are absorbing its energy in our energy field. This also is called the *aura*, also known as a human's *electromagnetic field*. Eloquently put, when we hold a crystal, mineral, or stone, we are working with the energy of that particular vibration/frequency, and it can enhance, balance, and adjust our bodies on a physical, mental, emotional, or spiritual level. This can create many feelings. The crystals' properties can change or influence our whole system—body and mind—to experience euphoria. I also call this beautiful feeling *unconditional love*, a feeling that some of you may consider a "high." I'm assuming that is where the expression *good vibes*, or *high vibes*, came from—from just feeling good!

Human Harmonizing and Crystal Harmonizing

There are a few ways you can understand what human harmonizing is. It can be when like-minded people get in a group and their values and mannerisms mesh well together. Another way is how each part of the human body synchronizes: our heart, our lungs, and our veins make the blood flow while we take in oxygen through our mouth and skin. Oxygen goes into our lungs and is carried though our bloodstream. This is an example of how humans harmonize with bodily functions. We are quite amazing beings.

Crystal harmonizing is using the energy/vibration of the crystal to release, adjust, change, or advance a person/object's energy into a more positive vibrational frequency. For most humans, placing crystals around or on the body—by wearing them, for example—can enhance our well-being. Each one of us is different: where we live, the way we grew up, our belief systems, the way we process our emotions and thoughts, our health, and what we were trained or taught make up our vibrational energy. It is what we are. All of us should want to be our ultimate best. We can't help what happens in everyday life because we can never control anyone other than ourselves, but we can adjust ourselves to deal with life and heal in positive ways. Using crystal therapies, such as crystal body layouts, wearing crystals, and gridding our home or spaces can keep us optimal. Harmonizing is key to keeping us and our spaces at their best.

You can also understand crystals as energy objects. Crystal vibrations can be measured with frequency equipment that calculates in hertz, an international system of measurement equal to one cycle per second. The movement or compression of the atoms in a crystal molecule can make an electric charge. This electric charge can create a current of energy flow; the frequency that is generated from the charge can be measured, and the measurement of that frequency is called the *resonance* of that crystal. Since crystals can be somewhat unique, it can be difficult to get an exact frequency number. That is why I created the vibe meter to make life easier for you as a crystal healer. If you can understand the feeling, vibe, or "charge" you may receive when using certain crystals for healing and adjusting purposes, you are good! Some examples of frequencies in common use include Quartz crystals, which are shaped and compressed to create a frequency that makes radios work, and the high-frequency "chips" our computers use to connect to the internet. Additionally, a tuning fork is tuned at certain frequencies that resonate to help people heal or balance; those frequencies can transmit throughout our bones and muscles to create healing vibes within our bodies. It is pretty incredible. All in all, crystals have positive frequencies, and that's how they harmonize with our physical and energy bodies.

Knowing What Crystals Harmonize with Each Other: Using the Appendix

As you read on, you may feel the need to go to the appendix section of this book, where you'll be able to look up crystals and their specific usage. For example, if you needed emotional healing, you could look in the appendix under *emotional*. You should then look within the appendix for a few more crystals that align with your goals and intentions. For example, if you wanted to use a stone for confidence and physical strength, you would look up *confidence* and *physical strength* to find the crystals that correlate with those keywords.

Once you start working with crystals and learning about your emotional, mental, and physical energy bodies, you can create the correct combinations for crystal healing layouts. They all come together like an easy puzzle. Plus, lucky you, the crystal appendix guides you on what stones are used for certain ailments, including physical, emotional, mental, and spiritual ailments, and their correlating chakras.

Chakras, Auras, and Crystal Healing

Crystal healing is a term used for healing the human physical body and the energetic body. In school, we learned about our physical bodies. The energy body is something that most people cannot see. Our energy bodies are equally important for our health and well-being.

Our energy bodies have layers. These layers are within the human aura, or the space between your physical body and about four feet away from your body. Our auras have positive, negative, and neutral charges, and balancing them is the key.

We are affected daily with other people's energy and environmental conflicts; these can unbalance our auras and our energy centers. Our seven main energy centers are called *chakras*. When your aura energy and your chakra energy centers are balanced, you will feel fantazmic and on top of your game.

We have over 144,000 chakras in our bodies. However, the seven chakras I am going to talk about are the biggest and affect us the most. Chakras are energetic wheels; visualize them as big spirals or vortexes of vibrational energy that run through and about four feet outside of our bodies. They are constantly moving. Each chakra can move in and out of balance depending on the thoughts we have and each emotion and experience we endure. Our chakras and aura work together as a dynamic duo. Our chakras and our aura cannot function without the other.

Your energy field is your aura. There are a few names for describing our energy that surrounds our human physical body: *aura, electromagnetic field (EMF), energy body,* or one's *etheric body*. It can get confusing since everyone may use a different name to describe the same concept, but know that I will be using these terms interchangeably throughout the book.

These seven bigger chakras can keep us balanced emotionally, physically, mentally, and spiritually, which is super important for us to generally feel good. When our chakras are off-balance, they make us off-balance too. In crystal healing, the goal is to balance the chakras and cleanse the auric fields of a person's body. We can do this using crystal layouts since crystals, minerals, and gemstones hold and/or emit certain vibrational frequencies and can enhance or help us heal and/or balance our chakras and auras.

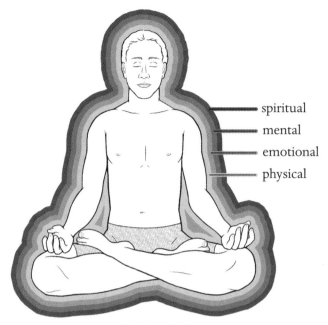

The Aura Body

There are four main layers to the aura. You may hear that there are more than four layers; it is all in what you believe or find to be true. The four layers I teach are eminent in your crystal healing practices. These are the physical, emotional, mental, and spiritual layers.

Closest to the body is the physical auric layer, and moving outward from there are the emotional, mental, and spiritual layers. They can be adjusted with crystals to help them vibrate at a higher frequency. This adjustment can make us feel better and balance our emotions. The balance of those frequencies within our energetic bodies can vibrate, hold, or emit negative and positive energies.

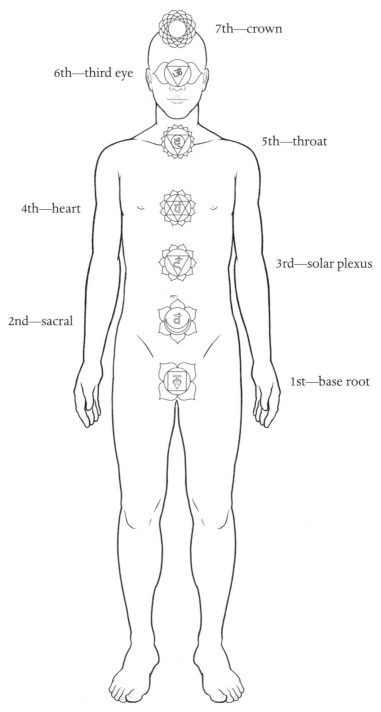

The 7 Chakras

Using the correct combination of frequencies that come from gemstones, crystals, and minerals can heal, adjust, balance and/or neutralize energy. These combined frequencies can also help us release unwanted energy that no longer serves us and change the frequency to what we need to be well. Crystals and gemstones induce wellness and healing of the human body's energy field. Many crystals and gemstones have mineral properties that help our energy fields balance and, therefore, can balance us on emotional, mental, physical, and spiritual levels. Many crystals contain elements such as silicon, aluminum, oxygen, magnesium, iron, titanium, boron, beryllium, sodium, potassium, calcium, fluorine, carbon, chromium, and manganese.

Minerals are grouped by what they contain. First are silicates. Some examples of silicates include Beryl, Amethyst, and Tourmalines. Second are oxides, which are compounds of metals or other elements and oxygen. Examples are Rutile, Rubies, and Sapphires. Third are carbonates, which contain carbon and oxygen. Examples include Aragonite and Calcite. Other groups of minerals are phosphates, which contain phosphorus; borates, which contain boron; and sulfides/sulfates, which contain sulfur. Phosphates also include halides, which contain chlorine. All of these work with the energy of our bodies and our energy fields. Crystals and humans work well together!

Learning about the auras can help you understand that placing a crystal in a certain layer of your electromagnetic field can make a difference in the outcome of your crystal layout session. In the diagram that shows the layers of your aura, you can see that these four major levels represent a big part of our being. For example, if I placed a crystal like Black Tourmaline in a person's spiritual layer, this would help them release from a past life, if you believe in that. Likewise, if I needed to focus, I would place a White Howlite stone on my forehead in the physical aura layer. This will ignite and/or balance the frequencies to keep my thoughts from scattering all over the place. I could lie down for 15 minutes with that White Howlite on my forehead and then get going on my goal.

When a crystal or gem is within four feet of your body, it can affect your body's energetic fields, which is good. However, if I want to use my special extra expertise, I would want to proceed with a crystal body layout to really do some adjusting, using the knowledge of the aura layers and what they represent to fix, alter, and balance anything I may need. This is what I provided for you in the crystal body layouts. If you want to become an expert junkie too, join me for a workshop or retreat; I can teach you.

Okay, enough of the science class for now. I know you want to get into the crystal layouts work—the fun part!

The Difference between Grids and Body Layouts

The energies of crystals and gemstones placed as layouts around the human body can be profound in moving and balancing energy. They surely make you feel stronger, brighter, lighter, and super cool, in my opinion. Many people can feel a deep connection to spirit, meaning a loved one that has passed, an Angel, or what one might call a God or Universal Source/higher power.

I personally love the feeling of my physical body and mind connecting. This is the connection of self. I call it *syncing up*. When I do a session with certain crystals, they make me feel intelligent. Not only do I feel super smart, but I always feel crystal energies bring self-love. Crystals can help our bodies heal—this is the major plus!

Crystal Grids

Crystal grids are educated and calculated ways to position crystals, minerals, and gemstones to create intentional frequencies and change the energy in a certain location or space. Crystal grid work is awesome because you can make grids in small or big spaces. Many people believe they can change Earth's energy by placing grids in different locations, and it's true; I can attest to this. Grids can be made of crystal, minerals, and other items, such as totems, to change Earth's energy and, hopefully, heal the earth. Some people create grids to raise vibes and become landing marks for aliens! All over the world, seen or unseen, there are grids.

Body Layouts

Body layouts are simply the way a crystal healer would place crystals and gemstones on the physical body or within the body's aura. The crystal healer would be certified or knowledgeable of how crystals harmonize, using these skills for a purposeful, successful session.

The Effect of Thought and Intention

Our own negative or positive thoughts can change our electromagnetic fields/ auras. It totally makes sense when you understand how energy works. You can prove how energy works from thought frequencies and also from voice frequencies by holding a pendulum. Once you have your pendulum steady by holding the end chain, the crystal point of the pendulum facing down, bring the crystal close to your forehead at the third eye. You should be holding the chain above the top of your head and the point three inches from your brow area. Stand in front of a mirror if you are doing this alone so you can see everything clearly. Now that you are ready, the idea is to not move the chain and pendulum's direction with your hand. The purpose is to use your mind's energy to move it. To do this, steady the hand on the chain, stare at the pendulum stone, and say with strong intent which way you want it to move. For example, I would say, "Move back and forth," in a strong voice. I would really say it like I mean it. Focus and visualize it moving the way you say, and it should move instantly! If you are having a hard time making it move, take a deep breath, exhale, and try it again. Know that you are powerful; say it with power and mean what you say. The pendulum will move. Some people who have a hard time speaking up in general may find it takes them a few times before they get the pendulum moving, but everyone can do it; we all have inner power! If you got it quite easily, that is great—you are rocking the crystal pendulum! Since you are an ace at it, try to make it move in a circle; you would say, "Move in a circle to my right." Woohoo! Amazing, right? Wait until you try it! You will see how powerful our human minds are. You will be showing off your newfound gift all the time. It is great to know your own power of thought and how it truly influences the energy fields of your body.

Intentions are what you desire and project. They are the thoughts, feelings, and actions of what you want to occur. It is good to set intentions while working with crystals. I have made a list of intentions to match each layout with specifics of the crystals for optimal results. This will guide you to advance, heal, or view the world in a new, positive way. You might also take a crystal trip somewhere out of this world. Really—I am not kiddin' on this one.

Other Influences and Enhancers during Crystal Healing Sessions

An activator is something that can connect with one or more of our five senses and trigger our awareness. Our five senses consist of sound, hearing; vision, color, and/or shapes; scents, smelling; touch, physical/feeling; and taste.

Everything has a frequency that we can use our senses to accept or reject. In crystal healing layouts, our goal is to harmonize and activate positivity for each particular experience, whether by releasing/going out of body or becoming advanced in self-healing. Activators such as essential oils, mandalas, mantras, crystals, music, or guided meditation can all be used for activating the utmost positive and harmonizing crystal healing experience possible.

Sound is one important activator. "Sound personality" is when we accept something we hear. We can always cover our ears or put earplugs in, but sound is a blessing. As we touched on earlier, sound frequencies are healing to humans if they bring positive harmonizing vibrations to the adapter. Sound can connect to our other senses and trigger emotions. The same goes with our other four senses. Activators can be good or bad depending on what each of us likes or dislikes. For example, you may love classical music and hate reggae, so playing soft classical music may make the crystal session more comfortable and positive, while playing reggae music may make you want to storm off. By the way, reggae is my all-time favorite music besides Elvis. Yeah, I know: weird combo.

With that said, there is no right or wrong, just different, and what is good for you might be bad for another person. All in all, we can accept or deny frequencies. If we accept the frequencies as information through our five senses and process them accordingly to help us delete, heal, adapt, and move forward in our lives, it is helpful and positive.

It is incredible that our bodies have so much more than we can see with the human eye. We are activated all day long by our environments. Our surroundings play a huge part in our systems to change and heal, relax, and balance us, but they also can make us unhappy, unbalanced and negative, or sick. Our goal is to be the best we can: full of vitality and zest. I hope you understand more of how our systems and energy, frequencies, and activators can be adapted as enhancers for crystal healing and our lives.

In crystal healing, you are choosing to create a positive, relaxing, safe environment by using activators that harmonize with the knowledgeable placement of the crystals. The ambiance itself is an activator: the sound, the visual enhancers, the essential oils, and the comfortable, clean, protected space all combine to create an optimal professional crystal healing session.

What to Expect from a Crystal Body Layout Session

Many people who are vivid dreamers actually see visions in their mind's eye or third eye, a.k.a. the 6th chakra, during crystal sessions. Some people can visualize or feel emotions of a past life, a parallel life, or future information. Many can see or sense Angels or spirit guides with their intuitive skills or natural psychic abilities. This is something you can come across with crystal work.

Some people can receive clarity on situations in their life during or after a session with crystals. Many people can see colors moving toward and away from them as their eyes are closed. Here are some examples of what people experience during sessions:

I saw my deceased mother! I saw myself flying! I was the emperor of Japan! I saw the inside of my body. I felt amazing and renewed! I let go of the fear! I felt my friend that passed hug me and hold my hand! My body was light; I felt like I was floating and was somewhere in space. I felt free. I connected with an Archangel! I spoke some language I don't know—I think Indian…

Some of these statements were from clients that had crystal sessions. Some statements were from my personal exploration of using crystals and gemstones. Some of these sessions were for healing and many just for fun.

However, not everyone can see inner visions or colors that glide in and out of their minds. Most people can feel and sense information through these crystal meditations. I ask you not to expect too much or place pressure on yourself when trying each of these layouts. The best part about trying these amazing combinations is that there is no stress—just relax, let go, and enjoy. What counts is when you feel and notice results. If you don't expect anything, then you won't be disappointed. Overthinking is usually the block; stop thinking about time or how much time you have. True meditation is when you forget about time.

Everyone that I have worked with reported that they felt relaxed and better than they did before they tried a crystal session! People who used crystal layouts for specific healing purposes have also had positive outcomes, noting relief and subsided physical and emotional symptoms. Some proclaimed they had been healed completely! I cannot make any claims, but I can repeat what was reported from clients. That was a mini disclaimer.

There is a lot that can go into an incredible crystal healing session. Knowing the energetic body is one key component. Understanding harmonizing and frequencies is also vital. Read on, and I will share all my secrets for the best results and make you closer to becoming a master at crystal healing.

Chapter 2
How to Select and Care for Your Crystals and Gemstones

Like I said, there is a lot that goes into a crystal healing session. Understanding how to use all your tools in the process is the difference between a good crystal healing session and a crappy one. Yeah, I'm just going to be blunt about it. I always say, if I need knee replacement, I'm not going to a heart doctor. This is the reason to specialize and be the best, knowing which layouts work best for which ailments. Knowledge is king. I teach you how to perform a professional crystal healing session. In order to attain this level, you'll need to first understand the basics of how to best select and care for your crystals and gemstones.

If you are new to holding and feeling a crystal's energy, let me give you a small test to try. This one-minute test can help you select the correct crystal you need for that day; it's super easy, no overthinking needed, because it's a feeling and sensing test. This simple test ensures that you are selecting the best crystal for your needs.

First, look at your selection of crystals or crystal jewelry. Choose the ones you feel drawn to look at and touch. Take those specific crystals and place them in front of you. Hold one crystal at a time up to your heart chakra, which is at the center of your chest. Hold that one crystal for one minute. You will sense a feeling of "yes" or "no." You may also feel impartial. Note that feeling, and then place the crystal down and away from you. Now try the next crystal, holding it the same way against the heart chakra. Again, take one minute to notice what you sense and feel. You will hold each crystal separately, doing this until your whole selection is complete. Then choose to wear or hold the crystals that had a "yes" feeling. This test proves your body knows what frequency is needed to harmonize and balance you for that particular day.

There are a few basic classifications for crystals and gemstones. In science books there are tons of classifications, but I like to teach it simply—we don't have to be full-fledged geologists to know crystal healing. Keeping it simple and detailed on the uses, placements, and vibe meter of each crystal is all you need for now.

Raw vs. Polished and "Vibe" Factors

Raw or polished? I like my crystals both ways. This is something that can be quite controversial to many crystal junkies out there in crystal healer land. Raw crystals mean they are not polished or dolled up with color sheens, infused color, chemical sprays, or adornments.

Rocks, crystals, and gemstones can be polished with or without chemicals or dyes. Polished rocks are by far prettier to look at and many times easier to put in your sock or bra because they are usually smoother. You will also hear them called "tumbled" stones. This is because raw stones are placed in a rock tumbler, or huge machinery, to polish them so you can see all the details of the stone. The tumbled or polished stones are just as powerful as raw crystals or gems, but many people believe less is more. Just like eating food, the fewer ingredients on the package, usually the healthier for you. Having more ingredients doesn't mean it's terrible or harmful; it's just a preference of purity.

I know you are thinking: But what if a stone is infused with color? Does that mess up the frequency of the stone? I would have to say that it can, usually slightly. It can change the stone's natural frequency, but, on the other hand, the stone can be infused with something that changes the frequency to something more positive as well. Their chemical makeup can be enhanced.

Each crystal has a unique variety of chemical elements and frequencies, either because of the faux color infusions or the natural water infusions from the time it was created. Each size can also hold a different frequency. As a stone is exposed to its environment, it releases or repowers its natural energy. Receiving sunlight or moonlight, or being placed in a frequency-enhancing crystal grid changes a crystal's energy. Nowadays, there are Rife machines and frequency generators to program specific frequencies within a crystal.

If a person releases some major negative vibes in a crystal healing session, this will make a difference to the crystal's energy. The crystals can absorb the negative vibes emitting from the person while changing or adjusting that person's overall frequency and clearing up any unhappy baggage. A skilled crystal healer can make all the difference in this negative energy exchange by intently placing harmonizing crystals that promote self-loving frequencies; this crystal body layout would be advantageous for both the stones and the person receiving the healing because they would feel better about themselves and overall more positive.

Just a note: if the crystal healing facilitator has no clue about the crystals placed around the receiving person and sets a grid of crystals that confuses the energy vibrations, the outcome of the session may not be so good.

I want you to relate to how crystals can work harmoniously with our human bodies and understand that the knowledge of crystal placements and their specific energies can contradict or synchronize with the holder or receiver of the crystals. I am saying this because if you bought a whole pile of beautiful crystals and set all of them on your nightstand, oh gosh, you may wake up more tired or have some wacky dreams! Learning which crystals and gems can enhance or otherwise is important, especially if you are performing a crystal healing session on other people. If you are experimenting on yourself, have at it! Experiments can be super sensational, but having an understanding of how and why each crystal works can make a great difference in what you were trying to accomplish.

Crystal Cheat Sheet

Later in the book is a detailed reference chart and list of 66 crystals that will help you choose the stones you want to work with. For now, here is a quick guide or cheat sheet to some important crystals for your collection and to help you find what crystals might work best for whatever circumstance.

Feel free to make multiple copies and share the knowledge. The crystal cheat sheet and mini crystal stash are kind of like an aspirin in your purse or a mini emergency kit—something you carry just in case. This quick pocket directory explains easily how crystals work with our bodies and includes a list of what each can do for you or for friends.

To use these crystals, set your positive intention of what you need your crystals for and give purpose to the energies. This means the crystals and your energy are working together, creating an equal energy exchange. When you set the intention of what you are utilizing the energy of the crystals for, you set the energy frequencies to work in harmony with your body's energy frequency, therefore accepting the healing. You can hold the crystals in your pocket or wear them as jewelry.

Manifest money: Jade with Citrine and Green Aventurine. These are the abundance trio!

Manifest self-love and compassion: Rose Quartz.

Manifest and attract love from others: Rhodochrosite. This pinky really works! This stone is the color pink, by the way.

Manifest goals: Meditate with a Rainbow Quartz Point or a Citrine.

Got a loved one that is losing their memory? Memory loss/dementia/confusion: Rutile Quartz, Unakite, Kyanite, Moss Agate, and Blue Lace Agate. This combo can ease their *who am I, where am I* syndrome.

Help with moods/depression and bring clarity of the thought process: Clear Quartz with Lepidolite. You could also hold a Botswana Agate.

Reduce stress and anger: Howlite and a Bloodstone together.

Release negativity: The trio of Blue Lace Agate with Black Tourmaline and Selenite. Citrine also is a strong crystal to bring positive energy into your life and release bad energy from around you and your space.

Need to get things done? A Ruby Zoisite will put some energy in your body to get you motivated.

Sciatica/backaches/skeletal issues: Garnets and Amazonite.

Are you on the emotional rollercoaster? Hold a Lepidolite and Amethyst or Purple Fluorite.

Trouble focusing? You need a Clear Quartz Point, Quartz Pyramid, or a White Howlite stone. These stones are great for studying, researching with clarity, and creating structure.

Need to dream better or more vividly? Herkimer Diamond, Super 7, or Auralite 23!

Selling a house or business? You need Citrine and Smoky Quartz. Additionally, Rose Quartz makes a home feel loving, and Amethyst makes it feel comfy and relaxing.

Just need to relax? Place an Amethyst on both sides of you.

Have an addictive personality? Iolite helps release old negative patterns as does Rutile Quartz; hold either or both with a Black Tourmaline.

Want to talk to Angels or feel them around you? Angelite or Celestite held with a Cavansite crystal.

Physical healing: Red Jasper, Green Fluorite, or a beautiful Malachite.

Feeling uptight or have a friend who needs to lighten up? Moldavite; a gram of this green relaxant gives a feeling of highness—not as a kingly feeling of strength or entitlement, but as a feeling of positive high vibes.

Need to speak up and talk clearly to others? A Blue Lace Agate, Chalcedony, or Aquamarine will get those words out!

Crystal Collection—My Favorite Crystals

A collection of crystals is a perfect blend of your most incredible stones. You can keep them in a cool wooden box or glass bowl. Anywhere you feel fit for your prized babies.

My Body Layout Stashes

Many of you may be just beginning with the whole crystal layouts extravaganza or crystals in general. That's totally cool. As you get more and more connected to their energies working with yours, you will want to have two crystal stashes. I repeat: two. You will want your first stash for your personal gem babies. These will only be used by you.

You will also need a second stash for your additional bunch of crystal babies. This is if you start doing crystal layouts for others or for a business. These you would only use with clients. No mixies.

If you start mixing stashes, your crystals can get crossed, and your precious babies don't like that. When you have intention of purpose with a gem or crystal, it is programmed with that intent or frequency. If you are using their crystal energies intently for you, they are hearing that. If the intent is for others, they can hear that statement too. The main concern is cleansing them routinely as needed. You can have transference with crystals that absorb their holder's energy. Transference is adapting the frequencies of another person or object. If your crystals are not cleared and someone else's negative vibes are on them, you can pick up or absorb that energy from the frequencies of the unclean crystals. Please make sure not to mix your crystals without cleansing or clearing them. It is important to frequently clean all of your crystals and gemstones!

My Secret Crystal Stash

I keep a secret stash of mini crystals in my purse. With it, I can let go, release, erase all my negative emotions, gain focus, and attract my desires. I named it my vita-rox-box, and it is travel-sized!

My secret stash is at my disposal; anytime I need a crystal, I can hold it, or put it in my bra, sock, or pocket. I stress that this tiny miracle box is unisex because anyone can work with these gemmie babies. I call crystals vitamins for the body and soul. Everyone can benefit from their incredible mineral powers. If you've got something going on, I have a stone for that right inside my purse! Unleash them and feel them work your aura into balance and bliss! Knowing your stashes and what they are for makes you impressive to others, especially if you are looking to make energy healing a career or part-time gig.

This is the emergency kit everyone needs. The vita-rox-box contains: Selenite, Black Tourmaline, Lepidolite, Tiger's Eye, Moldavite, Pyrite, Amethyst, Amazonite, and Rose Quartz. Why this combination of stones? Because …

… **Selenite and Black Tourmaline** protect you from absorbing negative energy from other people, computers, cell phones, and smart chips.

...**Lepidolite**, nicknamed *Ze' Prozac* stone, balances your emotions and mental thought processes.

...**Tiger's Eye** grounds you to the present moment and protects you.

...**Moldavite** allows you to let go and relax.

...**Pyrite** is your energizer stone; use in lieu of a Red Bull.

...**Amethyst** gives you better intuitive guidance and inner knowledge and aids in sleeping.

...**Amazonite** balances all your aura layers and chakras.

...**Rose Quartz** brings love and compassion within and to others in your proximity.

I beautifully packaged these crystal babies in a special mini stash box and keep them in my handbag. They are insanely effective in aiding us humans. They are Earth remedies.

My Top 11 Crystals:
Rockin' Remedies List for Use in Crystal Healings

This is a list of my most used crystals in healings. You'll notice each crystal is a holistic alternative remedy for common ailments. Here they are: my top 11 crystals from my rockin' remedies list, chock full of energy. When you read this list, you may say, "This chick talks crazy." If the language I use confuses you, I apologize. I express myself with nicknames and code. For example, if I were teaching a student to do a crystal body layout, I would say, "Grab two black beauties, *uno* of the *Ze' Prozac* stone, and three of the 'who am I, where am I' stones." I find I learn best when I associate crystals with a funny name or something to trigger my memory.

We all have our favorite crystals or gemstones to work with. Here are my top 11. All rock, but in different ways. These make up my infamous stash; when something is bothering you, I'm the first to say, "I gotta stone for that!"

1. **Lepidolite:** *Ze' Prozac* stone.
2. **Ruby Zoisite:** The getter done stone.
3. **Moldavite:** Uninhibited—"Dude, I feel good."

4. **Golden Calcite:** The sex stone.

5. **Citrine:** The moolah stone.

6. **Iolite:** "I need to be light."

7. **White Howlite:** Focus and clarity stone.

8. **Shungite:** The black beauty.

9. **Auralite 23:** Mack daddy multivitamin.

10. **Black Tourmaline:** "Nasty begone!" or the big blocker.

11. **Rose Quartz:** My lovey stone.

Here they are in more detail.

1. Lepidolite

Ze' Prozac stone (with a French accent, because it's fun). It is a harmonizer and balances your moods. It opens your third eye chakra and enhances inner wisdom. Moody? Grab one!

2. Ruby Zoisite

The getter done stone. It looks like candy, but don't eat it! A super motivator stone, it gets you moving in a positive direction. Many tasks can be completed when holding or wearing this stone of high vibration. Ruby Zoisite affects all of your chakras.

3. Moldavite

The meteorite that makes you feel uninhibited. It is a relaxer, releaser, and great for the heart and crown chakras. It releases unwanted emotions and can induce a spiritual out-of-body experience to make you feel floaty and powerful! Uptight? Moldavite is for you. Moldavite works on all chakras but mostly the heart and crown chakras.

4. Golden Calcite

Known as the sex stone, Golden Calcite is an aphrodisiac. It brings energy and awareness to your sacral chakra and enhances a positive connection with your sex organs and creativity. Need your sexy back? If you can't find Justin Timberlake, hold a Golden Calcite instead. Golden Calcite works on the sacral and solar plexus chakras.

5. Citrine

The moolah stone, or the happiness, abundance, and money stone. Lay one on your checkbook or wallet for manifesting *cha-ching* powers. Place Citrine in your home to change the energy to feel protected and positive. Citrine works on the solar plexus chakra, root chakra, and the crown chakra.

6. Iolite

"I need to be light." Iolite helps you get real and mindful. It can alleviate patterns and addictions, enhance your intuition, and help you release stress and unwanted energies. It helps you connect on a soul level and opens the sixth and seventh chakras. Iolite promotes understanding and clarity.

7. White Howlite

The stone for focus and clarity. White Howlite activates the root and third eye chakras. Great for studying, work, and being present in the moment.

8. Shungite

The black beauty for total protection. Shungite can be used as a water purifier and has antiaging properties. It can shield and protect our electromagnetic fields (auras) from cell phone waves, computers, and negative radiation. It allows and enhances a positive well-being.

9. Auralite 23

The mack daddy multivitamin. This one has the healing power of 23 mineral energies. Auralite 23 is mainly good for protection and healing; it's also good for DNA healing and cellular activation. Known as the stone that awakens all. Well then, I'll take one of these miracle crystals!

10. Black Tourmaline

"Nasty begone!" The big blocker. Black Tourmaline works with your root chakra. It can help you be present and grounded. It keeps negativity out of your aura and space and works as a barrier to block negative vibes from affecting you.

11. Rose Quartz

My lovey stone helps you emit and attract love. This pretty pink lady has the vibrations to guide you to smart choices in relationships. Want a happy home? Place a specimen of any size in your home and feel the loving energy emerge.

Considering the Size of Your Crystals

Sometimes size matters. Lots of people think they have to have humongous stones or crystals to make a difference in the power of the healing. Using multiple or bigger crystals can sometimes allow you to feel them stronger. However, I think of it as adding up the vibrations. If a stone like an Aragonite Star Cluster holds a Yowzer vibe and you have ten small (about the size of a penny) to midsize (about two inches rounded) Aragonites around your body, you're going to feel it more than one large Aragonite Star Cluster.

On the other hand, using a Moldavite Tektite piece of about three grams is just as powerful as using a big Moldavite. Again, this is assuming you learned which crystals and gemstones work and harmonize with one another and understand their purpose in the crystal healing session.

Choosing Power Stones

You might shop crystal stores and find power stones, or a crystal or gemstone that is the size of a baseball. They are biggies. I like to use them as paperweights and for meditation. You can hold one conveniently in your palm while meditating. They are powerful in the way of size. Like I said, size doesn't always matter, but some people like to feel a charge of energy with some literal weight. I particularly like these power stones because they are comfortable to hold when I want to do crystal sessions while sitting.

My five favorite power stones are Mookaite, Red Jasper, Unakite, Sodalite, and Tiger's Iron.

Mookaite is a form of Jasper. Mookaite is yellow and brown and has unique swirls within it. Mookaite is great for days when I feel down; it brings me self-confidence, self-worthiness, and helps me think of many ways to shift my emotions.

Red Jasper is strength of my body and mind; it also helps me stay grounded when I start too many projects and need some focus. Red Jasper brings me back to Earth when I'm floating out from too many tasks.

Unakite is a greenish-pink stone that is grounding and keeps me in line with my purpose. Unakite is for insight, prophecy, visions, stress relief, and creating positive change in one's mindset.

Sodalite, the blue beauty, opens my third eye and helps me seek truth when I feel confused or need direction respecting my needs and the needs of others.

Tiger's Iron is different from Tiger's Eye because it holds Hematite within it, making it appear with silver lines throughout the browns and golds of traditional Tiger's Eye. Hematite has metallic properties and brings grounding and shifts of thought. Tiger's Iron brings true balance in the mind and body. It syncs both to be more relaxed and centers one's thoughts.

Consider Your Sign

Another way you can choose stones is by astrological sign. I can tell you frankly that I constantly need grounding stones. Since I have so much Scorpio in my astrology chart, I take on a lot of emotions from others and myself. Grounding stones give me what I need to stay sane!

Since we are on astrology, let's make it fun and see which stones work best for your sign. Here are some traditional crystals and gemstones that correlate according to the knowledge I've acquired through crystal healing:

Aries: March 21–April 19—Herkimer Diamond, Rainbow Quartz

Taurus: April 20–May 20—Emerald, Pietersite

Gemini: May 21–June 21—Quartz, Sunstone

Cancer: June 22–July22—Ruby, Iolite

Leo: July 23–August 22—Peridot, Citrine

Virgo: August 23–September 22—Sapphire, Chrysocolla

Libra: September 23–October 22—Pink Opal, Cavansite

Scorpio: October 23–November 21—Topaz, Kunzite

Sagittarius: November 22–December 21—Turquoise, Auralite 23

Capricorn: December 22–January 19—Garnet, Amber

Aquarius: January 20–February 18—Amethyst, Celestite

Pisces: February 19–March 20—Aquamarine, Nirvana Crystal

Crystal Wands

When you are selecting your crystals, you might also consider trying a crystal wand. Crystal wands are crystals shaped to use for healing and holding in your hands. They are magical wands for they hold energy that can change your chakras and aura layers to be balanced and positive.

Wands come in varieties. Their shape and size make your sessions comfy. Holding a crystal wand eases the need to grasp or clench while having a crystal session. You want to be relaxed. You don't want to be tightly holding anything! The wands have sleek shapes that make for natural holds. You can find wands that are short or long, smooth or coarse. Some crystal wands have an indent to relax your thumb on.

There are zillions of types of wands. Some are made precisely for crystal healings. The ones you see most commonly are chakra wands. This means they have stones on or within them that balance the chakras of your body. These can be held by the user or facilitator. There are double-terminated wands, or wands with points on both ends. These are perfect for when you are looking to release and change the body's energy, allowing the good to come in and the negative to flow out. I suggest a Clear Quartz double-terminated wand for this type of crystal healing work.

Wands with only one point are beneficial as well; think of it as directing the energy flow from the body. If I were to hold a single-pointed wand in my hand and I wanted to release negativity from my energy fields, I would have the pointed end facing away from my body. If I wanted to bring positive flow of energy into my body, I would aim the point toward me. I could also aim the point toward my grid to fill the grid with positivity.

Now that you have learned about several crystal tools and how to use them, it is most important that you know how to cleanse all of your crystals. This includes cleansing and clearing your personal collection and the crystals that you may be using on other people for crystal body layouts.

Cleansing and Clearing Your Gem Babies

Can crystals get dirty? Can they hold negative energy? Sure they can! Well, all of them except Selenite. Crystals and gems can hold negative vibrations once they are used for a period of time. It's like wearing your socks multiple times; they sure are going to get stinky because they are soiled with dirt and grime. Yeah, they need a washing. Cleanse those smelly nellies. Same goes for crystals and gems—they can pick up or hold some yuck too!

There are so many ways you can clean your babies. Always use your positive intentions. Intentions are what you desire and project. These are positive thoughts that can clear the lower energy vibes around you and your crystals. It is best to clear and cleanse your crystals and crystal jewelry at least once a month.

You cleanse them by using the following:

1. Herbs / sage

2. Sunshine / moon rays

3. Water

4. Sound vibrations

5. Other stones such as Selenite

6. Salt

7. Breath

8. Positive intention

1. Use the herb sage to clear them.

Roll them in herbs, or, if it's a sage stick, you can burn the sage; the smoke around the crystals will clear their energy. The sage bush has been used for centuries by people looking to protect, clear, and cleanse. White sage is wild in Arizona and California and, of course, cultivated to sell. Some of you may not be familiar with using sage. To sage is to clear and cleanse a space or object, people, or anything you need or want to free from negative vibrations. If it feels bad, I say sage it! It's quite liberating and it's an easy process. You may also hear it called "smudging." These terms are synonymous in metaphysical terminology.

To purchase some sage, go online or to a metaphysical store and purchase white sage, mugwort (also called black sage), pine, cedar, juniper (healing sage), 5 directions, and/or love sage. There are many varieties and they mostly come bundled with a string. They are often called *smudge sticks* or *sage bundles*. You can also buy sage loose. Loose sage is good if you have an abalone shell to keep it in while it's burning.

Smudge sticks come in different sizes: mini, medium, large, jumbo—you get it. If you have a home of 1,000 square feet or less, the mini will do with plenty left over. Note that some sages are combined with other herbs. One of the most common combinations is white sage with lavender; this one smells amazing. The other popular type is called *5 directions sage*; this one is my favorite. It has five herbal scents that burn together and smell really great. It usually contains a bit of white sage, pine, cedar, mugwort, and lavender. All of these are combined in one bundle.

Now you need to know how to burn sage. Use a lighter or match to light one end of the smudge stick and hold the other end with your hand. Please know that sage does not ignite and become a huge flame; it is a smoldering herb that burns slowly and gets very smoky. If you have fire alarms, be mindful that they may be set off. The next step is to hold the lighted sage and state your intention that this space, home, office, or whatever or whomever you are cleansing is clean and clear and protected. Say this with your inner voice or out loud. Repeat it as you go into each room or around the object or person. If you're cleansing a home or space, you will walk in each room and use the smoking sage to faintly outline each door and window with smoke. Do not touch the walls or draperies. You are just doing an air outline of every entrance door and window while stating that the space is clean, clear, and protected. Go through the entire home; it should only take about five minutes unless you have a huge home.

If you are smudging your crystals, state the same mantra. The same goes for a person. Smudging crystals or people will take even less time than smudging a home. Make sure you do not get too close to the person; about three feet away is a perfect distance to sage. You don't want to get the smoke in their lungs or make them uncomfortable.

Take the remaining sage and snuff it out in a glass cup full of dirt or sand. This will stop the burning. You can put it out under running water, but if you want to use the herb again, be aware that water can cause mold. It is best to snuff it with sand. If you want to use loose sage, it comes in small pieces. You would need a three-inch or larger abalone shell to hold the sage leaves. Abalone shells are best because the holes in the shell allow the sage smoke to filter through. After you light the sage in the shell, you would use the same routine as described previously.

2. Leave your crystals or gems out in the sunlight or moonlight for at least four hours.

Your crystals can be charged and cleansed of negative vibes with sun and moon vibrations. Any crystal, even those with their own cleansing frequencies, can be enhanced by absorbing the vibrations of the moon and sun.

I prefer to charge my crystals in the sunlight. I feel this is because I am a morning person; I like to get up early and enjoy those awakening frequencies of the sun. I've noticed that people tend to resonate more with the moon if they're night owls. The sun and moon are equally good cleansing and charging forces, which is nice for those of us who want options while creating great energy vibes for our crystal stashes!

You may be thinking, "What is the best time of year to place crystals out in the sun or moonlight?" There is no bad time or month. I set my crystals out every month in the sunlight. I call it monthly maintenance for my crystals—the sun keeps them refreshed and cleansed.

3. Run them under water.

Please be mindful to not wash Selenite or salt stones. These stones will disintegrate in fresh or salt water. If they are tumbled stones or polished crystal jewelry, please note that salt water can take away the shine and harm the jewelry. In this case, use fresh water.

4. Use sounds of high vibration.

There are many ways to use sound to clear and cleanse your crystals and stones. You can use mantras, Tibetan singing bowls, crystal singing bowls, and tuning forks.

Mantras are chants or words with a positive high frequency that can clear your stones, body, and room. The words *love*, *gratitude*, and *ohm* are just a few that can raise your body's frequencies if said repeatedly. Clearing your stones with your voice is fun. I love to stretch the words out long and deep. *OHHHHMMM*. Try it. You will feel a positive shift in your body's energy.

Tibetan and crystal bowls are another great option for crystal cleansing. Tibetan singing bowls are made of metals and are tuned to have positive frequencies that balance and align all chakras and clear the aura of negative energies and low vibrations. You can also use a singing bowl to clear your space of negative vibrations. It is important to cleanse a room before and after a crystal healing session, before to get unwanted energy out, and after in case you or your client releases and leaves negativity in the space. Tibetan singing bowls can cost 40 US dollars or more depending on the size and if they are handmade.

Crystal singing bowls are made of pure crystals. The most common is made of clear or frosted Quartz. You can find specialty crystal bowls made of Moldavite, Rhodochrosite, and others. These bowls can be quite costly and are considered an investment. I have seen them range from 90 to 5,000 dollars. When you shop for a bowl, keep in mind that the bowl's size is not indicative of a louder sound or stronger frequency, but rather tailored for specific chakras. For instance, a Quartz bowl that is tuned specifically for the resonance of the third eye chakra is smaller than a bowl tuned to the frequency of the root chakra. The root chakra requires a much larger and thicker bowl to resonate. Overall, Tibetan and crystal bowls can be made and tuned for all chakras or a specific chakra, and the size will be created according to the needed resonance. I love the way these bowls sound; they are relaxing and create a sound bath that scrubs your crystals and your entire body inside and out. To clear your crystals, simply lay your crystals inside the bowl and play the bowl, or lightly tap the outside of the bowl with the wooden dowel to make it vibrate with sound. Just a few minutes of playing the bowl will cleanse you, your room, and the stones.

Tuning forks produce another type of sound you can use to cleanse and clear your crystals. They are made of aluminum or Quartz. Have you heard of tuning forks? Quite a few doctors use them for healing muscles, bones, and nerves. Tuning forks are tuned with pitch and frequency; they are two-pronged acoustic resonators. Each one can be tuned to a different resonance. There are tuning forks that are tuned to all the planets' frequencies. I have a whole set of planetary tuning forks that I use in healing sessions. Each one is tuned to a different planet: Mars, Earth, Pluto, Venus, Neptune, Saturn,

Jupiter, and Uranus. Each planet has its own hertz, the measure of frequency and tone, or resonance. Sound is healing because we as humans are made up of approximately 85 percent water, and sound travels five times faster through water than through any other substance. Through my research, I've found that the faster a sound wave travels through our human bodies, the faster we heal. Tuning forks can also "heal" crystals by cleansing them and restoring their pure frequencies.

5. Place a Selenite stone on top of or below your crystals.

As long as it is touching the stones you would like to clear, Selenite will automatically cleanse them instantly! You can find long, big pieces of Selenite, and these can be used as "clearing plates." I place all of my crystals on top once a month or after a crystal healing session to clear someone else's aura from them.

6. Use salt.

You can roll your stones and crystals in coarse sea salt or wash them with salt water. This includes the ocean. Remember what I mentioned about polished stones or metals! Salt can corrode the shine and luster.

7. Use your breath.

Think of something beautiful or powerful and simultaneously blow over your stones to cleanse them. This is an ancient way of clearing all negativity from one's body and items in hand. In shamanism rituals, breath is a way to cleanse and release. I use my breath to clear out negative energy from a person's aura during a crystal session; I imagine pulling the negativity from their auric layers and using my breath to vanish the energy that no longer serves their highest and greater good. I always make sure I use a breath mint. I am Italian. I love garlic. Garlic can scare away vampires and your clientele!

8. Use your intention.

Using intention with all of the cleansing methods above is the best way to clear and purify anything. State, "I am clearing and cleansing my stones and my space"; this mantra contains high vibrations. It is positive energy that is directed from your mind and will clear anything you wish, including your precious crystals!

Sometimes Crystals Need a Break

Sometimes crystals need a break. If you drop or break a crystal, do not worry, but know that this could be a sign. They still hold their amazing frequencies when broken; however, your energy fields or aura may not need that particular crystal or gemstone's offerings at that time. You were not listening to your little crystal buddy and kept on holding or wearing it. This can cause it to break or change colors. Think of it like this: If you are at your max of vitamin C, you can get sick from taking too much. Likewise, have you ever been around a person who takes every ounce of energy out of you? If you stay around them, you are likely to tell them off or explode with frustration. Well, that is your crystal. It's had enough of you for now. Give the crystal baby a break! Your crystal holds and emits frequencies to help you heal, balance, release, adjust, or advance. If you already got what you needed from it, its job is done. Let your crystal refresh and recover by getting charged by the sun or moon's positive energy. You may have overloaded it. Another explanation is you were just a klutz that day and broke it!

Choosing Crystal Frequencies: Combating Negative Energy

Sometimes you may want to select your stones based on their frequency. When we get into the section defining the 66 crystals that we will be using, you'll see that I've indicated the frequency level of each as a guide to help you choose which type of energy you're looking for.

Each crystal, gemstone, or mineral holds and emits these frequencies. Anything and everything that exists on Earth holds a vibration; basically, everything is "energy." This is why sound can be healing. Sound frequencies from tuning forks and crystal singing bowls can travel through our skin, blood, and bones, healing us from the inside out to some degree. Those vibrational frequencies travel through our entire bodies. Frequencies that our human eyes cannot easily see can help heal us.

An example of harmful frequencies are those of cellular phones. These little computers emit and transmit frequencies too. However, these vibrations are not positive for our human bodies and cause physical and mental degeneration. Some call these EMFs lower or negative vibrations. The best way I can explain this to you is that the electromagnetic field that surrounds our human bodies is permeable. This means that our strong auras (electromagnetic fields) can be penetrated by negative vibes that can cause damage to our energy fields. These harmful vibrations are frequencies that can be blocked or avoided, but, in today's world, it is hard. Almost every person owns a cell phone, computer, TV, dishwasher, and a power service connected to their home or apartment. It is tough to avoid negative frequencies, especially when every town has several huge cellular towers emitting 24/7. What can we do?

Well, honestly and realistically, all we can do is limit the closeness of those items. Here are some tips:

1. Keep your cell phone in a separate room when you sleep. Never sleep with a cell phone near your body. Limit your time using your phone when holding it to your head.

2. Situate your bed to be away from any power outlets or utility intakes. Most people sleep six to eight hours—think about intruding negative vibes in your sleeping space and energy field for that long. That is definitely not a good thing!

3. Most dishwashers, TVs, and computers have smart chips within them; this allows the electric companies to see your usage of energy and estimate how many people are in your home. These smart chips connect constantly to your main utility power box that is normally located outside an exterior wall of the home or apartment. The smart chips allow these frequencies to connect several hundred times on a day-to-day basis. I know—scary! These negative frequencies can make you very sensitive and may cause illnesses. Smart chips really can suck the life out of you.

4. To help alleviate some of those negative waves, place a stone called Shungite close to those items. Shungite can help block negative EMFs from your space and guard the body's physical and energetic body/aura.

Selecting a Healing Stone: Shungite

Okay, I have to talk about this miracle stone. There are so many uses for Shungite. Let me say—not super pretty or shiny. It looks like coal!

I once sat on a Shungite healing pad. It was crushed up Shungite made into a square material for placing anywhere on the body. So I sat on it. My butt was hurting, but I wanted to see if I'd feel different if I did something unusual with it. I was really feeling tingles in my butt, and then the energy of the stone went up to my spine, and then I felt it over my entire body.

It was an experience I will never forget. It moved within 20 minutes from my butt to all of me. It went from my lower back to my knees, then to my ankles and feet; the upward sensations went from my lower back through my arms and the entire front of my body up to my head. I felt my energy shift, and, knowing that Shungite is great for EMF protection, I admit I was in front of my computer all day before I decided to sit on it. Now I sit on it all the time when I'm working on my computer. It truly helps relieve pains and those nasty nugatory vibes that can harm my creative abilities. My friends say Shungite still does not help my spelling abilities, but that is something I can live with.

Shungite is found in Karelia, Russia. It is the only place on Earth with naturally occurring Shungite as far as geologists know to date. Shungite is formed in a shallow water area where carbonite is present. You can drink Shungite-cleansed water directly from Russia's Lake Onega! Shungite can purify water from just about everything that can cause us harm. It can cleanse water of bacteria, pesticides, and metals. That is pretty amazing.

Shungite has been used in medical treatments since the early eighteenth century. The Russian army used Shungite to purify their water for the troops. The antibacterial properties of Shungite have been confirmed by modern testing. I learned that Shungite was also used in the eighteenth century as paint. Neato!

I totally believe in the Shungite healing properties—big time. I use it for its properties in my drinking water. I have Shungite all over my home. I keep most of it hidden since it looks like black coal. It's not super pretty; however, they are making it in nice geometric shapes nowadays. I have Shungite behind my TV to protect my space from smart meter frequencies. I keep a chunk on my computer, my cell phone, and outside where my electric meter joins with my house. I placed a bag of Shungite chips around my home and yard. I'm protecting my aura as much as I can! I know it sounds like a lot, but seriously, I'd rather spend my money on Shungite than on frivolous things because Shungite is proven to benefit my body and environment.

Making Friends with Your Crystals

You will start to notice you will kind of make friends with your crystals. Some of you may hear them talking louder to you, telling you ancient stories and how to use them for healing and other information like that. This is not crazy talk; this is just part of you getting deeply connected to your energy buddies. This is the true sign that you are now a crystal junkie. Welcome.

I talk to my crystal buddies all the time. I know all of their names—common courtesy. Honestly, it's amazing to connect with energies that can help you heal and download information—crystals contain mega-knowledge. They can open new perspectives, change your bad thoughts to positive, take you out of a depression, and so much more! I'm telling you, these are your new buds. Treat them righteously.

Sharing is great. You will feel the need to give a crystal away once in a while. Your inner knowing will tell you when another person needs your crystal bud more than you do. It's also possible your crystal buddy will tell you to let go and stop being so needy, that they need to be cleansed or need to be alone for a bit. It's all good. Just honor the energies.

Chapter 3
66 Crystals and Their Level of Frequency

You will now be introduced to the fabulous 66 crystals that will enhance your life. I know you are eager to learn more. I list the crystals and give you sweet details of how you can use each. Along with this useful information, you will find the coordinating *vibe meter* to let you know the level of power each crystal gives off. If you have some of these crystals currently in your stash, it would be superb of you to hold them one at a time, for a minute or so, to notice what level you feel. Take a few notes about each of the crystals you held and felt. My personal vibe meter has four levels that gauge the frequency felt by me and other crystal users that I have performed crystal healing sessions with. Check it out!

Yowzer is the immediate and fast punch of energy. This means these crystals/stones have the highest vibrations that can kick your butt into gear quickly. Fast results arise from usage of this stone. This crystal used alone is super potent; this crystal used with others is a powerhouse of healing. You can feel these crystal babies right off the bat. If you use them long term (up to 60 minutes), you are going to be feeling high vibes for sure.

Grounded Chill is about recharging with a slow and steady energy. It can be for building energy, cleansing, or releasing. These particular crystals or gemstones feel extraordinary. They usually give a bit of instant feeling, but, as you work with them, their sensation becomes progressively stronger. It's a chill feeling because the stones gradually take you to the balance you need from them. Working with these crystals is definitely felt in the energy field. They are vibing at frequencies that can be recognized as slow, strong, and steady.

Mellow Soother is about calmness, relaxation, and finding soothing energy that acts "undercover," running subtly in the background. This means the crystal/stone is more Snoop Dogg's style—mellow and slow, but it works well. It's at its best when used with other crystals. Some people may not feel their vibrations in a strong manner, but the crystals are still working—just incognito. These crystals encourage good feelings and peacefulness.

Enlightened stones are those that connect you to higher realms, spirit guides, your source, and Angels. They can bring higher knowledge from other realms of existence. They give a feeling of unconditional love: a powerful yet beautiful light feeling. You may feel that your energy body is lifted up to the sky, safely and compassionately.

By the way, if you don't feel the same thing I feel from these crystals, that's cool. We all are equipped with different frequencies that make our soul's energy original. Check out each crystal and make your own cool crystal meter. It is fun to do.

Now, allow me to introduce you to your new crystal babies! These 66 crystals will rock your crystal body layouts and your everyday life.

1. Agate, Blue Lace

Vibe Meter: Mellow Soother

The Chakras: 5th throat

Light blue with streaks of white and an almost layered appearance, Blue Lace Agate is a beautiful stone that can be used on the throat chakra to open communications with others in human life. It can bring creativeness out and help you express your feelings in a truthful way. Blue Lace Agate helps you realize you can do anything if you put forth the effort. This stone is also wonderful for working comfortably with children. If you are a mother or teacher, professor or psychologist, this one is great on your office desk. Blue Lace Agate can help you gain better listening and communication skills. It gives you relief with calming energies to soothe your mood.

2. Agate, Moss

♣

Vibe Meter: Grounded Chill

The Chakras: 2nd sacral and 1st base root

Moss Agate is a true grounding stone, colored a light to dark green that sometimes will have flecks of white or brown. It heals the heart and brings balance and sensible thoughts. If you feel too spacey, keep this in your pocket, or use it for a choice meditation that brings balance and grounding to your body and thoughts.

3. Agate, Thunder

✷

The Shaman Stone

Vibe Meter: Yowzer

The Chakras: All—7th crown, 6th third eye, 5th throat,
4th heart, 3rd solar plexus, 2nd sacral, and 1st base root

Thunder Agate is a Yowzer because it really sets you straight in being grounded and feeling loved at the same time. It opens your crown chakra but keeps you aware of your surroundings. It brings a safe and powerful feeling. You may feel the energy of Native American spirits as you hold it; I have experienced this spirit energy on countless occasions. Thunder Agate contains Chalcedony and markings that can look like animals or picturesque scenery. I love to do group meditations and add Thunder Agates to the room. I make an event out of it. I create a nature grid in the center of the room. I set the chairs for the participants in a circle around the crystal and elemental grid. My main crystal is the Thunder Agate. I try to get a big one the size of a cantaloupe; it looks impressive. Plus, the frequencies it emits are grounding and connect to everyone's root chakra while simultaneously allowing the crown chakras to open. This is a very balancing type of meditation and grid to create. I then place the Thunder Agate in the middle of the circle. I use flower or rose petals for outlining a circle on the floor. The idea is to use earth, fire, water, wind, and metal to create elemental energies that synergize with our auras. Next, I add water to a wooden bowl and set three raw Quartzes inside. You could also use one bigger Rainbow Quartz Point. If you use the Rainbow Quartz Point/generator, place it in the water with the point aiming out of the water (at least the tip of it). Inside the petals circle is where I place all of these items. Then I add quarter-sized pieces of copper to the bowl of water with the crystal Quartz. Copper is a conduit of energy and will help connect the Quartz and water to super-duper amplify the frequencies that can be felt by the group. I now have the water, metal (copper), earth (crystals and flowers), and I will use fire to light my sage. I light the sage when I begin the meditation to clear the space of any negativity. My breath (wind) blows the lit sage out. I do all of these steps with intentions of a positive experience for all my attendees. If you try this in a group, you can enhance the session by having each person hold a crystal in their hands during the meditation. I suggest a Thunder Agate, a Tiger's Eye, or a crystal Quartz of any kind. Just one per person. All the crystals in the room, inside or outside the nature grid, will connect. My group sessions for crystal meditation are 60 minutes. I like to let everyone feel the crystal in their hands during the session. Some people may have visions or feel "visitors." When the meditation is completed, I ask the participants to step within the flower circle. This way they can feel the energy. One by one, I allow each person to stand inside. Many of them feel the extra-amplified energy inside the circle. Both inside and out have beautiful energy vibrations. One person may notice something stronger than another and share their experiences. It is enjoyable for everyone. I occasionally do a nature grid solo. I find it makes me grounded to Momma Earth and connected to my sources. I feel genuinely protected.

4. Agate, Various Colors

♣

Strength and Stability

Vibe Meter: Grounded Chill

The Chakras: 2nd sacral and 1st base root

Agates can be many colors: blue, brown, red, or yellow. Agates usually have banded formations or lines running through the various colors of the stone. You can sort of see through them. Agates hold great energetic properties: they encourage calmness and consciousness of life's experiences, promote inner growth and sensibility, and can balance the physical body and all the aura layers. One particular Agate, Zebra Agate, is black and white. This one is strong in balancing your physical, emotional, and mental auras. I think of it as the Yin and Yang stone balancing one's male and female aspects. Darker Agates, such as greens and browns, are generally root chakra stones; they ground and bring structure or order to one's life and thought process. You can get beautiful slices of Agates in a variety of colors. Agates are perfect for an office. They are picturesque, make great pieces of art, and bring dynamic qualities of success.

5. *Amazonite*

Balances All of You

Vibe Meter: Mellow Soother

The Chakras: All—7th crown, 6th third eye, 5th throat,
4th heart, 3rd solar plexus, 2nd sacral, and 1st base root

I call this stone Amazing-nite. It does so many great things; it aligns and balances all the energy centers in your body! Yeah, all 144,000 of them, including the top seven chakras! Amazonite jump-starts self-determination, helps discard feelings of victimhood, and encourages you to take charge of your life. It balances moods and dissolves sadness. Amazonite brings a person to self-realization and rational thinking. It can help harmonize the thymus gland and strengthen the nerves and brain. I particularly use Amazonite in my jewelry. Wearing Amazonite balances me and makes me feel happy. I have a unique bracelet made of it; it instantly soothes me from daily stressors.

6. *Amber*

Vibe Meter: Yowzer

The Chakras: 3rd solar plexus and 2nd sacral

Amber is a powerful orange-gold color, gradually formed from a tree resin that has aged millions of years. It was a healing stone and amulet for at least 1,000 years. It represents freedom, good luck, and happiness. Amber can help you be more flexible in thoughts and with others.

Amber helps with digestion, the spleen and kidneys, and helps joint problems. This may be too much information, but your digestion can be accelerated when wearing Amber. I've tried this, and boy does it work—super fast, by the way; at least it did for me! I wasn't trying to use it for that. I was in my shop trying on some new merchandise, one being an Amber necklace. I had it on for only 15 minutes, and I felt movement. It actually was kind of funny because I didn't realize it was the necklace until later. Amber is great for internal organ functions and for balancing them. Emotionally, Amber helps you be less judgmental or critical of yourself and others.

Amber accelerates the healing of wounds. For small children, it alleviates teething pains. Amber works best if the mother wears it while holding the child. This is a transference process. If you use it on a baby or small child, please tape the piece of Amber under the crib where the baby will not be able to grab or eat it. If you want to put a big piece in the baby's socks, make sure you double sock and place the Amber between the socks, because Amber can be sharp if broken. There are baby bracelets and necklaces with Amber beads, but be mindful if the baby chews or breaks the beads; you don't want them swallowing the Amber! The necklaces and bracelets should be double or triple knotted so they are more kid-proof.

7. Amethyst

Vibe Meter: Enlightened

The Chakras: 7th crown, 6th third eye, and 4th heart

Ah, Amethyst. It relaxes all of you. The words to describe Amethyst are *homey*, *loving*, *protective*, *calming*, and *super Zen*.

The world-famous purple crystal (part of the Quartz family) encourages spiritual awakenings, gives insight, helps alleviate sadness/grief, and quiets the mind. In meditation, Amethyst can be placed on the body or in the aura for healing. Ultimately, Amethyst relaxes the body and mind together. It encourages sobriety, rids pains, and releases tensions. It's great to put under the pillow for a restful night's sleep. Amethyst is perfect for everyone; you can't go wrong with giving an Amethyst as a gift. When I want to make a space feel welcoming, I add an Amethyst.

8. Angelite

The Connector

Vibe Meter: Enlightened

The Chakras: 7th crown, 6th third eye, and 4th heart

This stone is a dreamy light blue and brings communications with Angels and energies of the light realm. It helps with telepathic communication and astrological understandings. Angelite instills calm and compassion in one's being and soul. Angelite is perfect for any healing session.

9. Apache Tears

Vibe Meter: Mellow Soother

The Chakras: 4th heart and 1st base root

Apache Tears are native to Mexico and the southwestern United States. They are used in some cultures as tokens to help others with grief and all types of loss. Apache Tears are a variety of Obsidian, a glass-like volcanic rock formation, and are mostly black and roundish. They are semitransparent and can sometimes look as if some white powder is on them; this is sediment from where Apache Tears are found. Apache Tears can instantly ground you, assisting the root chakra and healing the heart chakra.

10. Apatite

Vibe Meter: Grounded Chill

The Chakras: 5th throat, 3rd solar plexus, 2nd sacral, and 1st base root

Apatite is bluish-green and is quite pretty. It is a mineral used in the medical field to build bone and enamels in the human body. It's also used for fertilizers.

This healing stone is wonderful for healing any bone issues, such as broken bones, and helps relieve pain in the "human casing" (body form). Believe it or not, Apatite is also being deployed to defend against radioactive material in the groundwater near the Columbia River.

Apatite is quite amazing to me since I have recently been receiving channeled messages about phosphate, the main component of Apatite. My Angel guides have been expressing that I should research phosphate and how it will help humans in the future. I received clairvoyant messages that Earth would become more and more contaminated with radioactive and environmental toxins, but would be able to recover using natural resources, such as crystals and stones, to counteract contaminants. I feel it's important to know how to use natural resources like Apatite to combat man-made pollution.

As of now, I am a big fan of Apatite. Imagine if we combined Apatite with Shungite stones—we would have an unstoppable positive healing weapon.

11. Apophyllite

Unicorn!

Vibe Meter: Yowzer

The Chakras: 7th crown, 6th third eye, and 4th heart

This is a gorgeous clear blue, green, or yellowish color. Apophyllites are actually naturally formed crystal pyramids. Apophyllite is very bright, light crystal that promotes reflection; it is great for grids, energy work, and meditation. Apophyllites magnify and focus energy through the apex of the pyramid shape and can enhance intuition. It's a wonderful crystal for the third eye and crown chakras by virtue of its bright clarity formed naturally into a pyramidal shape, exemplifying the high spiritual vibration of sacred geometry. It can connect one to the higher planes, bringing new wisdom through the subconscious. Apophyllites are in the Quartz family, which makes them amplifiers of goodness. Apophyllite crystals can help one increase intuition, connect with guides, and practice remote viewing and astral travel. Place this unicorn crystal on your third eye chakra (between your eyebrows) and float into another dimension. Here's the fine print of this crystal: Apophyllite is not recommended for wussies who can't handle possibly seeing a parallel dimension.

An Apophyllite is called an Apophyllite Pyramid as well. They, again, activate the third eye and crown chakras, making them more receptive to spiritual energies. Apophyllite's frequency can enable one to receive visions and insights about current situations, personal or otherwise. Meditating with an Apophyllite Pyramid on the third eye chakra can not only enhance one's psychic visions and clairvoyance, but it can also promote structure and organization in daily life. Apophyllite can help one to plan for one's future with certainty, despite any negative past experiences. While Apophyllite is predominantly a spiritual crystal, it does have physical healing properties as well. It can regulate bodily functions and improve memory. It also helps get rid of the habit of wanting too much.

12. Aquamarine

The Soother

Vibe Meter: Mellow Soother

The Chakras: 5th throat

Aquamarine is a form of Beryl. It ranges from green to light blue. Aquamarine clears up wishy-washy thinking and is a healing mineral that can harmonize the pituitary and thyroid glands, regulating hormone balance. This is also great for the throat chakra and for eye, ear, and throat health. Aquamarine is perfect for body layouts; it can be placed on or off the body. I use it on the eyelids for improvement of sight. I usually place a clean washcloth over the eyes then the Aquamarine on top. Aquamarine calms autoimmune disorders and is great to dissipate hay fever and allergies. You can substitute Aquamarine with a Blue Lace Agate in most cases. If your session calls for Aquamarine and you only have Blue Lace Agate, your crystal layout will harmonize fluidly with either. Both stones encourage spiritual growth, foresight, and clairaudience. They relieve stress emotionally and from the physical body.

Agate, *Blue Lace*

Agate, *Moss*

Agate, *Thunder*

Agate, *Various Colors*

Amazonite

Amber

Amethyst

Angelite

Apache Tears

Apatite

Apophyllite

Aquamarine

Aragonite

Auralite 23

Aventurine, *Green*

Azurite

Calcite, Yellow/Orange/Golden/Honey

Carnelian

Cavansite *(only the blue parts are Cavansite)*

Celestite

Chalcedony

Charoite

Chrysoprase

Citrine

Danburite

Dioptase

Emerald

Epidote

Fluorite

Garnet

Herkimer Diamond

Howlite, *White*

Jasper, *Ocean*

Jasper, *Red*

Kunzite

Kyanite, *Blue*

Lapis Lazuli

Lemurian Seeds

Lepidolite

Malachite

Moldavite

Moonstone

Nirvana/Ice Crystal

Obsidian, *Black*

Obsidian, *Snowflake*

Opal, *Pink*

Opalite

Pietersite

Pyrite

Quartz, *Clear*

Quartz, *Rose/Pink*

Quartz, *Rutile*

Quartz, *Smoky*

Rhodochrosite

Ruby Zoisite

Salt

Selenite

Shungite

Sodalite

Sunstone

Super 7

Tiger's Eye

Tourmaline, *Black*

Tourmaline, *Green*

Turquoise

Unakite

13. Aragonite

Vibe Meter: Yowzer and Grounded Chill

The Chakras: 2nd sacral and 1st base root

A wonder stone known as a star crystal. It has the appearance of coral and comes in a variety of colors, such as white, pink, yellow, green, or brown. Rusty orange-brown is the most common. Aragonite stabilizes spiritual developments that are moving too fast. It calms restlessness, brings flexibility in behaviors, stimulates muscular activity, and strengthens the immune system. Some people refer to Aragonite as a star cluster. This curative star cluster can help you ground. It helps with digestive complaints, makes one feel good in one's body, and can make you feel whole. I love Aragonite because it not only has all those great qualities, but it also seamlessly clears debris off your auric field. I feel the stone's power instantly! Take an Aragonite Star Cluster, place it by your feet for 15 minutes, and notice the grounding and clearing you receive.

14. Auralite 23

Vibe Meter: Yowzer

The Chakras: All—7th crown, 6th third eye, 5th throat,
4th heart, 3rd solar plexus, 2nd sacral, and 1st base root

Oh my gosh! Auralite 23 is all that and a bag of chips. This Canadian beauty can balance and align you and clear your auric field. It can immediately fill your energy/aura layers with positive vibes. I found it helps erase old negative patterns from someone's past, present, and all of their parallel lives on their soul level of existence (if you believe in that).

Auralite 23 has layers of Phantom Chevron Amethyst, which are the lines you see in its structure. One piece of Auralite 23 holds these minerals within: Amethyst, Citrine, Titanite, Cacoxenite, Lepidocrocite, Ajoite, Hematite, Magnetite, Pyrite, Goethite, and Pyrolusite, as well as gold, silver, platinum, nickel, copper, iron, Limonite, Sphalerite, Covellite, Chalcopyrite, Gilalite, Epidote,

Bornite, and Rutile. Auralite 23 supersedes any other crystal formation in my book! Many people feel it instantly cleanses them. I work with Auralite almost every day in my profession. I sit beside a four-pound chunk of Auralite 23 when I channel messages or meditate in order to be grounded and open at the same time; Auralite 23 makes channeling clear. Most people think that when channeling messages from nonhuman sources, like Angels or spirit guides, they solely need to open the crown chakra. It's possible to channel in this manner; however, in my career, I learned that being open at the crown, third eye, and root chakras is the best way to accurately receive messages and guidance from positive sources. It's important to remain connected to Earth through the root chakra while channeling higher knowledge through the crown and third eye so that we don't lose our Earthly presence and can use the insights we gain to benefit our Earthly lives. This is what I trust and believe. Overall, Auralite 23 is my go-to for protection, grounding, connection, enlightenment, trusting, and profound healing. It's everything packed into one!

15. *Aventurine, Green*

Vibe Meter: Mellow Soother

The Chakras: 4th heart

Green Aventurine is a stone formation that can fortify self-determination, bring relaxation, and help with regeneration and recovery. It helps in calming one's anger and intolerances, increases positive perceptions, and reduces judgments of self and others. It works with one's heart chakra and can regenerate the heart, possibly lowering cholesterol levels. It is also known to help with skin disorders and alleviate pains. Green Aventurine is a very comforting stone. If used with Citrine, it brings money and wealth by creating awareness of positive opportunities for abundance. I wrote a mantra for creating abundance: "Money comes my way easily. I can earn it, I can win it, I can be gifted it, and I happily accept it, because I deserve it." I will say this three times, and I can share that it truly works. I find that you have to know you deserve it to receive it.

16. Azurite

Vibe Meter: Yowzer and Enlightened
The Chakras: 7th crown, 6th third eye, and 5th throat

Azurite is a bright, brilliant azure-blue stone. It increases psychic ability and aids in meditation. Azurite is a copper mineral; it is occasionally found as prismatic crystals but is rarely ever faceted. More often it is found in massive form intergrown with Malachite. This is a result of the weathering and oxidation of copper sulfide minerals. It is a beautiful deep-blue stone that awakens the third eye, increases contact with your spiritual guides, and heightens your psychic awareness. The ancient Greeks and Romans used ground forms of the stone for medicinal purposes and for dye. I remember learning about King Tut and the Egyptians as a kid; my teacher said that Egyptians made their eye makeup from stones like Malachite and Azurite. In the hieroglyphic pictures, you can see the bright greens and blues of these stones. I learned in my later years that raw Malachite is poisonous to humans. I often wonder if that is one reason why many ancient Egyptians died at very young ages. If they were painting their eyes and faces with Malachite, then most likely. Just something to ponder.

Azurite is said to relieve arthritis, joint pain, and dizziness/vertigo. It is a liver stimulant and aids in detoxification. Azurite encourages activity of the brain, self-awareness, and inner knowledge. I use Azurite to open my third eye when I feel stuck in my ways. It opens my perception to new ideas and new visions.

17. Calcite, Yellow/Orange/Golden/Honey

Aphrodisiac

Vibe Meter: Yowzer
The Chakras: 5th throat, 4th heart, and 2nd sacral

Calcite activates the sacral chakra, or your sexual organs. This can heal and rev up that area in your body. It can also help you be creative in all aspects of life, love and relationships included. Calcite is an aphrodisiac and gets your motor running. *Bow chica bow wow.* This is a must-have; keep it handy for that hot date or new project.

18. Carnelian

Vibe Meter: Mellow Soother

The Chakras: 4th heart and 2nd sacral

Carnelian is an orange-red stone that is perfect to promote blood flow and invigorate you. Carnelian promotes vitality and creativity and reduces fears of not having enough, negative thoughts, and fears in general. Hold it when you are in need of finding new avenues to add fun and spontaneity to your life. Carnelian is also good for creating new projects and turning your sexual libido up a notch.

Carnelian is an intriguing general healing stone. It can restore the natural energy of your body, vitalize the circulatory system, and heal the heart. Carnelian can also calm angst and bring a sense of humor to your thoughts.

19. Cavansite

Clear Hearing Stone

Vibe Meter: Yowzer and Enlightened

The Chakras: 7th crown, 6th third eye, 5th throat, and 4th heart

Cavansite is a rare mineral made of sparkling bright blue crystals. It is found only in a small area of India and is difficult to mine, making it scarce and pricey. It sometimes forms in clusters within a brownish sediment. Those specimens resemble a robin's egg, but much smaller. Many clairvoyants use Cavansite as it helps strengthen the connection to source energy. I call Cavansite the *radio enhancer,* since I love using it for channeling intuitive messages.

Cavansite unites the throat and third eye chakras for clear insight, effective communication, and greater understanding. Cavansite is a stone of revelation and prophecy, stimulating spiritual breakthroughs and higher consciousness. It is amazing for channeling spiritual information and opening the door to infinite knowledge. It can also calm the nerves and emotions. Overall, one of my favorite stones!

20. Celestite

The Angel Communicator

Vibe Meter: Enlightened

The Chakras: 7th crown, 6th third eye, 5th throat, and 4th heart

Celestite ranges from white to light blue and is usually from Madagascar. Celestite promotes awareness and is said to bring Angelic presence. It clarifies the mind, grants clear communication skills, and can balance energies to calm and bring harmony to those who use it in meditation. Celestite is excellent for dream recall and astral travel. This is a great crystal to sleep or nap with. I suggest only a few times a week, though, because if you are astral traveling it can make you tired in your real life. In healing, Celestite replaces pain with loving light of the Angelic realm.

21. Chalcedony

Vibe Meter: Mellow Soother

The Chakras: 5th throat

Chalcedony is light blue and can have grayish tones and/or white bands. Chalcedony represents air and water and helps one to listen and communicate in an understanding way. It encourages communication with humans, animals, plants, and all energies of life. It improves one's perception of feelings and needs to promote self-awareness and lightheartedness. It is great for the throat chakra. This stone is perfect for children and adults who work with children because it helps with understanding, empathy, maintaining calm, and communication. Chalcedony brings you to enjoy and experience life without judgment;

it helps you stop comparing yourself to others and reduces jealousy. Chalcedony also aids telepathic and clairvoyant abilities.

22. *Charoite*

✳

Vibe Meter: Yowzer

The Chakras: 7th crown, 6th third eye,
4th heart, 3rd solar plexus, and 2nd sacral

Charoite is a fantastic purple stone. When I first laid eyes on this wonder of creation, I couldn't believe that nature had made such a gorgeous formation. I worked with this stone, and I found it works just as incredibly as its looks. I find all stones, minerals, and crystals have beautiful energies, as valuable as any energy on Earth because they are derived from earth. Charoite helps one cope with profound changes in life and overcome resistance; it brings quiet, refreshing energies, facilitates decision-making, and calms the nerves and heart. This is a good stone for relieving cramps.

Additionally, Charoite can ward off negative dreams and give protection in all realms of existence to the holder. One of my favorite attributes of this stone is that it helps a person know who they are without sugarcoating the reality of what they are currently doing or into, correcting bad behaviors and encouraging better actions.

23. *Chrysoprase*

≋

Vibe Meter: Mellow Soother

The Chakras: 5th throat, 4th heart, and 3rd solar plexus

Chrysoprase is a cool apple-green; it's an extremely intuitive stone and can bring in desires for change through new actions and motives. Chrysoprase encourages real actions, truth, and patience. It helps bring happiness to one's life as it emits a feeling of trust and security. It helps people avoid compulsive behaviors and replace them with new, healthier ideas. Chrysoprase aids in alleviating skin diseases and fungal infections when you use it with Smoky Quartz. It also stimulates fertility in women.

24. Citrine

Positive Energy and Money Maker

Vibe Meter: Mellow Soother

The Chakras: 7th crown, 6th third eye, 3rd solar plexus, and 2nd sacral

Citrine is a pale or brilliant yellow/gold crystal gemstone used to energize the mind. You will sometimes find it in a darker brown color. All shades of Citrine are positive. It has a wide variety of usages, which is why Citrine is loved by most people. It just feels great! I call it the *money stone* or the *happy stone*. I like to work with Citrine by first setting my intention of what I am using its wonderful frequencies for. Sometimes I use it for digestion and stomach issues such as diverticulosis. It can also help acute diabetes. Citrine can aid in mental and intellectual functions as it increases self-esteem, vitality, and energy. It is a must-have stone because it balances and dissipates negative energy. On top of all that, it brings wealth when worn or used with Green Aventurine. Citrine can also help you sell your home. You can place Citrine stones at the main entrance and in each room's corners. It is gorgeous as a decorative home accent; people love gazing at it.

I would like to share one example of why and where I use Citrine when I am administering crystal healing sessions. I have encountered over 40 crystal healings that I remember distinctively for a common issue we deal with in today's world. Many people, men and women of all ages, have issues with "not enough," or, in general, have fears of insufficient money or of being alone. These issues are the most common in my practice. Whether it be money, relationships, love, happiness, or self-worth, I can sense their fears intuitively or by using the handy pendulum over the root and sacral chakras of the physical and energy bodies to make an assessment. This assessment shows if they need Citrine's help to release negative energy and become positive in those chakra areas. Let me tell you how to do this adjustment. First, place a Black Tourmaline on the root and sacral chakras of the person's physical body. After 20 minutes, replace the Black Tourmaline with a combo of one Citrine and one Chrysoprase on both chakra areas until the session is completed. The Black Tourmaline releases old, fearful energy and feelings of inadequacy, and the Citrine replaces that void of energy with a positive, happy, filling vibe. Chrysoprase instills trust and security in those chakras and adjusts them to heal.

I wanted to share this because, as you learn that certain crystals can have many uses, you should understand that harmonizing crystals is crucial. Citrine has many uses; set the intention before your healing session, and Citrine can be your go-to gal for a happy crystal healing ending.

25. *Danburite*

The Stress Releaser

Vibe Meter: A Mega Yowzer

The Chakras: 7th crown, 6th third eye,
5th throat, 4th heart, 3rd solar plexus, and 2nd sacral

This magical baby is a powerhouse of immense energy that says, "I'm letting go! No ifs. No excuses." Any negativity you're holding is going to be gone. I'm gonna tell ya frankly that this one is no easy glide if you are ridding yourself of something harsh. It sure is a hardworking crystal for us humans. If you got—excuse my language—crap, it will be released! Danburite releases and brings you to a higher vibe of self-awareness and blunt understanding of your raw, true self and your higher self. Your Angels will feel the vibes of this Danburite stone and come to your rescue by guiding the junk out of your entire being of existence; you'll release negativity from the past, present, and future! Good riddance! Danburite is an incredible stone. It looks like a Quartz with a flat-angled tip; there is no other stone it can be mistaken for because of that feature. Very distinctive. Danburite is great for stress relief and connecting to other realms through channeling or telepathic communication. I love this stone. I use it with clients that have substance abuse problems or addictive personalities. Danburite will open them up to a new, better world; they can feel it, and soon they will want to adapt to that feeling they experienced. Danburite can be life-changing to those open to holding it. I do warn you that this is not a stone for wimps; you may have intense releasing before the changes occur within.

26. Dioptase

Vibe Meter: Yowzer

The Chakras: 7th crown, 6th third eye, and 4th heart

Dioptase is a beauty. It is a bright green color, and it helps heal matters of the heart. It helps with forgiveness of self and others and brings on compassion and understanding of all views of a situation. It encourages self-awareness, vivid dreams, hope, and creativity. Dioptase can relieve the pain of severe headaches and loosen your muscles if you have cramps. It has regenerative power for the liver. It can help enliven spirituality in one's life. If you believe in karma, this crystal will bring balance to you as it releases past abuses, self-inflicted or otherwise, from the soul's energy. It can give insight to past lives and your soul's purpose.

27. Emerald

≋

Vibe Meter: Mellow Soother

The Chakras: 7th crown, 6th third eye,
4th heart, 3rd solar plexus, and 2nd sacral

A legendary green stone that enhances memory and promotes clear, quick thinking. Emerald encourages positive actions by making your thought process positive. Healers use this to help all auric layers and chakras heal, promoting physical, mental, emotional, and spiritual wellness. Emeralds have been used since biblical times. They were in the breastplates of ancient Chinese warriors and used in countries around the world. The Emeralds were worn close to the heart to protect and create a sense of strength in the face of opposition. They were worn as signs of wealth, stature, pride, and privilege. Emerald comes in various grades; all carry energies that bring abundance and positive thought processes. Emeralds are great for the circulatory system, heart chakra, and emotional healing. Emeralds and Moldavite harmonize great together. Try placing a Moldavite on your third eye chakra and an Emerald on your heart chakra. You will feel the crystals connect energetically and may feel the energy throughout your body as well. This brings consciousness to the needs and wants of your subconscious, making them realities that need further action. I use this crystal combo when I need to sync up my goals and find it motivates me to rise to the occasion.

28. *Epidote*

The Attractor

Vibe Meter: Yowzer

The Chakras: All—7th crown, 6th third eye, 5th throat,
4th heart, 3rd solar plexus, 2nd sacral, and 1st base root

Epidote is a black, gray, and deep green magmatic rock. It can help dissolve false images to help a person recognize facades in life. It can regenerate the feeling for oneself. It strengthens any healing process. Epidote also amplifies energies. This I mention because, if you are not in a great mood, you might not want to carry this one. It will ignite your mood to be a stronger version of what you are feeling at the time. If you are sad, please use another stone, such as Black Obsidian, to release first.

Epidote helps you attract what you are putting out, so make sure you are putting out high positive vibes. I can attest to this one. Years ago, I purchased an Epidote necklace and wore it, not knowing what it could do. Boy, that was fun. I had a bad day, and then one negative thing came after another, and it was like I was swimming in negativity. I took the necklace off, and all balanced back. Since I'm a person who likes to experiment, I also wore it on a lucky day. I had won a small award that day and decided, "Hey, I should amplify this," and it worked! I won $20 on a lotto ticket, found a four-leaf clover in my backyard (no joke), and got an offer for a speaking engagement!

29. Fluorite

The Master Healer

Vibe Meter: Mellow Soother

The Chakras: 7th crown, 6th third eye, 5th throat,
4th heart, 3rd solar plexus, and 2nd sacral

Fluorite grows in a variety of colors: green, yellow, clear, pink, and purple. Some Fluorite stones have multiple colors within; I call these Rainbow Fluorites. All Fluorites are beautiful. Those with the greenest coloring work best for the heart chakra and healing on a physical level. The yellow or whitish Fluorite helps heal on the spiritual level or past traumas. The solid purple and/or pink Fluorite helps a person with emotional or mental issues that are blocking them, allowing the release in those chakras and aura layers. Fluorite is a perfect overall healing stone that gives determination, brings a sense of free spirit, activates a creative push, and is the gateway to the subconscious. Fluorite can help dissolve blockages or narrow-mindedness that prevents a person from moving forward in life. It stimulates fast thinking and helps one absorb higher knowledge. It can help regenerate skin, bones, and teeth, as well as help fix one's respiratory tract and posture. Fluorite can also help with joint problems and arthritis.

I have a beautiful piece of Rainbow Fluorite I use quite often in crystal healings. Since it has all the colors of the rainbow, I feel it helps a person adjust on all levels: physical, emotional, mental, and spiritual. The overall healer stone—you can't go wrong with one of these in your stash kit!

30. Garnet

Vibe Meter: Mellow Soother

The Chakras: 4th heart, 3rd solar plexus, and 2nd sacral

Stubborn and graceful and as compassionate and giving as my grandmother, who, fittingly, is also named Garnet. I love her on all levels! Garnet is a deep red and rich in powerful healing, courage, and love. Some Garnets are a higher grade, which means they are a better quality, and those are used mostly in jewelry or in specimen form and will be much costlier than the browner Garnets. The brighter the red, usually the more money. All are energetically equal in crystal healing purposes. Brown ones are just as potent to use in crystal layouts and grid work.

Garnet can bring protection to your body and your space. Physically, Garnet helps with the gallbladder and kidneys. This stone is the heart of strong love and helping you appreciate what you have. Garnet is great for assisting in healing the interior of the human body.

31. Herkimer Diamond

Vibe Meter: Yowzer and Enlightened
The Chakras: 7th crown, 6th third eye, 5th throat,
4th heart, 3rd solar plexus, and 2nd sacral

I call Herkimer Diamonds fantazmic! Yeah, that's a Jolie word. Let me introduce the Clear Quartz Diamonds that are only found in Herkimer, New York, in the good ol' United States, brought to you by planet Earth! The mine is extraordinary. Herkimer Diamonds are brilliant amplifiers of spiritual work. They are double-matrix crystals, which means both their ends are pointed and bring powerful energy. Herkimer Diamonds are superstar crystals—they can amplify the energy of any stone you pair them with! Try it with Moldavite and, boy, will you be flying high!

Herkimer Diamond spiritually advances you, opens the mind's eye, brings vivid dreaming, and cleanses the body. It can remove negative attachments in the energetic aura layers. Herkimers are strong *ka-boom* energy! I hold them to amplify meditation when I am asking for clarity and strong visions. These are great to pair up with Green Tourmaline to find your soul's purpose. Herkimers are perfect for manifesting and goal-setting. Keep one nearby when writing your dreams or bucket list. If you are a writer, Herkimer Diamonds can help you create wild, visionary stories from beyond with great detail.

32. Howlite, White

The Focus Stone

Vibe Meter: Grounded Chill

The Chakras: 6th third eye and 1st base root

This stone looks marbleized; it's white with gray swirled within it. White Howlite is magnificent for focus! It is perfect for studying or learning and keeps you on task. It calms a person to be grounded and have a better understanding of the present moment. It is made of calcium borosilicate hydroxide, which gives it its marbleized color. You will find that some Howlite is dyed a bright blue or pink to open up a person's senses to color. All are powerful, but the white or cream color is natural.

33. Jasper, Ocean

Vibe Meter: Grounded Chill

The Chakras: 3rd solar plexus, 2nd sacral, and 1st base root

Ocean Jasper is a stone of regeneration. It is a beautiful stone. I remember looking through a microscope when I was young and seeing the amazing shapes of amoebas and circles of green, peach, and white: a scenic cluster of living organisms. That's basically how Ocean Jasper looks. It's hard to give a perfect description, but this stone is something you have to see.

Think about the ocean; the ocean has healing properties, similar to Ocean Jasper, which can help the reproductive and endocrine systems and relieve stresses from your mind and physical body. It can keep you balanced and grounded and give you positive perceptions of life in general. The quality I love the most about Ocean Jasper is that it stops that feeling of Groundhog Day. Have you seen that movie? In it, the main character has such a monotonous life and he can't get out of it, so he lives Groundhog Day over and over and over. It's actually a hilarious movie if you like simple humor. Were we talking about crystals? I need a White Howlite to get my focus back… anyway, Ocean Jasper takes away that monotonous feeling so that every day is new and exciting.

34. Jasper, Red

Vibe Meter: Grounded Chill

The Chakras: 2nd sacral and 1st base root

Red Jasper comes in a variety of deep and browny reds. All Jasper stones can strengthen the physical body and fortify the auric layers. Jasper brings courage and willpower. Red Jasper allows the mind to be strong in decision-making. If you need confidence, Red Jasper has your back! I like to hold it when I work out for physical strength and when I am meeting someone new to feel extra present, confident, and on my game!

35. Kunzite

Vibe Meter: Yowzer

The Chakras: 7th crown, 6th third eye,
5th throat, 4th heart, and 3rd solar plexus

A crystal that is either white, pink, yellow, light gray, or light blue. Kunzite is a highly intuitive stone. The wearer of a Kunzite gemstone is believed to be blessed with good fortune. Kunzite is said to help one understand and interact better with others. In the Middle Ages, people believed that the cosmos was reflected in gemstones. Kunzite is assigned to the planets Pluto and Venus. The esoteric movement revived this ancient belief.

Kunzite is a clairvoyant amplifier and gives clarity to the user or holder. It can ease stress, overthinking, and negativity. It helps support the nervous system and brings powerful connections to your source. It holds some lithium in its composition, which helps with modern thinking and being receptive to newness and change. I use it often for strengthening my communication to the divine and to help me hear divine messages clearer. This may sound a bit kooky to you, but when I hold a piece of Pink Kunzite, I feel beautiful and strong. Try one and see what you feel or sense.

36. *Kyanite, Blue*

♣

Vibe Meter: Grounded Chill

The Chakras: All—7th crown, 6th third eye, 5th throat,
4th heart, 3rd solar plexus, 2nd sacral, and 1st base root

The perfect mineral, Kyanite is blue or blue-gray but can also be darker gray or black. Kyanite builds determination and balances the physical, mental, and emotional body. It helps improve the mobility of the physical body. Great for all the chakras and automatically aligns them; you can wear Blue Kyanite daily or use it in healing for balance. It can be worn to help those with nerve damage. It helps to dissipate dysfunctional life choices, and it enhances intuition. I love this mineral because it is perfect for anyone to wear or hold. I have experienced instant alignment of my chakras after holding a piece of Kyanite for 15 minutes. Grab a chunk and check your chakras with your pendulum; I'll bet you will become more balanced than you were 15 minutes prior. Make sure you check before and after holding a piece of Kyanite.

37. *Lapis Lazuli*

♀

Vibe Meter: Enlightened

The Chakras: 7th crown, 6th third eye, 5th throat, and 3rd solar plexus

Lapis Lazuli is a bright or deep blue with gold flecks. This stone expands the third eye for meditation and brings protection, healing, stability, and inner truth to the user. If you have trouble relaxing for meditation, place a Lapis stone over the third eye chakra, and you will feel the ease of opening yourself to the beyond.

I enjoy Lapis as jewelry. It makes me feel safe and mindful of my surroundings. I wear a chunky ring or bracelet when I travel since I may be in an unfamiliar place. Plus, I really love its telepathic enhancement. If you like to connect or chat with your guides, hold a Lapis power stone. You may be curious: How did it get the name Lapis Lazuli? In medieval Latin, *lapis* means "stone," and *lazuli* means "of the heavens." Therefore, stone of the heavens. Some ancient cultures considered Lapis a type of Sapphire that connected the spirit with the Gods of the sky.

38. *Lemurian Seeds*

Momma Help Me…

(These are strong-to-the-core formations of light!)

Vibe Meter: Yowzer and Enlightened

The Chakras: 7th crown and 6th third eye

Lemurian Seeds are preprogrammed crystals that can be clear or orange. They are of the Quartz family, but I like to categorize them separately. You will notice they have slight grooves and markings as if they've been chiseled in some areas. These groove marks are natural, for your information. The grooves are also called "records" that have been embedded within the crystals. In crystal junkie language, we call the grooves "record keepers" of knowledge. They are known to allow you to retrieve information from ancient Lemuria. If you are not familiar with Lemuria, let me introduce you to a myth or ancient healing legacy. The Lemurians were light beings, and they still exist in other dimensions. They have a strong desire to help all people. We all can learn how to self-heal with their ancient healing techniques, mainly utilizing Lemurian Seeds. Lemurians want humans to be more self-sustaining and allow us to use their higher knowledge, inviting us to connect to their portals of energy and decipher the frequencies embedded in each crystal to heal and adjust ourselves. They empower, not enable, with their healing. They don't want us to need them, but they share their knowledge to educate us so we can advance on

Earth. Pretty cool of them. The Lemurians say they are from Atlantis. I understand that they still reside there, but humans can't see them because they are in another dimension. Crazy cool!

I could go on forever about them; I channel their messages often. Some say each Lemurian Seed contains 10,000 messages. These sacred messages provide higher knowledge of the light and beyond.

Many people have told me that when they are holding a Lemurian Seed, they gain information that allows them to solve problems in their current life. I believe, and many others do as well, that each crystal seed instills you with understandings of modalities of healing from the Atlantis Lemurian existence. Ya know, mystical stuff like that. It's higher knowledge!

Seriously, I've totally downloaded knowledge on how to heal energetically from these Lemurian guides of light. I've held the crystals and meditated with them many times. The crystals have enabled me to help teach others to heal themselves. Call me crazy, but I learned a lot from these incredible energies. Try for yourself and meditate with one. It takes a few times to connect with the energies, but please continue working and meditating with them. These stones have the capacity to also allow contact with members of the Angelic realms as well as ancient teachings.

39. Lepidolite

Ze' Prozac Stone

Vibe Meter: Mellow Soother

The Chakras: 6th third eye, 5th throat, 4th heart,
3rd solar plexus, 2nd sacral, and 1st base root

Lepidolite has similar effects as the pharmaceutical mood stabilizer called Prozac. This is a unique pinkish-purple stone and is known as a healer of depression. This stone activates the throat, heart, solar plexus, sacral, root, and third eye chakras. Lepidolite is used for psychic protection and balances the psyche. It is great to keep in your purse. This way, if you have a negative day, you can counteract those negative feelings with this positive and productive mood enhancer. Lepidolite has lithium within it, so it can help with alleviating nervous or irrational thinking and balance a person's erratic behavior. It is actually made up of potassium lithium aluminum silicate.

I like to hold this stone when I have an off day. One of my good friends loves chaos, but she constantly claims she does not like the chaos of her life. I can tell you that she creates it! When she gets on her roller coaster of emotions, I hand her *Ze' Prozac* stone and literally tell her, "Hold this chill pill." We always laugh about it, and she says she really does feel structure in her head beginning to get her on track when she holds Lepidolite, or the chaos corrector.

40. Malachite

Heart Healer

Vibe Meter: Mellow Soother

The Chakras: 4th heart

Miraculous Malachite. It is a hardcore healer stone, especially for emotions and physical ailments of the heart, including those related to relationships and love.

Malachite is a rich green stone with darker green streaks. It's gorgeous; the swirls of light and dark greens naturally occur in Malachite. It is a copper carbonate mineral and forms naturally in mini, roundish masses; then, when it is cut by a lapidary, a professional stonecutter, you can see all its beautiful stripes. Malachite helps release negative emotions, brings powerful healing and protection, and enriches your thoughts for wellness and positive living.

I have some clients that have physical heart issues. They feel relief after sessions with Malachite. They claim it is calming to them and they feel less stress in the chest area. Malachite seems to make them more understanding of multiple perspectives and less self-critical.

41. Moldavite

Crippy Trippy Stone

Vibe Meter: Yowzer and Enlightened
The Chakras: 7th crown, 6th third eye, 4th heart, and 2nd sacral

Moldavite can get you to a higher frequency fast! This mysterious green gemstone harmonizes well with many gemstones, but it is particularly strong with Amethyst and Citrine. It is said that Moldavite will supercharge and spiritualize the energies of whatever stone one uses with it. Exposure to the Moldavite begins a process of energetic resonance in which the vibratory rate of our entire being is increased, which is why this is such a transformative gemstone. This stone or Tektite is said to be a meteorite that fell in the Czech Republic. As it landed, the heat and pressure of the meteor united with the earth and formed a green glass-like stone with cosmic powers. Scientists could not duplicate this stone because nothing is like it on our Earthly plane. Most people feel the stone's vibes instantly when they hold a piece. Moldavite can also give you an out-of-body experience. Many people claim they leave their physical bodies and take a "trip"!

When I hold a small piece of Moldavite, about the size of a dime, my heart beats fast, and I can feel a zip line of energy to my third eye chakra and then to my crown chakra. It takes me way up, and I feel stoned. I am not comfortable with that feeling since I don't like drugs or alcohol; it makes me feel I have no control over myself. I prefer structure and to be grounded since I am very intuitive. In my lifestyle, I need to be grounded—presence is great for being a conduit of messages and healing. However, when I do want to relax, unwind, and take a "trip," I love to add Moldavite to my crystal body layout, because Moldavite can whisk me into other dimensions easily. Moldavite is a favorite of many because lots of people love that feeling of escape, and it also helps them release and get enlightened. I like Moldavite to go out of body, but it's not an everyday stone for me to wear or hold. I just like to use it once a month to get my escape time and let it take me up to the stars and sky—I just feel like I am somewhere with no cares!

I do have many friends, healers, and clients who absolutely resonate with Moldavite and wear it daily. They say it makes them feel utterly fantastic. One of my friends actually wears rings and necklaces with larger inserts of Moldavite in the jewelry. One piece she has is larger than a half dollar. That's big! She vibes with Moldavite mostly because she is more of a type A personality. She feels it chills her down a few notches so she is not so uptight or overthinking, like she would be without wearing Moldavite.

I want to mention that using Moldavite intentionally to release any old patterns or negativity is mind-blowing; Moldavite makes everything come up and out of you. Not physically (as far as I know), but emotionally and mentally and spiritually. Moldavite brings you to see what you need and then helps you release anything that may be a crutch or negative energy, eliminating unproductive thoughts or blockages from your subconscious. It brings the dirt to the surface so that you can dust it off and get on with your life with better perceptions and actions.

Moldavite is a very costly Tektite for it is sold by the gram, but boy is it powerful! Some people who are a bit more hyper in everyday life seem to feel a balancing of their being, making them feel less controlling. Moldavite is truly amazing.

42. Moonstone

The Traveler Stone

Vibe Meter: Mellow Soother and Enlightened
The Chakras: 7th crown, 6th third eye, and 5th throat

Moonstone is a light taupe and/or creamy white stone that aids communication by promoting clear thinking and inspiration. Back in the 1900s, Moonstones were used for happy, safe travels. Moonstone assists in the fulfillment of one's own destiny. It has been long regarded as the gemstone of psychic abilities, wish fulfillment, and balancing emotion. In regard to wish fulfillment, Moonstone tends to work better on things that are needed versus things that are just wanted. Moonstone opens the intuition in all of us and works conjointly with cosmic forces, or the moon cycles. Believe it or not, it can help women regulate their menstrual cycles. It is a strong stone for enlivening divine and feminine energy.

43. Nirvana / Ice Crystal

✳ 💡

Vibe Meter: Yowzer and Enlightened

The Chakras: All—7th crown, 6th third eye, 5th throat, 4th heart, 3rd solar plexus, 2nd sacral, and 1st base root

This pinkish or white crystal has a unique appearance due to its formation under water. It was discovered when the ice melted in the Himalayan mountains due to global warming and the crystals were exposed. Their energy brings memories of the past and can also show us epiphanies of the future. Nirvana Crystals balance our male and female energy and bring inner enlightenment. When you hold one, it zaps you; well, I know it does that to me.

In the mining of these magical crystals, there have been whitish crystals and deeper, rustic-pink crystals. If you hold the pink in the left hand and the white in the right hand, you can feel a circuit of energies go through your body. This vibration is balancing from head to toe. It also creates a wave of vibes that harmonizes male and female, or yin and yang, energies. I will use myself as an example. Because I am an independent person, I come off at times as more male-dominant, especially in my work ethic. My female side is lacking at times because I work more than I play, so, when I hold the pink Nirvana in my dominating male side (the right hand), I start to feel more balanced and relate and articulate my life better once I receive my Nirvana adjustment. Some of you may be the opposite or in-between. If so, feel both the white and pink Nirvana, taking five minutes at a time trying each in your hands, and see how you feel or sense that energy flowing. It is really amazing. These crystals are pretty rare since there was only one mine found, so, if you can get your hands on them, keep them for your personal stash. If you can afford to get a set of two, go for it! They are worth every penny. I have three sets.

44. *Obsidian, Black*

Vibe Meter: Grounded Chill

The Chakras: 1st base root

Black Obsidian and Black Tourmaline have several properties in common: both release and protect you from negativity and self-judgments; both are true grounding stones, keeping you present in your body; and both Black Tourmaline and Black Obsidian look very similar and are sometimes hard to tell apart. All Obsidians are healing stones and are a natural glass that forms when molten lava is submerged in water. Black Obsidian absorbs and dissolves anger and criticisms. I call it *pure protection*. It is also known for transformation. Black Obsidian helps release the old and brings clarity to those who use it properly.

Obsidians come in an array of multicolored natural glass formations. There are shiny green, blue, and black Obsidians. All are for healing the total body inside and out. Obsidians are structures of elemental energies. They are formed of earth, fire, and water. These are the divine elements. Obsidians can promote greatness within the psychic and mental bodies for deep healing of a person's past or present.

45. *Obsidian, Snowflake*

Past Lives Time Travel Stone

Vibe Meter: Yowzer and Enlightened

The Chakras: 7th crown, 6th third eye, 5th throat,
4th heart, 3rd solar plexus, and 2nd sacral

Snowflake Obsidian is black with white beauty marks. It protects you from emotional draining, and it can bring past lives/parallel occurrences to the meditative mind. It's really fun to work with! Snowflake Obsidian gives us a broader perception of the concept of time and the dimension we live in. It may open our minds to parallel time lines and realities.

Obsidian is considered a mineraloid, since it is a mineral that was materialized from natural glass. Be mindful when shopping for any color of Obsidian because there is man-made glass sold as natural Obsidian. The difference is that true Obsidian is from volcanic composition, while man-made Obsidian is heated, sand-colored glass. Both can be beneficial, but, in crystal healing, the high-vibe volcanic properties are better!

46. Opal, Pink

Vibe Meter: Enlightened

The Chakras: 7th crown, 6th third eye, 5th throat, and 4th heart

Light to medium pink and opalescent, the Pink Opals are intuition-opening stones. They can be emotionally supportive in crystal healing by stabilizing good moods. They can help increase trust in one's feelings and passion, which promotes expression and zest for life. The Pink Opal contains manganese and helps with all heart ailments. This spiritual stone brings you to an elevated level of understanding and wisdom. As you work with this stone, you will feel the high vibrations of its beautiful energy lift you to self-trust. I use Pink Opal in meditations for self-connection. It helps me know what I truly want at that time in my life. My meditation is deep because the stone helps me get past my mind chattering and the negative or judgmental human experiences that cloud my inner knowing. Then I can fully access the all-knowing me and my soul energy.

47. Opalite

Vibe Meter: Mellow Soother

The Chakras: 7th crown, 6th third eye, and 4th heart

An opalescent, white stone sometimes with a rainbow-like appearance. Opalite opens the third eye chakra for meditation. It is an intuitive opening to connect with light or source energies. Opalite is man-made, but it's composed of natural

Dolomite and metal, which give it the opalescent, shiny, glassy look. It carries rainbows within, which connects to our human visual sense and creates a positive vibration from what we see, and, therefore, connects to our chakras as color frequencies. Noticing the rainbow colors in Opalite brings us success and happiness. I find it can also bring friendship and relationship harmony. I wear it when I meet new people; people always want to touch it and get closer.

48. Pietersite

Vibe Meter: Grounded Chill

The Chakras: 3rd solar plexus, 2nd sacral, and 1st base root

This blue-black, brown-flecked stone is nature and more. It is said to increase stamina; enhance fortitude, perseverance, and courage; and access the subconscious, all while assisting one in recognizing the soul's beauty. This stone is grounding and keeps me open at the crown at the same time, allowing transformation and growth in my present life. Pietersite can help you reorganize chaos in your life and is great for respiratory problems. If you are not present, meaning you think too far ahead or too far in the past, you need to hold this stone in your pocket for a few days. This will bring you to appreciate what you have in the present moment.

49. Pyrite

The Quicker Upper Energizer Stone

Vibe Meter: Yowzer

The Chakras: 4th heart, 3rd solar plexus, and 2nd sacral

Pyrite is made of iron sulfide, formula FeS_2. It has a beautiful shine and golden luster. Many call it "fool's gold." It is great for using in manifestations, especially for abundance and wealth, and for businesses. It encourages feelings of self-worth and makes positive feelings in the space for you and others. It can deflect negative energy and mend the aura if it has been punctured or torn.

Its healing abilities are stellar, especially for keeping negative toxins away from you. Pyrite is great for confidence, manifesting your goals to full fruition, and opening your gates to creative endeavors.

50. Quartz, Clear and Rainbow

Vibe Meter: Enlightened

The Chakras: 7th crown and 6th third eye

Clear Quartz is what I call the "mother of all crystals." It comes in various natural formations and cuts and is multipurpose. Clear Quartz is used for clarity, focus, and intention of positive admiration. It opens your mind if you feel stuck in thoughts that are not serving you in a positive way. Clear Quartz is an amplifier of healing energy, meditation, and self-realization. It is great for anyone to work with on all levels of healing and advancement.

There is another type of Quartz I love to work with called Rainbow Quartz. Rainbow Quartz is a mellow soother and affects all seven chakras. Rainbow Quartz has a clear but crackly appearance. The cracks within it sometimes look like Angel wings. Well, I think that is what they look like. Some specimens have rainbows you can see within them. All colors of the rainbow are the spectrum of all seven chakras. Rainbow Quartz brings vibrations of success. It is great for manifesting your desires and goals; hold one while you are meditating or use one as an office paperweight so its super vibes can sink into your aura and space! This Quartz's energies are positive and fulfilling!

51. Quartz, Rose / Pink

Vibe Meter: Mellow Soother

The Chakras: 7th crown, 6th third eye, 5th throat,
4th heart, 3rd solar plexus, and 2nd sacral

Rose Quartz ranges from dark to light pink; it's called both Rose Quartz and Pink Quartz. It is used to enhance unconditional love and protection. This is a well-known crystal; it is universal in projecting positive energy and great for a housewarming gift. Holding one fortifies or deepens existing love. It is perfect for self-acceptance and creating peace and love for self and others. It encourages strength, hope, and positive relationships. It is a perfect stone to give to your mother or to hold if you are one; it helps you with patience and compassion.

52. Quartz, Rutile

Pattern-Stopper

Vibe Meter: Yowzer and Enlightened

The Chakras: 7th crown, 6th third eye, 5th throat,
4th heart, 3rd solar plexus, and 2nd sacral

This is a pattern-stopper that helps people let go of physical, mental, and emotional addictions and negative behaviors. You on drugs? This can help stop the obsessive desire or self-destructive thought processes that lead to your next hit. It blocks the imprint of the habit or negative desire from the subconscious to help you be the real you. Negative mental and emotional patterns are also stopped as you work with this stone in crystal healings over a period of time. Are you passive? Well then, hold this one to get your power back. It helps you feel powerful, not powerless.

53. Quartz, Smoky

Bad Begone

Vibe Meter: Grounded Chill

The Chakras: 1st base root

A grounding stone. Sometimes it's very light gray in color; sometimes you can find really dark, smoky points. I feel the darker ones are stronger in protecting. All shades of Smoky Quartz can help reduce depression and negative emotions. Smoky Quartz helps us through hard times, brings relaxing effects, helps concentration, protects against radiation, fortifies the nerves, and can help alleviate back problems. It can make you connect the Earthly, present realm to the spiritual realm; I call Smoky Quartz a porthole or communicator to your soul and light energy, such as Angels or your source. Smoky Quartz is a strong protector of your personal space and energy, keeping the area clean of negative vibes. I also find that if I am irritated or ornery, I can hold one to release my own negativity.

54. Rhodochrosite

The Love Attractor

Vibe Meter: Mellow Soother

The Chakras: 4th heart, 3rd solar plexus, and 2nd sacral

Rhodochrosite has pink tones and some brown specks or lines. This stone brings love into one's life. This includes self-love. It brings out the mindfulness to remain calm in all situations of the heart. It is powerful enough to release psychological issues, fears, and anything related to stress.

I made this wonderful concoction for a client; she wanted to have positive self-love and attract someone in her life. I added a bag of lavender, a Rhodochrosite stone, and a mantra: "Love comes my way; I accept and attract what I desire." After two weeks of carrying the concoction in her purse, she met her new boyfriend; he was a keeper!

55. Ruby Zoisite

The Getter Done Stone

Vibe Meter: Yowzer

The Chakras: 5th throat, 4th heart, 3rd solar plexus, and 2nd sacral

A green crystal with beautiful flecks of pink, Ruby Zoisite looks almost like a wonderful piece of candy (but don't eat or ingest this beauty)! Ruby Zoisite is a motivator stone. It is great for recovery after illness, helps you realize your own ideas, stimulates fertility, and makes you creative. It helps you with awareness, positive self-esteem, and makes you feel you can support yourself and what you need to do in life. I call it the *getter done stone*. When I use it, I feel like I have a personal coach putting fire under my butt to get me going: vitality galore!

Years ago, I had a load of stones and crystals, and I picked out Ruby Zoisite around 7:30 a.m. when I got up. I placed it in my pocket and began my day. Mind you, I do not drink coffee. By 10 a.m., I had washed my car (myself), gone to the grocery store, mowed my lawn, picked weeds, washed all of my dirty clothes, folded and put them away, and washed my two dogs. I was saying to myself, "Dang, girl, you are Superwoman today," as I walked into the ladies room. Seconds later, as I pulled down my jeans, the Ruby Zoisite stone rolled on the floor in front of me. I said, "Ruby Zoisite, you did all this!" I had forgotten that little motivator was in my pocket. It's been my go-to gal for getting things done ever since.

56. Salt

Vibe Meter: Mellow Soother
The Chakras: 5th throat, 4th heart,
3rd solar plexus, 2nd sacral, and 1st base root

A natural cleanser for your aura and the space you live in. Himalayan salt, especially salt lamps, emits a number of ions into the surrounding atmosphere when heated by an external source, like candles or electricity. Heat from the lamp breaks down the sodium chloride in a process known as ionization. You can feel the clean energies of salt just by holding a piece. The salt lamp also makes breathing easy and can help with asthma. If you walk into a room with multiple salt lamps, you can instantly feel the cool, clean ion charges in the air; you most likely will breath cleaner and notice a big difference in the feeling of the room. The lamps are gorgeous for positive ambiance.

Natural pink Himalayan salt is great for baths; it cleanses negativity and toxins, but it can be drying. I use salt crystals when I shower; I grab a handful from my bathroom salt dish, add some lavender or geranium essential oils, and slowly rub the salt over my arms and body. It's super refreshing and relaxing after a day of meetings and energy healings. I know you want to lick it to see if it tastes the same as table salt. I did that for you. Imagine me with a big smirk on my face; yeah, I did that. Pink or white Himalayan salt is the purest. It's totally different from Morton table salt. Natural Himalayan salt is said to relieve migraines and improve the body's adrenal functions.

57. Selenite

✳

The Cleaner and Vison Maker

Vibe Meter: Yowzer

The Chakras: 7th crown, 6th third eye, 5th throat,
4th heart, 3rd solar plexus, and 2nd sacral

I love this formation. Selenite is white or orange and is naturally opaque; if hollowed out as a lamp, light passes though it with a nice glow. Selenite is flaky, meaning it can disintegrate easily and break. You can use Selenite for past life regressions or parallel lives. I make crystal grids with Selenite and Apophyllite to induce past recall sessions. You can call back a current life situation by releasing and have vivid dreams or astral experiences. It is great to place near your television, computer, or any negative electronic-wave-producing device. You can see changes as it is utilized, and most people can feel the area change immediately. The Selenite's color may become milkier over time. Selenite cannot be washed with water—it will dissolve! Fortunately, Selenite is self-cleansing. You can place one of these in a pile of your other gemstones, and it will cleanse them all for you. I place some of my stones on top of my Selenite lamp; it looks artistic and it cleanses my stones!

Selenite, or calcium sulfate, helps you create your inner knowing, connect to your soul, be trusting and open to new ideas, release negative thought patterns, and feel lighter. It helps ease chronic pains, fatigue, and skeletal/skin disorders. Overall, Selenite is a winning mineral. It adjusts and cleanses you, instills peace, and is great for spiritual work and meditations.

I have huge bricks of Selenite that are 20 pounds and over three feet long. I use them to make room grids for meditations and to clean my room and clients. Selenite will clear what no longer serves a person in the past and present.

58. Shungite

The Black Beauty EMF Protector

Vibe Meter: Mellow Soother

The Chakras: All—7th crown, 6th third eye, 5th throat,
4th heart, 3rd solar plexus, 2nd sacral, and 1st base root

This is an extremely lightweight stone that has the appearance of coal or metal. It looks similar to Hematite, but it has a purifying energy and clears your space. This means it is an EMF protector. It cleanses your aura and protects you from harmful frequencies emitted by cell phones, the electric waves from your power company, computers, and harmful electronics that have smart meters within them. It is used in hospitals in Russia to accelerate healing for patients and for absorbing toxins such as radiation. Believe it or not, this Shungite stone is also ground up and used in facial creams to keep you youthful! It has fullerenes that are healing and regenerative for humans. Everyone should have a piece of this for their cell phone or office. If you are an active facilitator of healing modalities, you should have several in your stash kit; I advise at least eight small pieces and a Shungite body pad to use with your clients. I set up an entire grid with Shungite if I am facilitating crystal healing for a client that has had an MRI, X-ray, or chemotherapy. I have Shungite near every TV, computer, and smart meter item in my home. I'm thinking that, in the year 2030, we will be making Shungite body suits to wear around town; it is an overall protection and cleansing stone. SHHHHHungite! I love to say that!

59. Sodalite

Vibe Meter: Mellow Soother

The Chakras: 7th crown, 6th third eye, and 5th throat

A must-have gemstone! Sodalite is royal blue with some white rays. Many people confuse this stone with Lapis because they are the same color blue. The trick is that Sodalite has some white minerals in it, and Lapis has gold Pyrite within it. Now that you know how to spot the difference, you will never mistake the two again.

Sodalite got its name from its high sodium content; Sodalite purifies your aura and protects you from negative energy. It also opens up the third eye for meditations. I use it in several basic body layouts to open my clients' third eye. If I feel they have a hard time relaxing during a healing session, I will place Sodalite on their third eye, which is just between their eyebrows. Sodalite is a staple stone for your stash box.

60. Sunstone

Vibe Meter: Mellow Soother

The Chakras: 7th crown, 3rd solar plexus, and 2nd sacral

Sunstone is from the Feldspar family and is mostly orange with dark pieces of Goethite and Hematite within it. It's a beauty to hold and place on the sacral and solar plexus chakras for healing emotional issues, especially those related to relationships, sex, and inner feelings of unworthiness. Sunstone heightens intuition and instills happy thoughts and confidence; it also brings power, wealth, and insight into acquiring wealth. Sunstone represents the phoenix, the symbol of rebirth and newness. With its sunny disposition, Sunstone awakens us to our presence on Earth.

61. Super 7

The All-in-One Crystal!

Vibe Meter: Yowzer and Enlighted

The Chakras: All—7th crown, 6th third eye, 5th throat,
4th heart, 3rd solar plexus, 2nd sacral, and 1st base root

Supahhhh 7! Also known as Sacred 7 or Melody's Stone, this baby is formed of seven different minerals that grow together naturally. This formation is rare, which is why it costs a bit more than your average crystal. The seven components are Amethyst, Clear Quartz, Smoky Quartz, Cacoxenite, Rutile, Goethite, and Lepidocrocite. It has healing properties of seven stones! It is said to be a sacred stone and is found in the Espírito Santo (Holy Spirit) area of Minas Gerais, Brazil.

You gotta feel this one! It is a powerhouse that encourages all psychic abilities, including telepathy, clairvoyance, channeling, and telekinesis. It can help you visually see auras. It purifies and energizes all of our chakras and energy fields and aligns them to the highest positive vibrations. This stone is the mac—it harmonizes and stimulates the body's natural healing system, including our cellular memory. It protects and makes you feel unconditional love from your guides and all that exists. Get this—it never needs to be cleansed or cleared! It's like seven vitamins in one.

62. Tiger's Eye

The Protector

Vibe Meter: Grounded Chill

The Chakras: 7th crown, 6th third eye,
3rd solar plexus, 2nd sacral, and 1st base root

This stone is brown with gold sashes. I love this beautiful stone; it reminds me of an inner tree trunk and its stripes of strength. Tiger's Eye is pure protection.

When I was a kid, I held it every night because I was feeling things I was unsure of. There were spirits or energy around me that I was not educated about, especially because I couldn't see, only feel, the presence of a visitor. Tiger's Eye totally warded off that energy so I could sleep. Tiger's Eye is also great for eye health, grounding, courage, and peaceful emotions.

63. Tourmaline, Black

The Absorber

Vibe Meter: Grounded Chill

The Chakras: 1st base root

A true black stone that keeps you grounded. Black Tourmaline absorbs negativity and will ground and realign the chakras; it is perfect for psychic protection and is used to ward off negative energies from other people or your own thoughts. It cleanses and purifies the energy fields. I love to set a big chunk of raw Black Tourmaline at the base of the spine, which is the location of the root chakra, during a crystal healing session. I place one there and one piece below the client's feet. I do this because most people release quite a bit of negative energy through their feet, so the Black Tourmaline is there to absorb it. The same goes for the root chakra area.

Another great place for Black Tourmaline is at your front door as it protects and can energetically intimidate an unwanted visitor or repel a negative attitude someone may have. I'll never forget when I placed a piece at my crystal store's front door because we had a few undesirables hanging around the day before. The following day, I saw those same undesirables come to the door, open it two inches, then immediately close it. It was great because other people with positive, respectful attitudes came in all day long! Black Tourmaline, you are the prize rock!

64. *Tourmaline, Green*

The Find Your Purpose Stone

Vibe Meter: Yowzer and Enlightened

The Chakras: All—7th crown, 6th third eye, 5th throat,
4th heart, 3rd solar plexus, 2nd sacral, and 1st base root

Green Tourmaline is usually captured inside a White Quartz formation. Natural Green Tourmaline has a rod-like, clear, glassy appearance. It is a heart chakra empowerment stone. I use this often with all healing and especially for love issues. It can help you find one of your soul's purposes. We have many purposes in a lifetime, and Green Tourmaline helps us see ourselves for who we are and connects our physical bodies to our souls. This means being synced and balanced in life and on Earth. Use one in your meditations when you feel you are a bit lost or that you need novelty. Green Tourmaline helps when a person is looking for new opportunities and a new identity. You can specifically use it to connect to your soul's purpose at that particular time in your life. When you are in transformation or feeling lost in life, hold this mineral with a Herkimer Diamond—the Herkimer will amplify the energy and bring clear visions of what is and what is supposed to be. Green Tourmaline keeps your thoughts rational and goal-oriented. The best of life is dreaming big while living in reality and knowing reality and dreams can be one and the same if you focus on your purpose; Green Tourmaline helps with all of that.

65. *Turquoise*

Vibe Meter: Grounded Chill

The Chakras: 5th throat, 3rd solar plexus, 2nd sacral, and 1st base root

Turquoise is most related to many Native American tribes; it can be found in Mexico as well as various places in the United States. Turquoise can be blue, green, or purple depending on where it is mined. It brings luck and happiness, attracts friendships, and releases shame and guilt. It is a general healing stone. Turquoise is protection and has elemental powers. I love to wear it as jewelry—it makes me feel my soul energy is awakened and ready for anything that comes my way. To make sure you are purchasing authentic Turquoise, look closely at the piece you are interested in, and see if you notice something that looks like it has been dyed. Many retailers sell dyed Howlite and pass it off as Turquoise. Since I am a feeler, I hold the Turquoise in my hand and up to my heart chakra and say, "Is this positive for me?" I will instantly feel a yes or no. The yes to me is a positive feeling while no feels unsure or uncomfortable. You can use this simple feeling/intuitive technique with anything you want to purchase or utilize. The key is noticing how you feel while holding the item.

66. Unakite

The "Who Am I, Where Am I?"

Vibe Meter: Grounded Chill

The Chakras: 1st base root

This is a gazer stone; when I say this, I mean this stone has so many pinks and greens within it that I can't stop looking at it! These stones have mesmerizing energies that vibrate quite high for all healing use. Unakite promotes balance and emotional stability; it can transform negative emotions to positive. The best part about Unakite is that it can ground you and help you be in the present moment. It gives you self-realization and super clarity. If you are feeling out of your head and forgetful, this stone is for you. It gets you out of the beer-goggles vision and into reality. It helps you know who you are and where you are.

That was all 66 crystals! I hope you have a huge stack of crystals that you have been able to observe, feel, and take notes on. If you did start noticing where in your body you were likely to feel something and made a note about it, then you are doing grand, my friend! This is pivotal in crystal healing: know thyself, and know thy crystal gem babies.

Part 2

Crystal Body Layouts

Chapter 4
Prepping for Your Crystal Body Layout Sessions

Before your session, you'll choose one of the 26 amazing crystal body layouts, which you will learn more about in the next chapter. Each layout includes the number of crystals needed, positive intentions to internalize or verbalize, and meditation directions that you will follow.

Some of the layouts are for specific ailments. If you know someone who can benefit from a crystal healing, share this information or perform a healing to assist them if you are trained properly. Pick a layout you need for the current day, read and follow the instructions, and then go for it!

Before you dive into the sessions, we are going to cover some preparation work that will be helpful to know. The components of a crystal healing session include making an assessment, checking the chakra centers and the four aura layers, journaling your findings, attending to your space, and tracking your progress.

Make Your Assessment

Before you lie down to start your journey, it is best to check your chakras. This will help to gauge your healing and successes. If you are not familiar with doing this, I will explain how to perform this easy assessment.

You learned earlier that your aura and chakras work best when they are synced up. We can check the chakras easily with a tool called a *pendulum*.

Pendulums are basically a piece of stone, crystal, metal, or wood hanging from a chain or string. You can use a necklace if you like. Once your pendulum is clean of any old energies, it's ready to use.

How to Use a Pendulum for Checking the Seven Chakras

You can clear and cleanse your pendulum in many ways (see chapter 2). The easiest way is to simply place your pendulum in a mini Tibetan singing bowl; play the bowl with the wooden dowel and let the vibrations / sound cleanse your pendulum.

Once your pendulum is cleansed, hold it by the string or chain. Use your other hand to hold the hanging crystal or item still. When the pendulum is still, hold it over your base root chakra (look at the chart on page 18 to know where it is and what it represents).

Notice how the pendulum starts moving: it could move right to left, left to right, back and forth, clockwise, or counterclockwise. You may also notice that the pendulum sits almost still but vibrates. At this time, just make a note of how it moves.

In every crystal chart, you will have a space to list your chakra movements. It's important to log the movements of your pendulum to more easily track your progress and results.

Each one of these directional flows tells you which way your or another person's energy moves within that particular chakra. As you check each chakra, hold your pendulum approximately four inches away from the body over that chakra and note the pendulum's movements.

Since our chakras can change with a single thought, you can make them move however you want. You can do this by projection, using your mind's energy on the pendulum and willing it to move. Focus on it and visualize it moving the way you want. Please do not sway it with your hand—that is not the point of this. The point is to show you how powerful your mind is and that every thought and visualization is energy, whether verbalized or telepathically projected. Some call this *telekinesis*, or the psychic ability to move objects with your mind. Telekinesis is different from checking your chakras because telekinesis is using your intentions to move an object. Using the pendulum to check your chakras is about allowing the pendulum to move naturally as each chakra area influences it to match its flow. The pendulum's natural flow should not reflect your mind's wishes, but rather your body's chakra and aura vibrations.

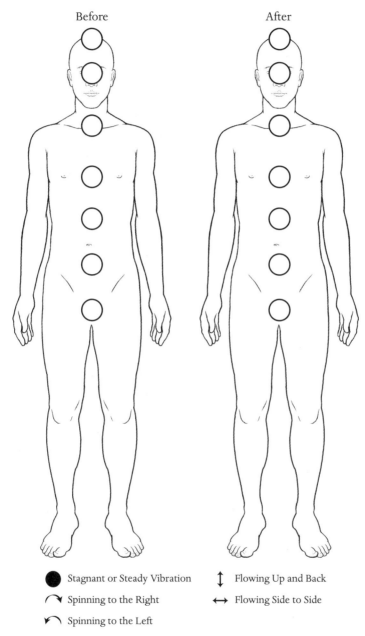

Before   After

● Stagnant or Steady Vibration   ↕ Flowing Up and Back
↱ Spinning to the Right   ↔ Flowing Side to Side
↰ Spinning to the Left

Chart Your Energy Shift

If you check your chakras weekly over a period of three weeks and find there are one or more chakras that are constantly unhealthy or still, that can mean there is an irregularity in your energy flow. This information is very telling of what is going on with your physical or energetic body. To learn more, you can take an energy healing class such as Reiki or read books that provide insight on energy healing modalities.

When checking the chakras, you want to check each one separately. Focus on the area of your body representing that individual chakra, then hold the point of the pendulum close to the chakra. Allow your pendulum to swing however it wants to naturally. Try not to stare at it to avoid influencing its movement with your intentions. It is best just to gaze down once the pendulum starts moving.

If your pendulum stands still over a chakra location, this could mean that chakra may have very little or stuck energy. In some cases, the pendulum may look as if it's vibrating in one place, neither moving in a circle nor swinging. If it stands still or vibrates in one location, this can mean little or no energy is flowing there. The goal is to help the energy flow clockwise in a healthy circle. A circular flow in the healthy direction for your location of living is important. (If your pendulum is moving clockwise and you are on the northern side of the equator, this is a healthy sign. I mention this because some of you reading this may live in Australia; therefore, a healthy chakra would spin counterclockwise, and an unhealthy chakra clockwise.) Circular motion is a sign that the vortexes in your chakras are freely flowing and discarding anything that's negative and keeping the positive. This is why it is important to understand the flow of your body's energy.

If you feel you have stuck or stagnant energy, you can realign your chakras and balance them with these crystal body layouts. I suggest Layout #1: Chakra Healing—Alignment and Balance (see chapter 5).

The main goal of checking/assessing your chakras is to chart the movements for vitality before and after a session of crystal layout healing. This way, you can document if you are balanced, releasing, and advancing in positive ways.

If your chakras are healthy and have good vitality, you will feel your optimal, balanced self on a physical, emotional, mental, and spiritual level. This is what we all strive for—to feel good, healthy, and balanced!

Take note if your chakras are open; if so, the pendulum will spin at a good speed, the circles the size of a baseball or larger. Having your chakras open and spinning in large circles shows you are balanced and well. However, remember that there are four layers of our human aura that coordinate with our seven chakras: the physical, the emotional, the mental, and the spiritual. Checking each level of your aura within each chakra with your pendulum is crucial to a deep understanding of your energetic health. To check the physical, emotional, mental, and spiritual auric layers, you would hold your pendulum above any chakra at two inches, six inches, 12 inches, and 16 inches, respectively, and note the pendulum's movements. Knowing which layers are blocked or unhealthy can help you determine which crystals to work with during a crystal body layout session. This insight can correct and/or adjust that chakra for health and overall wellness.

If any of your chakras are spinning unhealthily, this can mean you are having thoughts that are closed or unwell. This does not necessarily mean a negative flow of energy—you might just need some adjustments to redirect and balance the flow of energy in that chakra. This can be done by allowing yourself to let go of unwanted stressors in life. Holding on to negative occurrences and rethinking them is like reliving them over and over. To let go means releasing negativity and replacing it with positivity. Imagine bringing blissful energy into your thoughts and your life in general. Think of a beautiful item like a flower and notice its details. This can change the flow of energy instantly for some people.

If your pendulum swings back and forth or left to right, this is just showing you the flow of energy of that particular chakra. It does not mean bad or good. It can be just a neutral swing. However, chakras are best and balanced as discussed in the previous paragraphs.

Exceptions of Pendulums

If the swing changes in gauging your assessment of each chakra, remember where on Earth you are. If you are on the south side of the equator, counterclockwise would be healthy, and vice versa.

Please note that a woman's menstrual cycle can affect the spin of the sacral chakra—it can be healthy, but its spins may show otherwise.

Always check your or others' chakras without any jewelry or crystals on the body. Jewelry can change the current flow of the chakras and energy in general. Always check your chakras before and after a crystal session. This way, you can assess the changes.

Just to recap, go to each chakra, check the movement of the pendulum, and make a note of each. Check all seven chakras. Once you complete the charting of the seven energy centers, it's time to place your crystal layout for your session. Please remember that after you have had your entire crystal healing layout session, you should recheck all seven chakras to see what balanced or changed. It's fun to assess and gauge your body's energy.

Exercise: Your Chakra Assessment

Let's practice by doing this exercise. Pick up or make a pendulum and cleanse it in whatever way you prefer. We will now use it to check your seven main chakras.

Use the intention that the picture on page 97 is your body while focusing on checking your personal chakras. You can do this by stating your full name while looking directly at the picture. Now your intention is set.

Start at the base/root chakra, and, one by one, work your way up, separately checking each chakra. Notice if your chakras are spinning counterclockwise or clockwise, if they are forward- or backward-flowing, vibrating, or still. Make a note next to each of your chakras.

Remember when I taught you about the four auric layers in the electromagnetic field that surrounds your body? This tidbit of information will make you the best crystal healer in your town. Once you know the layers and what they represent in your energy body, you can place additional crystals to adjust what is needed in each auric field.

Now you can do the same assessment with all four auric layers in each chakra location. Neato! You can use the same chart to check each aura layer in each chakra zone. Each aura layer is approximately four inches thick. Start with the physical auric layer, which is two to four inches from your actual skin; from there, the next four inches are the emotional layer, followed by the mental layer, and last is the spiritual layer.

If you checked all your chakras and each of the four auric layers within that chakra and found that your heart chakra in the emotional and mental auric fields was counterclockwise, this could mean you are holding on to something other than a high positive vibration. It could be that emotionally you are upset with someone or yourself concerning a relationship. The counterclockwise spin in the heart chakra emotional auric layer indicates this. Also, if the mental aura layer of the heart chakra runs counterclockwise, this indicates that the way you process those emotions may not be positive, and you should look into how you are judging that situation.

When you are checking the four aura layers with a pendulum to receive this information, is not always 100 percent accurate. Take that into consideration, because we do change our energy, our chakras and aura vibrations, from second to second. I mean this literally. However, if you check them several times and find the same chakras, the same auric layers, consistently spinning in an unhealthy direction, I would look into that. It shows that you can take action to change or adjust so you can be healthier in those aspects of your life. How can you help as a crystal healer? Well, it's easy. Knowing how to check your energy centers and energetic layers will add to your knowledge of placements and crystal properties so you can adjust each area by choosing the appropriate harmonizing crystal. You'll pick those particular crystals that assist in adjusting or releasing the energy in each area as needed. You could use your crystal remedies list and look up what ailment, under the physical, emotional, mental, or spiritual levels, connects with the harmonizing crystals and adjust that need. Just place the crystals on the appropriate chakra to begin the crystal healing process for positive change.

How to Prepare for and Chart Your Crystal Body Layout Session

Preparation and Setup

When you first start out, you will need to pick a crystal layout from the 26 selections that you will learn about in the next chapter. Next, check out the items listed on the "What you need" list for that particular body layout. Purchase or gather your gems and crystals for the meditation.

If you bought the monthly subscription for the crystal layout kits from my website, www.CrystalJunkie.com, you will have all you need—essential oil included. If you would like to add the guided meditations by *moi*, you can purchase and download them anytime from my site as well. If you want to try essential oils with your crystal layout session, grab your oils. These are optional but make the experience top notch. You will see I emphasize the specific crystal combinations that work best with each essential oil.

I provide the crystal placements for the body and off the body, the intention, a high-vibe mantra, and a color enhancer. All of these components together are syncing energies to adjust you and make your experience grand!

You can make your crystal layout session flawless if you have a few more things. Get a clock or timer to set an appropriate time for your session. I suggest at least 25 minutes per crystal session. Most people take 15 minutes just to relax their bodies. In my sessions, I prefer 45 to 60 minutes.

If I set the timer, I can totally let go for that session and explore wherever my mind takes me. I find I'm not rushed or uneasy knowing I have to be at work or have errands to do because the timer is on. Try to have your crystal layout location/space where there's the least amount of electronics. If the vibes are of lower frequency, they can disrupt your peaceful healing.

Tracking Your Progress

I suggest that with each crystal layout you try, you should…

… write a list of the stones and crystals used. Describe their shapes and note if they are raw or polished. I write all of this, including the names of the gems and crystals.

… draw out your placement of the crystals or use the diagrams shown in this book. This will be your guide for when you want to compare notes as you practice with your layouts. You may in the future want to amp up your layouts by adding other stones that you feel work with your specific energies and create new layouts of your own.

… mark the date of your session and experience. Add the duration time. This will also help you gauge the meditations.

… have a pen and notepad to write what you felt, saw, or experienced. When my timer goes off to finish the session, I can write down and remember all that went on in my body and mind. Many times, I will take notes throughout the day and night as I receive more insight about my session. I always write down what comes to my mind.

…list on your notepad how you feel before and after a session using a scale of one to ten, one being the worst and ten the best. You can check your chakras before and after the session to gauge your healing. Note that if you are participating in a releasing session, you most likely will be emotional and letting out some negative stuff—so understand we let go and release before we feel great. Give adequate time for that particular type of session. I suggest at least 30 to 45 minutes and 60 is best. Remember to give additional time to ground after your session. Record your feelings accordingly using the one to ten scale. I also use a happy face, super happy face, or googly-eyed face. Just saying.

…use the body outlines. You can make copies of this to keep track of your layouts. I suggest you make ten copies. You can gauge your success and experiences on the back of the body layout. List and describe on the body part the emotional or physical feelings or sensations. If you are a healer, this is a great assessment to give your clients as well as keep for your records.

…journal your findings. I journal my findings on the back side of the body chart. You can make copies of the body charts to use along with the crystal layout diagrams and journal on the flipside of the paper. Here is an example of how I journal my findings:

- **Date of session**
- **Purpose**: **Indian Meditation—Finding Soul's Purpose**
- **Session**: #1 (if it was your second time doing this session, you write #2)

…list if this is your first time doing this particular session or if it is the second time, etcetera. Notice how you may have changed over a period of time with that layout. After a few times, did it help you move on from that particular issue and advance?

Attending to the Space

First things first: make certain that your crystal healing session space is clean and clear. Take three minutes and sage the space or say positive mantras to clear it of any negative vibrations. You can simply say, "My space is clean and clear; it is filled with love and gratitude." I always repeat the words *love* and *gratitude* three times to make the space full of positive vibrations.

Next, lie down flat and faceup in a comfortable, quiet place. If you want, you can put an eye pillow or dry wash cloth over your eyes. Sometimes this helps you relax and keeps the light dim. Have all your crystals placed in the appropriate places as shown in each layout diagram. The crystals can be under you or on top of you. If you are on a massage bed, you can lay the crystals on the body or under the bed if you have an adjustable bed set to a low level; the crystals can be up to three feet away from the body, but no farther. This is because the crystals and stones would be outside the auric field and have a lessened effect on the body's energy.

Burning some incense or herbs can enhance the crystal session. I love to use a water diffuser with organic essential oils to relax. A candle is fine too, but make sure it's in glass or self-contained. If your session goes longer than expected, you won't have that candle worry in the back of your mind. Be sure to use organic and nonsynthetic chemicals for aromatic sensitivities.

My Experiences vs. Yours

Please remember we are all different. One crystal layout session may suit you better than me or vice versa. Make sure when you write out your experiences and findings that they are purely what you truly felt or sensed. That is the importance of you experiencing the layouts. If you think that my experience will influence yours, then please do not read the details until after you do the crystal healing. The same goes for comparing with friends. It's fun to share—share and also enjoy the differences. If you get into these meditations often, notice which crystals your body works with best. Remember that as your life changes, your body has different needs—be open to positive change.

Purpose: Achieving my goals, finding my soul's purpose (chapter 6, Layout #5).

Things I saw in visions: I saw myself and two other people with me signing books and speaking to large audiences.

Any particular part of my body I felt most? I felt my throat and my heart. My heart felt overjoyed in the success I saw and felt in that vision. I felt healthy.

Any lesson or insight revealed? I learned that I can complete a dream goal. I felt the real connection of my goal reached in my visions.

Overall experience: How did I feel? Positive!

What were my thoughts immediately after the session? I had ideas for new subjects to write and speak about.

That night, did I have vivid dreams? Yes—more of what I will accomplish.

Did I receive any other important information from this or new revelations throughout my day? I felt empowered all day.

Do I feel like I should do this session again? Yes. I will do a monthly maintenance of this to keep me on track to reach my goals and to keep ideas flowing.

Where I was (location in vision or experience): I felt I was in north Florida but had traveled to speak.

Was it completely quiet? Was there music on? If so, what was it? I had relaxing music called "Relaxing Waves."

Did I burn incense? Nope.

Did I use any essential oils? Yes, just a dabble of frankincense on my third eye area and lavender on my wrists.

What color clothing was I wearing? I was wearing an orange top and blue jeans. (This is something to note because colors can reflect chakras and also our emotions/moods; I also found that colors can be subconsciously telling—orange represents creativity, for example, and I became creative in this vision of my crystal layout.)

Always give yourself ample time after a session. You may feel a bit heavy or light-headed. This is normal with crystal layout sessions. Give yourself at least five to ten minutes to ground yourself, or to bring yourself into a comfortable state of being, allowing your body and mind to be back here on good Earth!

One way to ground is to hold a Black Tourmaline in both of your hands. Keep both feet on the ground and uncrossed. You can sit or stand. This will give you stability and ground you quicker. Remember—no immediate driving after high-vibe sessions!

Time to Experience

Many of the meditations are for relaxing. You may find that you experience astral traveling, insightful messages, and colorful visions. Some of you may fall asleep, and so forth. It is all okay. There is no wrong, but there is a guided suggestion. Remember that no matter what you experience, you are still receiving the healing energies of the crystals.

You can use the crystal layouts with or without the guided meditations. The recorded meditations make it easier for those who need some imagery and guidance. With or without them, you will feel amazing—all you have to do is relax. You may feel tingles and heat or coolness; this is normal. You may feel sensations of floaty-ness or heaviness with some combinations of crystals. This is also normal. In my research, I have experienced feelings of euphoria, complete connection, and incredible visions. You can experience countless sensations during a crystal healing.

An important point to mention is that setting an intention before the session is mandatory. An intention is what you desire and project. It is best when you start your healing to keep your thoughts positive. Thoughts are powerful; only use positive thoughts in your crystal healing. You are enabling yourself to sync your body and mind connection to accept the vibrational exchanges.

On each layout page, I list all the crystals and gemstones you will need for these amazing high-vibe crystal layouts. Each meditation has a format to follow that is best for your experience with that particular layout grid. If you are a novice, I advise you to try these on yourself before using them on others so that you know and feel the experience personally. This way, if you decide to try crystal grids on someone else, you can share your experience. It will also help you as a practitioner choose which grid is best suited for your client or friend.

In every crystal layout, I will remind you of the basics. I made a whatcha' need list:

• The best essential oil for the purpose. You can learn more about each essential oil in the appendix.
• A specific diagram of where to place your crystal gem babies.

• A positive mantra to raise you to high vibes before and after your session.

• A section to chart your chakras using your pendulum.

Remember to cleanse your crystals before and after your session. Use the Tibetan singing bowl or any option from the chapter about cleansing and clearing. Keep a notepad and pen near you to journal about your sessions. After your session, you can log everything you felt, saw, or experienced during your crystal healing session.

If you are a trained healer or high-vibe-crystal-certified facilitator, you should chart a client or friend's progress; it's great for them to see this information. It helps to take notes on what you felt while administering the crystal healing session and listen to your client afterward to record what they experienced as well.

Please note: Turn off your cell phone, computers, and nearby devices; their negative EMFs can disrupt the frequency harmonization of the crystals and your aura.

Start Here

I always state, or have my client state, verbally or mentally, "I am and I allow myself to relax. Love surrounds me—I am love. I am always safe and protected." I do this to raise my vibes and place a positive thought before I travel or journey to wherever the heck I'm going with my crystals.

Please forget about time and all that stuff—just vibe out with your crystal gem babies. That being said, when working with others, I suggest you use a structured order for every session. Order shows your professionalism and demonstrates the integrity of your crystal healing service.

Now that you have perfected the ambiance of your space, cleared the energy in the room, and placed your chart of crystals and your journal next to you, you are ready to go! Good job!

Chapter 5

Body Layouts for Healing and Wellness

Early on in this book, I talked about how crystals can work together, kind of like people who get along. I also discussed how, like people with different personalities, crystals and gemstones hold different frequencies. As people, we can be different but understand each other and have fun together. Crystals are similar in that they emit unique frequencies but can harmonize to be great teammates or buddies for each other. Crystals are remedies that assist us in general healing and in cleansing home grids or crystal body layout sessions. I list the perfect crystal buddies for specific uses ranging from ailments to out-of-body fun. Each layout has harmonizing crystals specific to the purpose of each session. If you need to purchase crystals for your layout, find a local rock shop or go online to get the whole kit we provide for easy use.

Crystal body layouts are listed according to usage and numbered for your convenience. Simply follow the diagram and directions. Crystal layouts are powerful; keep in mind that you may be a bit sensitive after a session. Please give yourself at least five minutes to ground afterward.

In this chapter of body layouts for healing and wellness, you can balance your physical and energetic bodies. I crafted four layout sessions to optimize your entire body. Start with aligning and balancing your chakras; that is a staple crystal layout. Then move up to the next level to improve your mindfulness of the physical body in the polarity session. As you find time for a relaxation and general healing session, you may receive visions. Lastly, I added a calming layout for ADHD. I find it's a growing condition that a crystal session can bring solace to as it lessens overthinking or mental overprocessing. Each layout is unique and refreshing.

The layout choices include:

1. Chakra Healing—Alignment and Balance
2. Polarity Balance—Sync Your Mind and Body
3. Relaxation and General Self-Activation of Healing
4. Calming ADHD

Layout #1: Chakra Healing—Alignment and Balance

The purpose of this crystal layout:

Awaken your senses and perceptions to feel a positive high vibration over your entire body; release stress and bring the *ahhhh* into your whole being. This layout is one of my favorites. This crystal layout is for those who want to become balanced physically, mentally, emotionally, and spiritually and clarify their thinking and choices.

What you need:

1 Amazonite

1 Kyanite

1 Sunstone

1 Quartz Point

1 Red Jasper

1 Citrine

1 Opalite

Why these crystals harmonize together:

Amazonite and Kyanite balance all of you and physically, mentally, emotionally, and spiritually connect you. Kyanite can regulate and align your chakras and clean your aura layers. Citrine and Sunstone erase negative emotions and replace them with positive vibes in the lower chakras, or the sacral and solar

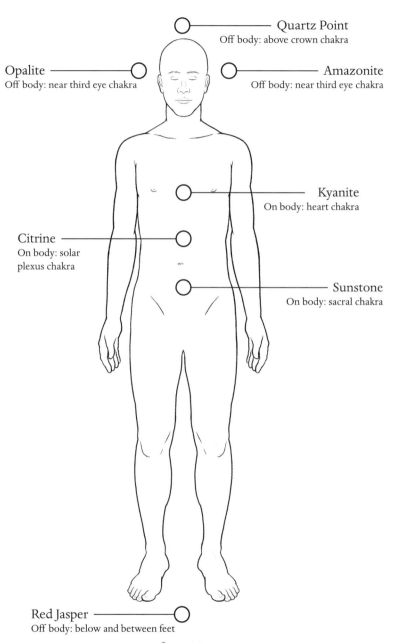

Quartz Point
Off body: above crown chakra

Opalite
Off body: near third eye chakra

Amazonite
Off body: near third eye chakra

Kyanite
On body: heart chakra

Citrine
On body: solar
plexus chakra

Sunstone
On body: sacral chakra

Red Jasper
Off body: below and between feet

Layout 1

plexus. Red Jasper keeps your root chakra and body feeling safe and strong. Quartz Point opens the connection to your source, bringing unconditional love into your whole body, inside and out. Opalite guides the all-knowing you, or the inner self, to feel and / or know that you are balanced and understand the mind-body connection.

Best essential oils for this session (optional):

Lavender oil. I dab it on the third eye chakra and on both wrists.

High-vibe mantra (repeat it three times):

Ohmmmmmm

How long should I lie with this crystal layout?

30–45 minutes is best.

Reminder:

You should always sit or lie with your crystal layout for at least 20 minutes to receive proper balancing and harmonizing. Longer sessions (up to 90 minutes) are positive for you as well. If you need to set an alarm for your session, please do. Place all cell phones or electronic devices in a nearby room or hallway; they should be at least eight feet away from you and your crystals. Cellular phones, computers, and power outlets create negative energies for meditation and healing.

Crystal Body Layout

1. Find a quiet, Zen place to lie down. You can add light music if you prefer. I enjoy the light music of Llewellyn's "Return to the Temple" tracks.
2. Make yourself comfortable. Lie faceup.
3. See the diagram on page 111. This is where to place the crystals; this layout is placed on your physical body.
4. Set a specific intention; say it aloud or in your mind as you are ready to close your eyes and relax. Intention means what you desire and project with your thoughts. Here are two intentions; you can use one or both. **Intention one:** *"I am and I allow myself to completely relax. I am healing my body physically, emotionally, and mentally. I accept this healing and am always*

protected by the light that surrounds me." **Intention two:** *"I give myself permission. My session today is just to relax and release stress."* If you need to heal/erase/let go of something, state the specifics and allow yourself to heal.

5. If you are a visual person, as you close your eyes and state your intentions, try to imagine a white or gold healing light moving over your entire body. Just relax, and if you fall asleep, know it is just fine to do so.

6. When you wake or open your eyes after the session is complete, focus on your feet and imagine them as roots going into the ground like a tree. This visualization will help you feel more alert and return to your physical body. Say in your mind or aloud, "I am perfectly fine and well, and my body is self-healing. I am balanced and feel great." As you open your eyes and state you are balanced and well, you will notice both of your feet. This helps you come back into the present moment and ground. Take a few minutes before you get completely up, and slowly arise when ready. Please drink water to hydrate.

Layout #2:
Polarity Balance—Sync Your Mind and Body

The purpose of this crystal layout:

This layout is for those who have mind chatter, think too fast or too slow, and need to balance mind with body and connect both in synchronicity; also for those who need to balance their male and female sides (yin and yang). This is a meditation where you begin to notice every part of your body, enhancing your yin and yang and fortifying your mind-body connection equally. Your conscious and subconscious are joined and have perfect understanding of what brings you positive balance in life.

What you need:

4 Lepidolites

4 Rose Quartzes

2 Amethysts

1 Azurite

3 Zebra Agates

1 Aragonite

Why these crystals harmonize together:

Lepidolite balances the emotions to resist chaos and disorder and keeps you relaxed. Rose Quartz brings love and harmony of the body and organs. Amethyst protects and balances while the Azurite connects your male and female sides to equally balance the right and left brain. The Zebra Agates work in harmony to sync all emotions, and the Aragonite makes all of the above known in the present moment—as you arise from this meditation, you will take action toward balancing your lifestyle and physical body.

Best essential oils for this session (optional):

Peppermint and lavender mixed together or rose oil alone. I dab the oil on the third eye chakra and on both wrists.

High-vibe mantra (repeat it three times):

Lahhhhhhhhh Mayyyyyyyyyyeh

How long should I lie with this crystal layout?

35–45 minutes is best.

Reminder:

You should always sit or lie with your crystal layout for at least 20 minutes to receive proper balancing and harmonizing. Longer sessions (up to 90 minutes) are positive for you as well. If you need to set an alarm for your session, please do. Place all cell phones or electronic devices in a nearby room or hallway; they should be at least eight feet away from you and your crystals. Cellular phones, computers, and power outlets create negative energies for meditation and healing.

Crystal Body Layout

1. Find a quiet, Zen place to lie down. You can add light music if you prefer. "Reiki Sleep Gold" by Llewellyn is the perfect amount of time at 43 minutes.

2. Make yourself comfortable. Lie faceup.

3. See the diagram on page 115. This is where to place the crystals; this layout is placed on your physical body.

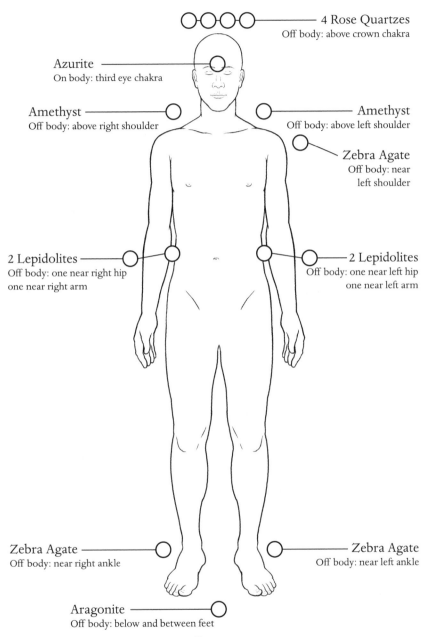

4 Rose Quartzes
Off body: above crown chakra

Azurite
On body: third eye chakra

Amethyst
Off body: above right shoulder

Amethyst
Off body: above left shoulder

Zebra Agate
Off body: near
left shoulder

2 Lepidolites
Off body: one near right hip
one near right arm

2 Lepidolites
Off body: one near left hip
one near left arm

Zebra Agate
Off body: near right ankle

Zebra Agate
Off body: near left ankle

Aragonite
Off body: below and between feet

Layout 2

4. Set a specific intention; say it aloud or in your mind as you are ready to close your eyes and relax. Intention means what you desire and project with your thoughts. Here are two intentions; you can use one or both. **Intention one**: *"I am and I allow myself to completely relax. I am healing my body physically, emotionally, and mentally. I accept this healing and am always protected by the light that surrounds me."* **Intention two**: *"I give myself permission. My session today is to heal/erase/let go of ..."* State the specifics and allow yourself to heal by focusing on any afflicted body parts for at least two minutes.

5. If you are a visual person, as you close your eyes and state your intentions, try to separately imagine the right side of your body and then the left side of your body, starting from the top of your head and slowly moving down to your feet. Then, after noticing each side separately, focus on each chakra in the middle of your body. Start from the crown chakra at the top of your head and move down to the third eye chakra, the throat chakra, the heart chakra (center of the chest), the solar plexus chakra (stomach), the sacral chakra (just below the navel), and the root chakra at the base of your spine. After feeling or visualizing, just relax, and if you fall asleep, know it is just fine to do so. If you need healing in one or more chakra areas of your body, you can focus on that chakra and its color; the colors that represent each chakra are listed on your chakra pendulum practice sheet.

6. When you wake or open your eyes after the session is complete, focus on your feet and imagine them as roots going into the ground like a tree. This visualization will help you feel more alert and return to your physical body. Say in your mind or aloud, "I am perfectly fine and well, and my body is self-healing. I am balanced and feel great. I am well." As you open your eyes and state you are balanced and well, you will notice both of your feet. This helps you come back into the present moment and ground. Take a few minutes before you get completely up, and slowly arise when ready. Please drink water to hydrate.

Layout #3:
Relaxation and General Self-Activation of Healing

The purpose of this crystal layout:

Many of us need a jump-start to activate ourselves and to have a better understanding of our purposes in life, but—dammit man—sometimes we need some time to just be. This crystal layout enhances self-healing on all levels: physical, emotional, mental, and spiritual. You will relax and feel an energetic healing of the body, mind, and soul and bring in energies of light, which can adjust or help heal while fortifying the immune system. This meditation also releases stress or uneasiness in one's life.

What you need:

4 Black Tourmalines

4 Selenites

2 Green Aventurines

1 Amethyst

1 Emerald

2 Fluorites

1 Garnet

1 Green Obsidian

1 Herkimer Diamond

1 Citrine

Why these crystals harmonize together:

Selenite and Black Tourmaline bring absorbing energy to erase patterns and cleanse them from your aura layers. Green Aventurine enables love to fill in for the old patterns that were brushed out. The Amethyst brings composure and healing energy to your mind and physical body while the Emerald can help heal the heart. The Fluorites regulate your adrenal glands and body to function well; place them on or near the thymus gland just above the heart chakra and below the throat chakra. The Garnet adjusts all the organs, and Green Obsidian brings

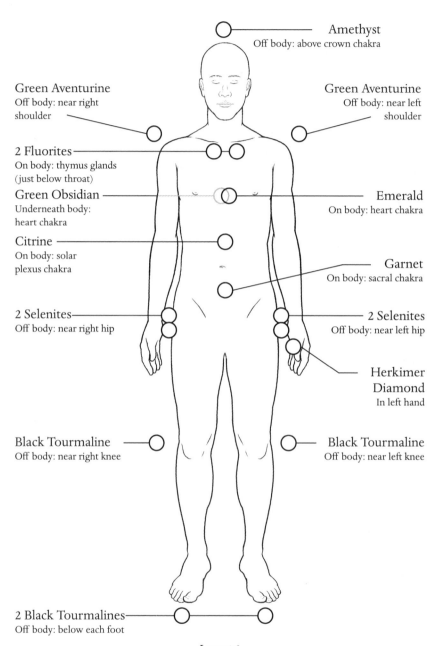

Amethyst
Off body: above crown chakra

Green Aventurine
Off body: near right
shoulder

Green Aventurine
Off body: near left
shoulder

2 Fluorites
On body: thymus glands
(just below throat)

Green Obsidian
Underneath body:
heart chakra

Emerald
On body: heart chakra

Citrine
On body: solar
plexus chakra

Garnet
On body: sacral chakra

2 Selenites
Off body: near right hip

2 Selenites
Off body: near left hip

Herkimer
Diamond
In left hand

Black Tourmaline
Off body: near right knee

Black Tourmaline
Off body: near left knee

2 Black Tourmalines
Off body: below each foot

Layout 3

the power of light to ensure optimism and hope. The Herkimer Diamond brings vivid messages and visions and amplifies all healing power to make one well-balanced and relaxed. The Citrine changes the vibes in the solar plexus from negative to positive, enlightening your emotions.

Best essential oils for this session (optional):

Lavender oil. I dab it on the third eye chakra and on both wrists.

High-vibe mantra (repeat it three times):

Laahhhhhhhhhhhhhhhhh

How long should I lie with this crystal layout?

30–90 minutes is best.

Reminder:

You should always sit or lie with your crystal layout for at least 20 minutes to receive proper balancing and harmonizing. Longer sessions (up to 90 minutes) are positive for you as well. If you need to set an alarm for your session, please do. Place all cell phones or electronic devices in a nearby room or hallway; they should be at least eight feet away from you and your crystals. Cellular phones, computers, and power outlets create negative energies for meditation and healing.

Crystal Body Layout

1. Find a quiet, Zen place to lie down. You can add light music if you prefer. I love playing Angel-inspired music for this crystal healing. I love Angel energy!
2. Make yourself comfortable. Lie faceup.
3. See the diagram on page 118. This is where to place the crystals; this layout is placed on your physical body.
4. Set a specific intention; say it aloud or in your mind as you are ready to close your eyes and relax. Intention means what you desire and project with your thoughts. Here are two intentions; you can use one or both. **Intention one:** *"I am and I allow myself to completely relax. I am healing my body physically, emotionally, and mentally. I accept this healing and am always*

protected by the light that surrounds me." **Intention two:** *"I give myself per-mission. My session today is to relax and release overthinking."*

5. If you are a visual person, as you close your eyes and state your intentions, try to imagine a beautiful pink healing light moving over your entire body. Just relax, and if you fall asleep, know it is just fine to do so.

6. When you wake or open your eyes after the session is complete, focus on your feet and imagine them as roots going into the ground like a tree. This visualization will help you feel more alert and return to your physical body. Say in your mind or aloud, "I am perfectly fine and well, and my body is self-healing. I am balanced and feel great." As you open your eyes and state you are balanced and well, you will notice both of your feet. This helps you come back into the present moment and ground. Take a few minutes before you get completely up, and slowly arise when ready. Please drink water to hydrate.

Layout #4: Calming ADHD

The purpose of this crystal layout:

When we are unable to calm the mind, our bodies and emotions can become unruly. If you find it hard to concentrate, this layout is for you. This meditation harmonizes the body on all levels to comfort the mind and soul and to align and balance; this meditation will also adjust the frequencies in your aura that have been keeping you awry.

What you need:

2 Blue Lace Agates

1 Kyanite

4 Lepidolites

1 Moldavite

1 Moss Agate

1 Rutile Quartz

4 White Howlites

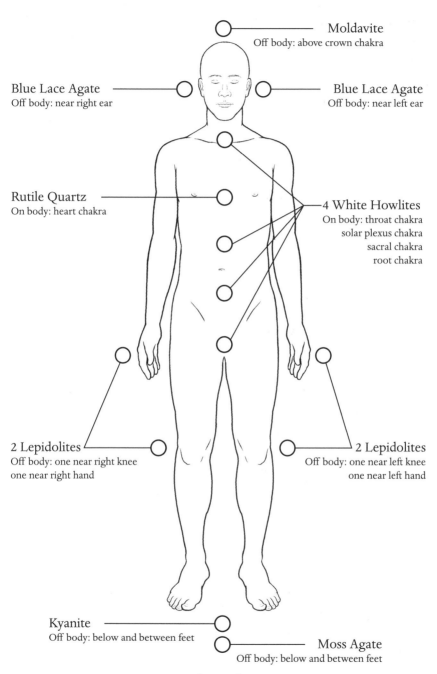

Moldavite
Off body: above crown chakra

Blue Lace Agate
Off body: near right ear

Blue Lace Agate
Off body: near left ear

Rutile Quartz
On body: heart chakra

4 White Howlites
On body: throat chakra
solar plexus chakra
sacral chakra
root chakra

2 Lepidolites
Off body: one near right knee
one near right hand

2 Lepidolites
Off body: one near left knee
one near left hand

Kyanite
Off body: below and between feet

Moss Agate
Off body: below and between feet

Layout 4

Why these crystals harmonize together:

The Blue Lace Agates calm mental chatter and bring a calm, safe feeling to keep one peaceful during this session. The Kyanite balances and aligns all the energy of the chakras while the Lepidolite soothes the moods to be stable. Moldavite allows a flow of relaxing energy into the mind and body, releasing tension and stress from overthinking. The Moss Agate grounds the thoughts, and Rutile Quartz helps rid the person's patterns, or irrational/abrupt behaviors, as White Howlite extends focus.

Best essential oils for this session (optional):

Lavender or chamomile oil. I dab the oil on the third eye chakra and on both wrists.

High-vibe mantra (repeat it three times):

Ahhhhh

How long should I lie with this crystal layout?

25–40 minutes is best.

Reminder:

You should always sit or lie with your crystal layout for at least 20 minutes to receive proper balancing and harmonizing. Longer sessions (up to 90 minutes) are positive for you as well. If you need to set an alarm for your session, please do. Place all cell phones or electronic devices in a nearby room or hallway; they should be at least eight feet away from you and your crystals. Cellular phones, computers, and power outlets create negative energies for meditation and healing.

Crystal Body Layout

1. Find a quiet, Zen place to lie down. You can add light music if you prefer. My fav is "Reiki Gold" by Llewellyn.
2. Make yourself comfortable. Lie faceup.
3. See the diagram on page 121. This is where to place the crystals; this layout is placed on your physical body.

4. Set a specific intention; say it aloud or in your mind as you are ready to close your eyes and relax. Intention means what you desire and project with your thoughts. Here is the intention you can use: *"I am and I allow my mind and body to slow down so I can relax. As I relax, I am noticing my heartbeat and my breathing. This makes me feel peaceful and comfortable. I hear my body, and it is soothing to me."*

5. If you are a visual person, as you close your eyes and state your intention, try to imagine a white or gold healing light moving over your entire body. Just relax, and if you fall asleep, know it is just fine to do so.

6. When you wake or open your eyes after the session is complete, focus on your feet and imagine them as roots going into the ground like a tree. This visualization will help you feel more alert and return to your physical body. Say in your mind or aloud, "I am perfectly fine and well, and my body is self-healing. I am balanced and feel great." As you open your eyes and state you are balanced and well, you will notice both of your feet. This helps you come back into the present moment and ground. Take a few minutes before you get completely up, and slowly arise when ready. Please drink water to hydrate.

If you found that at least two out of the four body layout sessions in this chapter have balanced your total being, you have succeeded! It is important that everyone balances and strengthens the mental and emotional energy fields/aura layers with positive frequencies. The physical aura layer and spiritual connections are affected strongly when the mental and emotional layers are unhealthy. Using one or more of these body and wellness crystal layouts for monthly maintenance can keep you on track.

Chapter 6
Layouts for Achieving Your Goals

Layouts for achieving your goals are critical if you want to reach them in a realistic time period. Try using one or all of these layouts. If you are a goal-setter like me, you will have a ball with these five layouts. I personally have one big goal per month; I make a date to hit that goal and place it on my refrigerator. There is no missing my list; I see it at least three times per day, embedding it in my conscious and subconscious to push for those achievements. Many people have a tough time getting started on their goals, usually because they just don't know how. I laid it all out for you—literally—with the crystal grids.

It's time you connect with at least one purpose per month. Because our purposes change often, it is good to state in your mind and write on paper what goals you want to reach. The goals can be small, such as completing a shopping list, or big and substantial, such as creating a lifestyle abundant with love, money, or self-improvement/health. Attracting like-minded love is a goal all in its own, but you can adjust your love intent for a relationship, for family, or for friendship. The money, luck, and abundance layout is something we all can accept easily. The new beginnings session can be for your various life changes, from a new work attitude to a new life. If it's fertility you are after, that session brings you to gain the positive mindset and physical health necessary for a new child. Lastly, the rational mind layout is something we all need to be mentally sound and logical.

Layout #5:
Find Your Purpose

The purpose of this crystal layout:

This crystal layout is for those who want to find one of their purposes at this time in their life. This layout helps practitioners trust themselves and feel loved, protected, and important.

What you need:

> 1 Thunder Agate
>
> 2 Green Tourmalines
>
> 4 Quartzes, tumbled or raw
>
> 1 Quartz Point
>
> 1 Cavansite

Why these crystals harmonize together:

The Thunder Agate brings Earth energy to release unwanted toxins of life, from thoughts to daily actions, to bring one back to nature, a healthy lifestyle, and honoring oneself and nature. Thunder Agate keeps your body grounded, which guides your Earthly body to acknowledge what your higher self believes is the best course of action. You receive this information on a conscious and subconscious level with the Green Tourmaline's energy. Green Tourmaline heals all wounds of the soul while Quartz clarifies the intent and purpose of your healing and provides insight into correcting your path. The Quartz Point draws the sky's strong energy within and around your auric fields to protect the shared knowledge from your soul's energy (the core of your existence) and transmit the knowledge to your physical body. The Quartz and the Cavansite give you the high frequencies to "hear" the information clearly and/or vividly through visons or feelings, and Cavansite enlightens you to new directions and finding your soul's purpose.

Best essential oils for this session (optional):

Rosemary oil or tangerine oil. I dab the oil on the third eye chakra and on both wrists.

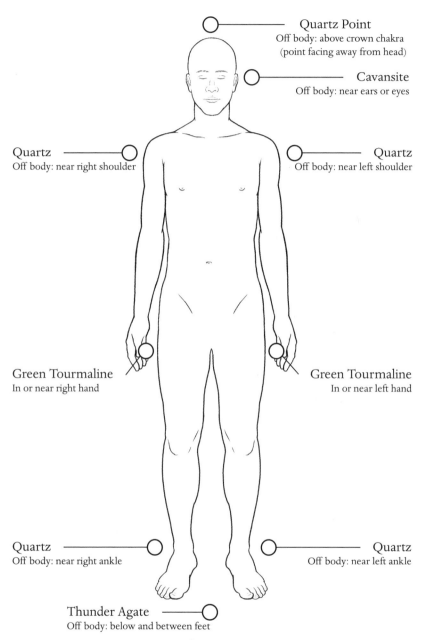

Quartz Point
Off body: above crown chakra
(point facing away from head)

Cavansite
Off body: near ears or eyes

Quartz
Off body: near right shoulder

Quartz
Off body: near left shoulder

Green Tourmaline
In or near right hand

Green Tourmaline
In or near left hand

Quartz
Off body: near right ankle

Quartz
Off body: near left ankle

Thunder Agate
Off body: below and between feet

Layout 5

High-vibe mantra (repeat it three times):
Ohhhhhhhhha rhiiiiiiiiiiii

How long should I lie with this crystal layout?
30–60 minutes is best.

Reminder:
You should always sit or lie with your crystal layout for at least 20 minutes to receive proper balancing and harmonizing. Longer sessions (up to 90 minutes) are positive for you as well. If you need to set an alarm for your session, please do. Place all cell phones or electronic devices in a nearby room or hallway; they should be at least eight feet away from you and your crystals. Cellular phones, computers, and power outlets create negative energies for meditation and healing.

Crystal Body Layout

1. Find a quiet, Zen place to lie down. You can add light music if you prefer. I like any Native American tribal drum or flute music for this one.

2. Make yourself comfortable. Lie faceup.

3. See the diagram on page 127. This is where to place the crystals; this layout is placed on your physical body.

4. Set a specific intention; say it aloud or in your mind as you are ready to close your eyes and relax. Intention means what you desire and project with your thoughts. Here are two intentions; you can use one or both. **Intention one:** *"I am and I allow myself to completely relax. I am healing my body physically, emotionally, and mentally. I accept this healing and am always protected by the light that surrounds me."* **Intention two:** *"I give myself permission."* Focus on your third eye chakra between your eyebrows. This allows you to open that chakra and clarifies any inner knowing you receive. Next, bring your focus to the crown chakra at the top of your head. This focus will allow you to feel and sense. Continue by invoking the universe, your guides, or your higher self: *"Please allow me to see, sense, or feel a clear message of what one of my current purposes is at this time in my life, year 20___. Gratitude; I am open to receive this positive information now."*

5. If you are a visual person, as you close your eyes and state your intentions, try to imagine a white or gold healing light moving over your entire body. Just relax, and if you fall asleep, know it is just fine to do so.

6. When you wake or open your eyes after the session is complete, focus on your feet and imagine them as roots going into the ground like a tree. This visualization will help you feel more alert and return to your physical body. Say in your mind or aloud, "I am perfectly fine and well, and my body is self-healing. I am balanced and feel great." Ask again what your purpose is at this time in your life. After this session, many people feel at peace and like they've gained insight into their goals or making purposeful lifestyle changes that will benefit them in the immediate future. Writing down what you saw, felt, or experienced during this session is extremely useful and insightful. As you open your eyes and state you are balanced and well, you will notice both of your feet. This helps you come back into the present moment and ground. Take a few minutes before you get completely up, and slowly arise when ready. Please drink water to hydrate.

Layout #6:
Attract Like-Minded Love

The purpose of this crystal layout:

This crystal layout is for those who want to bring in love from sources other than the self. This could mean attracting a new relationship, lover, significant other, or respect from others, such as family, coworkers, etcetera. You will also feel energies of unconditional love from your source energy using these high frequency crystal combinations. The intention is to gain newfound love and respect and attract what you want and desire. The goal is to also become balanced physically, mentally, emotionally, and spiritually, and clear in thoughts and choices. If you are doing this crystal layout for emotional or mental reasons, imagine green or pink and hold your hands over your heart chakra as you voice your intention.

What you need:

2 Rhodochrosites

4 Rose Quartzes

1 Charoite

3 Carnelians

1 Lapis Lazuli

3 Red Jaspers

1 Quartz Point

Why these crystals harmonize together:

Rhodochrosite brings in love from sources of light and sometimes loved ones in spirit realms; Rhodochrosite attracts what you desire, while Rose Quartz gives you appreciation, compassion, and self-love. The Charoite stone helps one find the source of their needs and new perspectives that guide them to attain what they desire. The Carnelians activate creativity and energetically reset the reproductive organs. Lapis protects you on all levels of existence, opens the senses, and awakens the third eye. Red Jasper gives one strength and security. The Quartz Point allows clarity and amplifies all of the crystals to harmonize with good intent.

Best essential oils for this session (optional):

Rose or lavender oil. I dab the oil on the third eye chakra and on both wrists.

High-vibe mantra (repeat it three times):

Looove ahhhhhhhhhhh

How long should I lie with this crystal layout?

45–90 minutes is best.

Reminder:

You should always sit or lie with your crystal layout for at least 20 minutes to receive proper balancing and harmonizing. Longer sessions (up to 90 minutes) are positive for you as well. If you need to set an alarm for your session, please do. Place all cell phones or electronic devices in a nearby room or hallway; they should be at least eight feet away from you and your crystals. Cellular phones, computers, and power outlets create negative energies for meditation and healing.

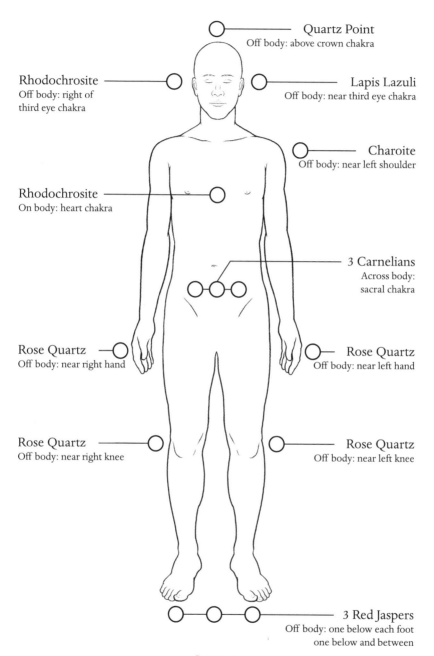

Quartz Point
Off body: above crown chakra

Rhodochrosite
Off body: right of
third eye chakra

Lapis Lazuli
Off body: near third eye chakra

Charoite
Off body: near left shoulder

Rhodochrosite
On body: heart chakra

3 Carnelians
Across body:
sacral chakra

Rose Quartz
Off body: near right hand

Rose Quartz
Off body: near left hand

Rose Quartz
Off body: near right knee

Rose Quartz
Off body: near left knee

3 Red Jaspers
Off body: one below each foot
one below and between

Layout 6

Crystal Body Layout

1. Find a quiet, Zen place to lie down. You can add light music if you prefer. I love some low volume serenity spa music for this session.

2. Make yourself comfortable. Lie faceup.

3. See the diagram on page 131. This is where to place the crystals; this layout is sweet—it rocks!

4. Set a specific intention; say it aloud or in your mind as you are ready to close your eyes and relax. Intention means what you desire and project with your thoughts. **Intention:** *"I am and I allow myself to release any old relationships that no longer serve me. I allow myself to replace that voided energy with positive love for myself. I choose to love. I deserve love. Love that I know is matching my understanding and definition of love."* You can additionally say what you want in respect to your love life, what you want for someone you love and/or who loves you, or what you want to be.

5. If you are a visual person, as you close your eyes and state your intention, try to imagine the real heart or the green or pink heart. Just relax, and if you fall asleep, know it is just fine to do so.

6. When you wake or open your eyes after the session is complete, focus on your heart and notice how it feels: Is it heavier or lighter? Do you feel relief? Make notes. Next, focus on your feet and imagine them as roots going into the ground like a tree. This visualization will help you feel more alert and return to your physical body, or ground you. Slowly wiggle your fingers and toes before you sit upright. Make sure you drink plenty of water to hydrate and replenish the body after the crystals' energy and your own have synthesized.

Layout #7: Money, Luck, and Abundance

The purpose of this crystal layout:

Money, luck, and abundance. Need I say more. This is self-explanatory. The purpose of this meditation is to attract money and manifest luck and goodness with equal energy exchanges; the practitioner will meditate for abundance, which can be abundance of money, love, happiness, and health. Regarding money, remember: you can earn it, you can win it, and you can be gifted it and happily accept it, because you deserve it.

Set your intention. Make it clear what you desire and project and then create and allow positive opportunities for good fortune in your life. This includes attracting the energy that will manifest in wins, money, gifts, and earning through good endeavors. After this crystal session, your aura will say, "I accept good things—bring them my way! I am a lucky human!"

What you need:

6 Citrines

4 Green Aventurines

1 White Howlite

1 Amber

1 Blue Lace Agate

Why these crystals harmonize together:

The combination of Citrine and Green Aventurine brings abundance, especially money abundance. The Green Aventurine also instills the frequencies of confidence and action. The key to success here is when the subconscious and conscious parts of you sync with an understanding of what you are intently working to achieve. It's important that your soul knows you deserve this good exchange of energy so that you can accept the money and positive opportunities that come your way. White Howlite gives you the focus and clarity to accomplish your goals, Amber activates the ego in loving ways, and Blue Lace Agate helps you hear and sense the ideas that your source is sending you. The Green Aventurine brings luck, prosperity, and options for success.

Best essential oils for this session (optional):

I dab bergamot or geranium oil on my third eye, sacral, and solar plexus chakras and on both wrists. If the pure oils are too potent for your skin, please mix them with a carrier oil.

High-vibe mantra (repeat it three times):

Tuuuhhhhhh maaaaaaaaayyyyyyyy

How long should I lie with this crystal layout?

40–90 minutes is best.

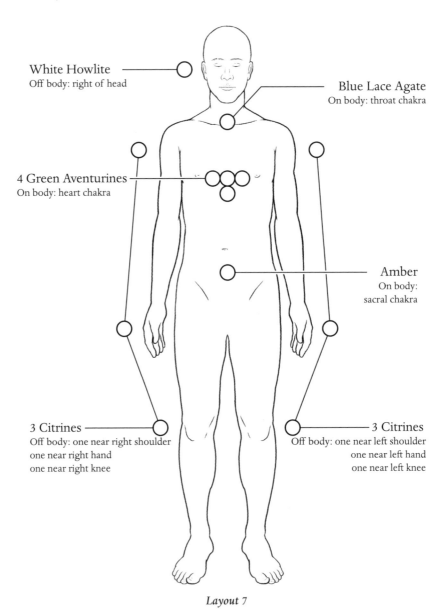

White Howlite
Off body: right of head

Blue Lace Agate
On body: throat chakra

4 Green Aventurines
On body: heart chakra

Amber
On body:
sacral chakra

3 Citrines
Off body: one near right shoulder
one near right hand
one near right knee

3 Citrines
Off body: one near left shoulder
one near left hand
one near left knee

Layout 7

Reminder:

You should always sit or lie with your crystal layout for at least 20 minutes to receive proper balancing and harmonizing. Longer sessions (up to 90 minutes) are positive for you as well. If you need to set an alarm for your session, please do. Place all cell phones or electronic devices in a nearby room or hallway; they should be at least eight feet away from you and your crystals. Cellular phones, computers, and power outlets create negative energies for meditation and healing.

Crystal Body Layout

1. Find a quiet, Zen place to lie down. You can add light music if you prefer.

2. Make yourself comfortable. Lie faceup.

3. See the diagram on page 134. This is where to place the crystals; this layout is placed on your physical body.

4. Set a specific intention; say it aloud or in your mind as you are ready to close your eyes and relax. Intention means what you desire and project with your thoughts. Here are two intentions; you can use one or both. **Intention one:** *"I am and I allow myself to completely relax. I am healing my body physically, emotionally, and mentally. I accept this healing and am always protected by the light that surrounds me. I give myself permission. My session today is to allow myself to be abundant in*—state your desire specifically, or say—*all ways in this Earthly life."* For your information, abundance can be of health, money, friends, family, lovers, business, and so on. **Intention two:** *"Money and good fortune come my way easily. I can earn it, I can win it, I can be gifted it, and I happily accept it because I deserve it."* Feel in your body that you're deserving. To guide yourself toward this deserving feeling, place your hands on your heart chakra as you say the second intention. This helps you to literally feel and can be what you need to make your conscious and subconscious understand that you do deserve love, money, health, and all that you desire.

5. If you are a visual person, as you close your eyes and state this intention, try to imagine a green or gold healing light moving over your entire body. Just relax, and if you fall asleep, know it is just fine to do so.

6. When you wake or open your eyes after the session is complete, focus on your feet and imagine them as roots going into the ground like a tree. This visualization will help you feel more alert and return to your physical body. Say in your mind or aloud, "I am perfectly fine and well, and my body is self-healing. I am balanced and feel great. I am abundant [say in what or all you desire], and I deserve this abundance to come to me this year of 20__, Earth dimension." This makes a difference—I'm totally serious! As you open your eyes and state you are balanced and well, you will notice both of your feet. This helps you come back into the present moment and ground. Take a few minutes before you get completely up, and slowly arise when ready. Please drink water to hydrate.

Layout #8:
New Beginnings and Fertility

The purpose of this crystal layout:

New beginnings and fertility is for those who want to invite a new soul into the Earthly realm or allow newness into one's life for fulfillment and joy. This is a jump-start of a person's cycles to promote new awareness and enhance the chances of fertility. Please use the specific intention for your goal.

What you need:

  4 Moonstones

  1 Ruby Zoisite

  2 Sunstones

Why these crystals harmonize together:

Moonstones promote healthy body cycles, and Ruby Zoisite brings forward movement. Sunstone represents creation, new life, fresh thoughts, and readiness for lifestyle changes.

Best essential oils for this session (optional):

Lavender oil. I dab it on the third eye chakra and on both wrists.

High-vibe mantra (repeat it three times):

Neeewww

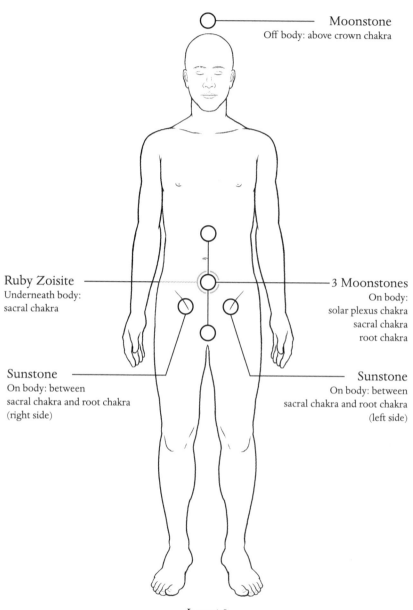

Moonstone
Off body: above crown chakra

Ruby Zoisite
Underneath body:
sacral chakra

3 Moonstones
On body:
solar plexus chakra
sacral chakra
root chakra

Sunstone
On body: between
sacral chakra and root chakra
(right side)

Sunstone
On body: between
sacral chakra and root chakra
(left side)

Layout 8

How long should I lie with this crystal layout?

30–60 minutes is best.

Reminder:

You should always sit or lie with your crystal layout for at least 20 minutes to receive proper balancing and harmonizing. Longer sessions (up to 90 minutes) are positive for you as well. If you need to set an alarm for your session, please do. Place all cell phones or electronic devices in a nearby room or hallway; they should be at least eight feet away from you and your crystals. Cellular phones, computers, and power outlets create negative energies for meditation and healing.

Crystal Body Layout

1. Find a quiet, Zen place to lie down. You can add light music if you prefer. My fav is "Reiki Gold" by Llewellyn. It's about one hour in length.

2. Make yourself comfortable. Lie faceup.

3. See the diagram on page 137. This is where to place the crystals; this layout is placed on your physical body.

4. Set a specific intention; say it aloud or in your mind as you are ready to close your eyes and relax. Intention means what you desire and project with your thoughts. Here are two intentions; you can use one or both. **Intention one (for all aspects of life):** *"I am ready for new beginnings. I allow myself to move forward with my life in all aspects. I allow the changes to be positive."* **Intention two (for fertility):** *"My body is ready to accept a seed to new life—I want, desire, and allow myself to be a parent pregnant with a healthy child."*

5. If you are a visual person, as you close your eyes and state your intention, try to imagine a white or gold healing light moving over your entire body. Just relax, and if you fall asleep, know it is just fine to do so.

6. When you wake or open your eyes after the session is complete, focus on your feet and imagine them as roots going into the ground like a tree. This visualization will help you feel more alert and return to your physical body. Say in your mind or aloud, "I am perfectly fine and well, and my body is self-healing. I am balanced and feel great." As you open your eyes

and state you are balanced and well, you will notice both of your feet. This helps you come back into the present moment and ground. Take a few minutes before you get completely up, and slowly arise when ready. Please drink water to hydrate.

Layout #9:
Rational Mind

The purpose of this crystal layout:

Having trouble with everyday decisions? Overthinking or overevaluating? The rational mind grid is available for you to test out; it instills focus and steady rationalization.

What you need:

  1 Azurite

  4 Lepidolites

  6 Quartzes

  2 Unakites

Why these crystals harmonize together:

Azurite opens the third eye chakra for better visions in the meditative state. The combination of the four Lepidolites around the body incorporates steady vibrations of calming energy that penetrate through the physical, emotional, and mental levels of the auric layers. Adding the Quartz amplifies this focus of energy to make a person completely relax, let go of worries, and just be, releasing the chaotic thoughts and indecisions that come with overevaluating. The Unakite stones help reveal inner truth and desires.

Best essential oils for this session (optional):

Rosemary oil. I dab it on the third eye chakra and on both wrists.

High-vibe mantra (repeat it three times):

Meeeee

How long should I lie with this crystal layout?

30–40 minutes is best.

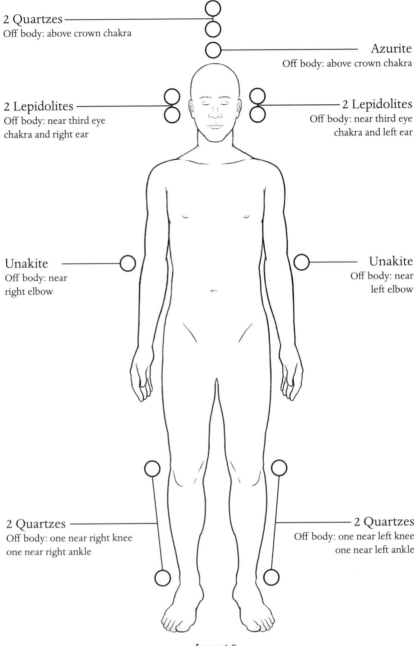

2 Quartzes
Off body: above crown chakra

Azurite
Off body: above crown chakra

2 Lepidolites
Off body: near third eye
chakra and right ear

2 Lepidolites
Off body: near third eye
chakra and left ear

Unakite
Off body: near
right elbow

Unakite
Off body: near
left elbow

2 Quartzes
Off body: one near right knee
one near right ankle

2 Quartzes
Off body: one near left knee
one near left ankle

Layout 9

Reminder:

You should always sit or lie with your crystal layout for at least 20 minutes to receive proper balancing and harmonizing. Longer sessions (up to 90 minutes) are positive for you as well. If you need to set an alarm for your session, please do. Place all cell phones or electronic devices in a nearby room or hallway; they should be at least eight feet away from you and your crystals. Cellular phones, computers, and power outlets create negative energies for meditation and healing.

Crystal Body Layout

1. Find a quiet, Zen place to lie down. You can add light music if you prefer. My fav is "Crystal Labyrinth" by Stone Age Music; it adds soft sound healing to the session.

2. Make yourself comfortable. Lie faceup.

3. See the diagram on page 140. This is where to place the crystals; this layout is placed on your physical body.

4. Set a specific intention; say it aloud or in your mind as you are ready to close your eyes and relax. Intention means what you desire and project with your thoughts. **Intention:** *"I am and I allow myself to think clearly and accurately. My mind is balanced and healthy. I make positive, rational decisions."*

5. If you are a visual person, as you close your eyes and state your intention, try to imagine a white or gold healing light moving over your entire body. Just relax, and if you fall asleep, know it is just fine to do so.

6. When you wake or open your eyes after the session is complete, focus on your feet and imagine them as roots going into the ground like a tree. This visualization will help you feel more alert and return to your physical body. Say in your mind or aloud, "I am perfectly fine and well, and my body is self-healing. I am balanced and feel great." As you open your eyes and state you are balanced and well, you will notice both of your feet. This helps you come back into the present moment and ground. Take a few minutes before you get completely up, and slowly arise when ready. Please drink water to hydrate.

Now you are a champion goal-setter; you've enabled yourself to have an abundant life of love, money, and success—all while thinking rationally! Wow, you should have some incredibly grounded energy; kudos. Please, share the knowledge with others. There is plenty abundance for everyone!

Chapter 7
Layouts for Attending to Your Spirit Self

You are now in my favorite zone of crystal body layouts: attending to your self-spirit! These make me imagine a bird soaring out of my physical existence to accept freedom, explore new dimensions, and access different lives. We can learn so much from seeing through new eyes or open perspectives. Once you relax in this type of session and trust the unknown, you become an ultimate human being. If you aren't quite there yet, you will release the toxins of stuck energies with self-exorcisms/entity removal, and then you'll move forward to the elemental balance meditation after heading out of your body.

Layout #10:
Spacey Fun Out-of-Body Experience

The purpose of this crystal layout:

This trippy Moldavite meteor/spacey fun out-of-body experience is for someone looking to release from the heart chakra and escape from the Earthly world for a bit. This crystal body layout totally induces a stoned sensation. You gotta love this one, but don't drive until you ground yourself after embarking on this Galileo space odyssey! This layout is great for those who want to astral travel and explore space and the beyond.

What you need:

> 1 Moldavite Tektite
>
> 8 Selenites
>
> 1 Smoky Quartz
>
> 1 Clear Quartz

Why these crystals harmonize together:

Moldavite helps you release anything you need to let go of from the conscious and subconscious. Moldavite can lift you out of the body with stellar effects. The Selenite will keep you clear of any aliens—ha! I mean your crazy subconscious thoughts or visions. Selenite will also cleanse the space of your session and your auric layers. Smoky Quartz keeps you protected and safe while journeying outside the body. Clear Quartz brings you clear visions and amplifies your senses. All these harmonize to make you feel connected to the cosmos. It is peaceful and, for some travelers of space and the beyond, educational.

Best essential oils for this session (optional):

Moldavite, sage, or rose oil. I dab the oil on the third eye chakra and on both wrists. I like to smear a dab of rose oil on my ankles for this session as well.

High-vibe mantra (repeat it three times):

Ohhhhhhhhha rhiiiiiiiiiiii

How long should I lie with this crystal layout?

30–90 minutes is best.

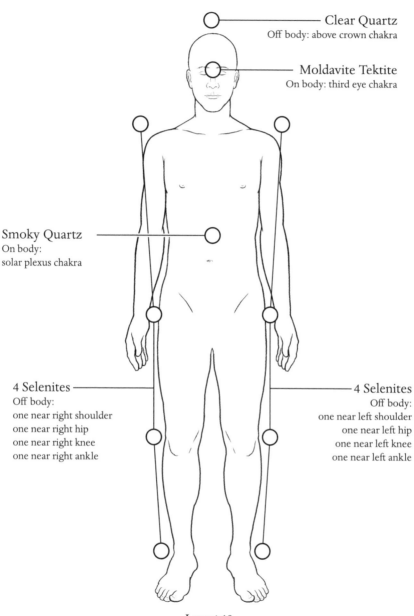

Clear Quartz
Off body: above crown chakra

Moldavite Tektite
On body: third eye chakra

Smoky Quartz
On body:
solar plexus chakra

4 Selenites
Off body:
one near right shoulder
one near right hip
one near right knee
one near right ankle

4 Selenites
Off body:
one near left shoulder
one near left hip
one near left knee
one near left ankle

Layout 10

Reminder:

You should always sit or lie with your crystal layout for at least 20 minutes to receive proper balancing and harmonizing. Longer sessions (up to 90 minutes) are positive for you as well. If you need to set an alarm for your session, please do. Place all cell phones or electronic devices in a nearby room or hallway; they should be at least eight feet away from you and your crystals. Cellular phones, computers, and power outlets create negative energies for meditation and healing.

Crystal Body Layout

1. Find a quiet, Zen place to lie down. You can add light music if you prefer. It is best to use ambiance music with no words unless you are using the specialized guided meditation that was made specifically for this crystal layout.

2. Make yourself comfortable. Lie faceup.

3. See the diagram on page 145. This is where to place the crystals; this layout is placed on your physical body.

4. Set a specific intention; say it aloud or in your mind as you are ready to close your eyes and relax. Intention means what you desire and project with your thoughts. Here are two intentions; you can use one or both. **Intention one:** *"I am and I allow myself to completely relax. I am healing my body physically, emotionally, and mentally. I accept this healing and am always protected by the light that surrounds me."* **Intention two:** *"I give myself permission to astral travel or float in a positive place and/or space."*

5. If you are a visual person, as you close your eyes and state your intentions, try to imagine a white or gold healing light moving over your entire body. Just relax, and if you fall asleep, know it is just fine to do so.

6. When you wake or open your eyes after the session is complete, focus on your feet and imagine them as roots going into the ground like a tree. This visualization will help you feel more alert and return to your physical body. Say in your mind or aloud, "I am perfectly fine and well, and my body is self-healing. I am balanced and feel great." As you open your eyes and state you are balanced and well, you will notice both of your feet. This helps you come back into the present moment and ground. Take a few minutes before you get completely up, and slowly arise when ready. Please drink water to hydrate.

Layout #11:
Astral Travel and Exploring Safe Portals

The purpose of this crystal layout:

This crystal layout is the safest way to travel outside your body! There are many places to visit in the worlds—yes, I said worlds! We never know until we experience, so take an inexpensive trip to another dimension or travel through a time you want to explore. The layout of crystals keeps you safe and keeps the portal open to automatically pull you back down to Earth when your session is completed.

What you need:

> 1 Apophyllite
>
> 6 Amethysts
>
> 2 Herkimer Diamonds
>
> 1 Turquoise
>
> 1 Smoky Quartz

Why these crystals harmonize together:

The Apophyllite crystal opens the mind and the crown chakra to allow travel and exploration outside the body and beyond Earth. The Amethyst keeps your energy smooth and easy to travel on high frequency. The two Herkimers are needed to amplify the uplifting frequencies to allow takeoff from the Earthly plane. Turquoise keeps you safe, and the Smoky Quartz keeps you in safe atmospheres with positive energy.

Best essential oils for this session (optional):

Lavender or rosemary oil. I dab the oil on the third eye chakra and on both wrists.

High-vibe mantra (repeat it three times):

Hummmmmm

How long should I lie with this crystal layout?

40–90 minutes is best.

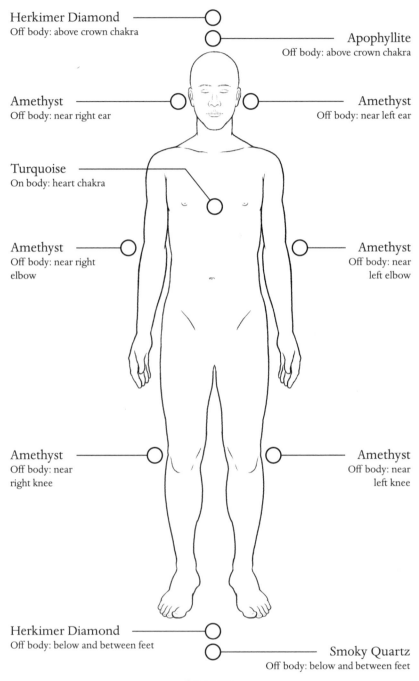

Herkimer Diamond
Off body: above crown chakra

Apophyllite
Off body: above crown chakra

Amethyst
Off body: near right ear

Amethyst
Off body: near left ear

Turquoise
On body: heart chakra

Amethyst
Off body: near right elbow

Amethyst
Off body: near left elbow

Amethyst
Off body: near right knee

Amethyst
Off body: near left knee

Herkimer Diamond
Off body: below and between feet

Smoky Quartz
Off body: below and between feet

Layout 11

Reminder:

You should always sit or lie with your crystal layout for at least 20 minutes to receive proper balancing and harmonizing. Longer sessions (up to 90 minutes) are positive for you as well. If you need to set an alarm for your session, please do. Place all cell phones or electronic devices in a nearby room or hallway; they should be at least eight feet away from you and your crystals. Cellular phones, computers, and power outlets create negative energies for meditation and healing.

Crystal Body Layout

1. Find a quiet, Zen place to lie down. You can add light music if you prefer. My fav is "Reiki Gold" by Llewellyn or "Crystal Labyrinth" by Stone Age Music.

2. Make yourself comfortable. Lie faceup.

3. See the diagram on page 148. This is where to place the crystals; this layout is placed on your physical body.

4. Set a specific intention; say it aloud or in your mind as you are ready to close your eyes and relax. Intention means what you desire and project with your thoughts. **Intention:** *"I allow myself to travel outside of my body form, using my mind and energy to astral travel out of the Earth dimension to explore and sense, then bringing my whole self back to Earth dimension; I am safe and protected and only travel in safe portals."*

5. If you are a visual person, as you close your eyes and state your intention, try to imagine a white or gold healing light moving over your entire body. Just relax, and if you fall asleep, know it is just fine to do so.

6. When you wake or open your eyes after the session is complete, focus on your feet and imagine them as roots going into the ground like a tree. This visualization will help you feel more alert and return to your physical body. Say in your mind or aloud, "I am perfectly fine and well, and my body is self-healing. I am balanced and feel great." As you open your eyes and state you are balanced and well, you will notice both of your feet. This helps you come back into the present moment and ground. Take a few minutes before you get completely up, and slowly arise when ready. Please drink water to hydrate.

Layout #12:
Past Life/Parallel Life/Alternate Life Journey

The purpose of this crystal layout:

This crystal layout is for exploring a past life, a parallel life, or an alternate life journey. Depending on your belief system or curiosity, you can choose which-ever resonates with you and explore that realm. I've explored them all many times. I set my intention to travel through a past life, then another day I will take a parallel journey!

What you need:

6 Snowflake Obsidians

1 Quartz

1 Apophyllite

4 Selenites

Why these crystals harmonize together:

The Snowflake Obsidians open dimensions to explore while keeping you safe. The Quartz gives you clarity, amplifies all other stones in the grid, and helps you remember your visions, journey, or anything you sense from this crystal session. The Apophyllite opens your inner knowing, the third eye chakra, and becomes a portal for viewing. The Selenites absorb negativity, keeping your ride positive so you can explore fully.

Best essential oils for this session (optional):

Frankincense or lavender oil. I dab the oil on the third eye chakra and on both wrists.

High-vibe mantra (repeat it three times):

heiiiiiiiiiiiahhhhhhhhhhhhh (hee-y-ah)

How long should I lie with this crystal layout?

30–90 minutes is best.

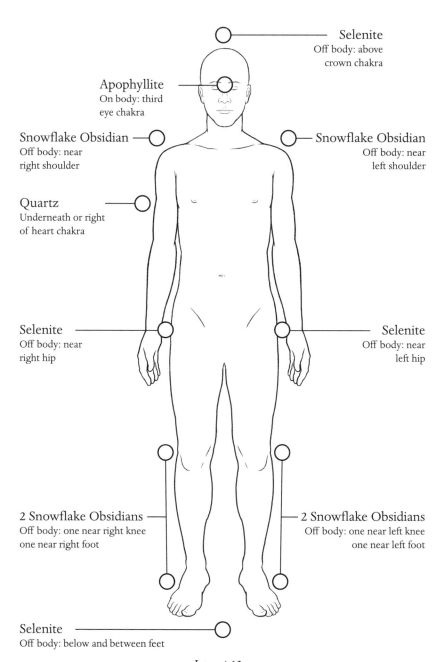

Selenite
Off body: above
crown chakra

Apophyllite
On body: third
eye chakra

Snowflake Obsidian
Off body: near
right shoulder

Snowflake Obsidian
Off body: near
left shoulder

Quartz
Underneath or right
of heart chakra

Selenite
Off body: near
right hip

Selenite
Off body: near
left hip

2 Snowflake Obsidians
Off body: one near right knee
one near right foot

2 Snowflake Obsidians
Off body: one near left knee
one near left foot

Selenite
Off body: below and between feet

Layout 12

Reminder:

You should always sit or lie with your crystal layout for at least 20 minutes to receive proper balancing and harmonizing. Longer sessions (up to 90 minutes) are positive for you as well. If you need to set an alarm for your session, please do. Place all cell phones or electronic devices in a nearby room or hallway; they should be at least eight feet away from you and your crystals. Cellular phones, computers, and power outlets create negative energies for meditation and healing.

Crystal Body Layout

1. Find a quiet, Zen place to lie down. You can add light music if you prefer. My fav is "Reiki Gold" by Llewellyn or "Crystal Labyrinth" by Stone Age Music.

2. Make yourself comfortable. Lie faceup.

3. See the diagram on page 151. This is where to place the crystals; this layout is placed on your physical body.

4. Set a specific intention; say it aloud or in your mind as you are ready to close your eyes and relax. Intention means what you desire and project with your thoughts. Here are two intentions; you can use one or both. **Intention one:** *"I am and I allow myself to completely relax. I am healing my body physically, emotionally, and mentally. I accept this healing and am always protected by the light that surrounds me."* **Intention two:** *"I give myself permission. My session today is to heal/erase/let go of/astral travel, past or parallel life."* State the specifics of what you want and allow yourself to heal by focusing on any afflicted body parts for at least two minutes.

5. If you are a visual person, as you close your eyes and state your intentions, try to imagine a white or gold healing light moving over your entire body. Just relax, and if you fall asleep, know it is just fine to do so.

6. When you wake or open your eyes after the session is complete, focus on your feet and imagine them as roots going into the ground like a tree. This visualization will help you feel more alert and return to your physical body. Say in your mind or aloud, "I am perfectly fine and well, and my body is self-healing. I am balanced and feel great." As you open your eyes and state you are balanced and well, you will notice both of your feet.

This helps you come back into the present moment and ground. Take a few minutes before you get completely up, and slowly arise when ready. Please drink water to hydrate.

Layout #13: Self-Exorcisms/Entity Removal

The purpose of this crystal layout:

If you have been feeling like something negative has been following you around or bad luck just won't leave your side, you may or may not be alone. You can easily pick up negative vibrations from a hospital, an office, or from someone who dislikes you. Do not fret, my friends—these negative vibes are easy to dispel. This rockin' grid will wipe all negativity from your energy and your space. On this grid, the intention is absolutely required! Bad vibes begone!

What you need:

2 Black Obsidians

3 Black Tourmalines

1 Danburite

1 Herkimer Diamond

Salt (a chunk the size of a quarter or larger)

4 Selenites

1 Tiger's Eye

3 Rutile Quartzes

Why these crystals harmonize together:

Placing Black Obsidian and Black Tourmaline at the lower extremities creates a pull of energy to release negative vibrations through the feet area. Black Tourmaline eases the excess out and away from the body's energy fields to cleanse and clear the aura. Danburite is a magnificently strong adhesive to patterns or low frequency energies, negating anything "clingy" in a person's aura or low vibration entities that have negative effects on a person's life or psyche. Together, Danburite, Black Tourmaline, and salt deeply cleanse every part of one's existence, including the spiritual layer of the aura, which includes past/parallel lives that can have a negative rollover into this current life. Rutile Quartz keeps

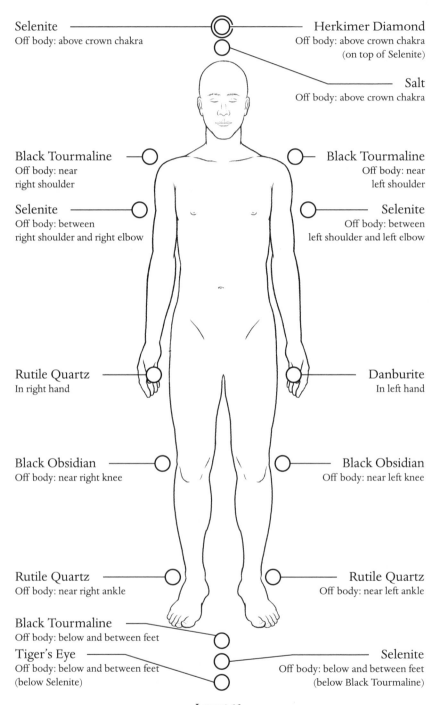

Selenite
Off body: above crown chakra

Herkimer Diamond
Off body: above crown chakra
(on top of Selenite)

Salt
Off body: above crown chakra

Black Tourmaline
Off body: near
right shoulder

Black Tourmaline
Off body: near
left shoulder

Selenite
Off body: between
right shoulder and right elbow

Selenite
Off body: between
left shoulder and left elbow

Rutile Quartz
In right hand

Danburite
In left hand

Black Obsidian
Off body: near right knee

Black Obsidian
Off body: near left knee

Rutile Quartz
Off body: near right ankle

Rutile Quartz
Off body: near left ankle

Black Tourmaline
Off body: below and between feet

Tiger's Eye
Off body: below and between feet
(below Selenite)

Selenite
Off body: below and between feet
(below Black Tourmaline)

Layout 13

a person from absorbing negative patterns or fear. Using a Herkimer Diamond always brings high intensity vibrations and powerful visions that can help a person see what is no longer needed in their life or lives. Selenite around the body cleanses and keeps that unneeded energy off the auras and physical body in this session. Tiger's Eye is for protection from the beyond's unknown energies, letting them know this session is wiping them away to never return.

Best essential oils for this session (optional):
Sage oil. I dab it on the third eye chakra and on both wrists.

High-vibe mantra(repeat it three times):
Oh Lam Ehh Ohhh Lahhh

How long should I lie with this crystal layout?
60 minutes is best.

Reminder:
You should always sit or lie with your crystal layout for at least 20 minutes to receive proper balancing and harmonizing. Longer sessions (up to 90 minutes) are positive for you as well. If you need to set an alarm for your session, please do. Place all cell phones or electronic devices in a nearby room or hallway; they should be at least eight feet away from you and your crystals. Cellular phones, computers, and power outlets create negative energies for meditation and healing.

Crystal Body Layout
1. Find a quiet, Zen place to lie down. You can add light music if you prefer. My fav for this session is "Keep Calm and Relax" by Llewellyn.
2. Make yourself comfortable. Lie faceup.
3. See the diagram on page 154. This is where to place the crystals; this layout is placed on your physical body.
4. Set a specific intention; say it aloud or in your mind as you are ready to close your eyes and relax. Intention means what you desire and project with your thoughts. **Intention:** *"Anything other than the light will go out of my body, out of my energy fields, and into the earth to be recycled and renewed.*

I allow my fear to dissipate as it no longer serves me. I am strong, and I am whole."

5. If you are a visual person, as you close your eyes and state your intention, try to imagine a white or gold healing light moving over your entire body. Just relax, and if you fall asleep, know it is just fine to do so.

6. When you wake or open your eyes after the session is complete, focus on your feet and imagine them as roots going into the ground like a tree. This visualization will help you feel more alert and return to your physical body. Say in your mind or aloud, "I am perfectly fine and well, and my body is self-healing. I am balanced and feel great." As you open your eyes and state you are balanced and well, you will notice both of your feet. This helps you come back into the present moment and ground. Take a few minutes before you get completely up, and slowly arise when ready. Please drink water to hydrate.

Layout #14:
Elemental Balance

The purpose of this crystal layout:

Sometimes we all can feel out of whack and unbalanced in our bodies or minds. Some can be totally off with how they process their thoughts. Elemental balance brings all of the universe that completes us to become more balanced in life. This crystal combination allows physical, emotional, mental, and spiritual connection to the five elements: earth, air, water, fire, and metal.

What you need:

1 Amber

1 Amethyst

1 Kyanite

1 Lapis Lazuli

1 Ocean Jasper

1 Thunder Agate

A glass or bowl of water (optional)

A plant or flower in a pot with soil (optional)

Why these crystals harmonize together:

Amber allows the sun's energy in the solar plexus, releasing any old emotions and renewing energy in that area of the body. The Amethyst brings relaxing, pure energy vibes, and Kyanite aligns all of your chakras to balance you. Lapis Lazuli protects your being and opens your mind to a healthier perception of your life and environment. The Ocean Jasper brings mindful visions as the Thunder Agate roots you to feel what is happening now in your life. Each element balances your conscious and subconscious with properties of the world near your body for this session. This is why I like to have a potted plant with soil and a bowl or glass of water in the room for this elemental healing session.

Best essential oils for this session (optional):

Sandalwood oil. I dab it on the third eye chakra and on both wrists.

High-vibe mantra (repeat it three times):

Ohhhmmmmm

How long should I lie with this crystal layout?

60–80 minutes is best.

Reminder:

You should always sit or lie with your crystal layout for at least 20 minutes to receive proper balancing and harmonizing. Longer sessions (up to 90 minutes) are positive for you as well. If you need to set an alarm for your session, please do. Place all cell phones or electronic devices in a nearby room or hallway; they should be at least eight feet away from you and your crystals. Cellular phones, computers, and power outlets create negative energies for meditation and healing.

Crystal Body Layout

1. Find a quiet, Zen place to lie down. You can add light music if you prefer. My fav is "Glimpse of Paradise" by Llewellyn.
2. Make yourself comfortable. Lie faceup.
3. See the diagram on page 158. This is where to place the crystals; this layout is placed on your physical body.

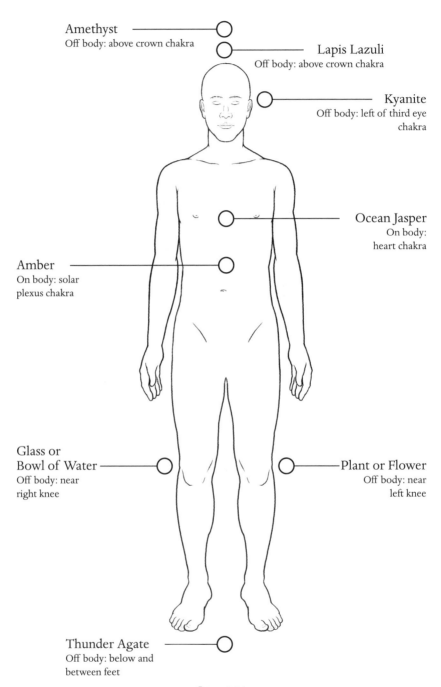

Amethyst
Off body: above crown chakra

Lapis Lazuli
Off body: above crown chakra

Kyanite
Off body: left of third eye
chakra

Ocean Jasper
On body:
heart chakra

Amber
On body: solar
plexus chakra

Glass or
Bowl of Water
Off body: near
right knee

Plant or Flower
Off body: near
left knee

Thunder Agate
Off body: below and
between feet

Layout 14

4. Set a specific intention; say it aloud or in your mind as you are ready to close your eyes and relax. Intention means what you desire and project with your thoughts. **Intention:** *"I am one with the universe—earth, air, fire, water, and metal. All of me is balanced."*

5. If you are a visual person, as you close your eyes and state your intention, try to imagine a white or gold healing light moving over your entire body. Just relax, and if you fall asleep, know it is just fine to do so.

6. When you wake or open your eyes after the session is complete, focus on your feet and imagine them as roots going into the ground like a tree. This visualization will help you feel more alert and return to your physical body. Say in your mind or aloud, "I am perfectly fine and well, and my body is self-healing. I am balanced and feel great." As you open your eyes and state you are balanced and well, you will notice both of your feet. This helps you come back into the present moment and ground. Take a few minutes before you get completely up, and slowly arise when ready. Please drink water to hydrate.

———

By now you have completely explored the options of this Earth dimension and beyond. Attending to your spirit self activates your senses and allows you to find inner strength from your mindful adventures. You may have realized that there is more to our lives than our cities and towns have to offer. Connecting to spirits or source is divinely positive: this connection brings self-awareness and expands the mind to conceptualize magical places. I hope you continue to move outside your box using your mind's power and loving intentions. Please share this knowledge with a few friends and help them explore!

Chapter 8
Layouts for Personal Transformation

Personal transformation layouts are by far the most used in the crystal healing business because they touch on what everyone needs and desires: they erase junk from all of you on a soul level and on all dimensions. Personal transformation layouts are also amazing as they take us on a journey to nature and guide us to epiphanies, self-love, trust, and to our all-knowing, pristine selves. In our world today, it is a struggle to be present and have appreciation for others, ourselves, and what we have. Gratitude and grounding are needed. The Mother Earth Grounding layout changes your vibe so powerfully that others will notice your positive changes. If you are feeling overburdened or physically tired, take part in the body rejuvenation crystal layout. Inside, all around, and out, you will feel full of vitality. If you wonder if you will ever be content, the levels of contentment session encourages self-understanding and creates a fulfillment factor in your life. Each body layout connects to a person's imperfections, sensibly and joyfully allowing acceptance along with sustainable avenues to promote positive change.

Layout #15:
Erase and Release Negative Patterns for Positive Vibes: Soul Talking[1]

The purpose of this crystal layout:

Erase and release patterns that no longer serve you and let go of addictions, self-sabotaging thoughts, old attachments, and resentments for self or others. This layout will cleanse, clear, and replace the negative energy with positive vibes. You should do this layout at least once every three months to get rid of that junk you accumulate. This is an especially unique crystal healing because it includes a lengthy, guided meditation. This meditation is very potent for releasing negative energy and replacing it with positive, new energy.

What you need:

- 2 Rutile Quartzes
- 1 Clear Quartz
- 2 Auralite 23s or 2 Charoites
- 1 Aquamarine
- 1 Unakite
- 1 Black Tourmaline or Black Obsidian
- 1 Danburite of any size

Why these crystals harmonize together:

The Rutile Quartz, Danburite, Black Tourmaline, and Black Obsidian allow one to release any old patterns. The Charoite and Unakite bring self-realization to the soul, and Aquamarine makes this realization heard on all levels of the person's existence—past, present, and future. Auralite 23 and Quartz amplify frequencies; the high vibes are instilled within the aura and chakras to make them balanced and healthy.

As the crystals synergize, each one works to balance, pull out negativity, and then replace it with positive, balanced frequencies for the auric fields and chakra flows—optimal healing!

---

1. Jolie DeMarco, *Soul Talking and Relationships* (Self-published, 2014), 74.

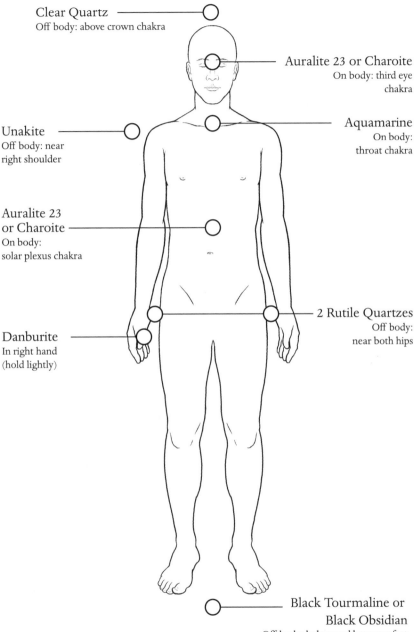

Clear Quartz
Off body: above crown chakra

Auralite 23 or Charoite
On body: third eye
chakra

Unakite
Off body: near
right shoulder

Aquamarine
On body:
throat chakra

Auralite 23
or Charoite
On body:
solar plexus chakra

2 Rutile Quartzes
Off body:
near both hips

Danburite
In right hand
(hold lightly)

Black Tourmaline or
Black Obsidian
Off body: below and between feet

Layout 15

Best essential oils for this session (optional):
Geranium or frankincense. I dab the oil on the third eye chakra and on both wrists.

High-vibe mantra (repeat it three times):
Looooovvvve

How long should I lie with this crystal layout?
40–90 minutes is best.

Reminder:
Check your chakras before and after the session. You should always sit or lie with your crystal layout for at least 20 minutes to receive proper balancing and harmonizing. Longer sessions (up to 90 minutes) are positive for you as well. If you need to set an alarm for your session, please do. Place all cell phones or electronic devices in a nearby room or hallway; they should be at least eight feet away from you and your crystals. Cellular phones, computers, and power outlets create negative energies for meditation and healing.

Crystal Body Layout

1. Read the guided mediation (provided below). Find a quiet, Zen place to lie down. You can add light music if you prefer. I love Llewellyn's "Relaxing Sleep"; it's about 43 minutes—perfect.

2. Make yourself comfortable. Lie faceup.

3. See the diagram on page 163. This is where to place the crystals; this layout is placed on your physical body. If you feel uncomfortable with the crystals on your body, you can place them underneath your bed or as close as you can to the locations shown in the picture.

4. Set a specific intention; say it aloud or in your mind as you are ready to close your eyes and relax. Intention means what you desire and project with your thoughts. Here are two intentions; you can use one or both. **Intention one:** *"I am and I allow myself to completely relax. I am healing my body physically, emotionally, and mentally. I accept this healing and am always protected by the light that surrounds me."* **Intention two:** *"I give myself permission. My session today is to heal/erase/let go of …"* State the specifics of

what you want and allow yourself to heal by focusing on any afflicted body parts for at least two minutes. Imagine them healing with green light.

5. If you are a visual person, as you close your eyes and state your intentions, try to imagine a green, white, or gold healing light moving over your entire body. Just relax, and if you fall asleep, know it is just fine to do so.

6. When you wake or open your eyes after the session is complete, focus on your feet and imagine them as roots going into the ground like a tree. This visualization will help you feel more alert and return to your physical body. Say in your mind or aloud, "I am perfectly fine and well, and my body is self-healing. I am balanced and feel great." As you open your eyes and state you are balanced and well, you will notice both of your feet. This helps you come back into the present moment and ground. Take a few minutes before you get completely up, and slowly arise when ready. Please drink water to hydrate.

Guided Meditation

This is an additional instruction to read beforehand. This is specifically for the Soul Talking crystal layout; this guided meditation will help you visualize and understand how to have optimal results.

Soul Talking with you: The term "soul talking" is a process that teaches people how to cleanse all their unwanted habits, thoughts, and emotions from past, parallel, and present lives. Here are the steps for this technique:

1. "I am [say your full name]; I allow my true soul, the energy of me, to engage with my human self, body and mind, to soul talk with my true soul energy, 'all that I am' energy, on all dimensions, all parallels, anywhere my energy exists—all energies of me in all locations."

2. Take 11 deep breaths in and 11 long breaths out.

3. Now, if you can, try to sense or feel an energetic band of golden light from the center of your stomach (solar plexus chakra—represents your ego).

4. Visualize connecting that golden light to your heart chakra. This is a golden light of healing energy. The heart chakra is located in the center of your chest.

5. Connect that same energetic golden light to your third eye chakra between your eyebrows.

6. Connect another golden light from the third eye to the top of your head; this is the crown chakra. The crown chakra connects your mind to the energetic golden light—to the all-knowing you, or your higher self. All of these points are energetically connected with a golden light.

7. Imagine small arches from one point to the next. Try to feel or imagine a flow of light in this golden string of vibrations. Feel or imagine the gold vibes flowing back and forth. All of these connected points are communicating, accepting and exchanging energy. This is the human you connecting with your true soul. The true soul is the energy of you; when a human passes into the light (deceases and leaves their life on Earth), the energy of the soul lives on. Energy is infinite. Whether you believe your energy goes to heaven, to another dimension, or is reborn, the energy of the soul goes somewhere. If you agree to that, you understand the way energy travels. Energy is vibrations that can be in places that we as humans cannot necessarily see with our human eyes. Vibrations do exist because they are a form of energy. Vibrations resonate over time and space. Okay, back to the meditation…

8. If you have a hard time visualizing the golden light, it is okay to skip that part. After reading this last paragraph, I think you understand connecting energy and how it connects the human you with the energy of your essence.

9. State, "I am to be of pure energy. I, [your full name], at this time, year 20__, Earth dimension, bring only love into my pure energy; I release all blocks—all thoughts other than the light. I release all judgments of me and others that are not light. Any and all habits that are not light, I release and exchange with positive energy."

10. At this time, specifically say what you would like to replace with positivity. It can be a thought, vision, or pattern. You should feel or sense the exchange and visualize or state your specifics aloud. For example, if I had a pattern of attracting people who take advantage of my niceness, I would allow myself to release that pattern and replace it with attracting people who respect me in all ways. If you have more than one habit or pattern to release, focus on one at a time. Remember to make it your intention that you truly change and exchange negative patterns with positive.

11. Once you have gone over your list and replaced each of the negatives with positives, read and say this statement: "I only see myself as pure and high vibration energy, which means happy, healthy, and loving. I only allow loving relationships in my energy. I only allow loving energy around me. I am always safe and protected by loving energies. I allow myself and I deserve to have only positive, equal energy exchange with all beings of energies and all that is energy, including myself. I allow and accept these changes in my life to be of goodness and advancement. I only allow the light within, around, and in my thoughts on this year, 20__, Earth dimension, including all of where I exist, existed, and reside—in all my forms, human and beyond."

12. Once again, take 11 deep breaths in and 11 long breaths out—with every exhale, really try to release. Lastly, give gratitude to yourself and all energies of life.

13. To complete this soul talking crystal body layout, drink a glass of water and place your feet flat on the floor or ground. This will bring harmony and help you feel stable after any meditation. Some people call this *grounding yourself* and *returning to your physical body*. If you continue to feel floaty, hold a Black Tourmaline in your hand for five minutes and repeat in your mind, "I allow myself to be present in my body, back on Earth."

14. Most people will feel great as the emotional weight is lifted from their bodies. You may feel a bit tired or released of emotions; please rest and allow your body to relax.

Layout #16:
Self-Realization Wilderness Journey
with Nature Guides

The purpose of this crystal layout:

Follow the path of inner knowing. Relax as you take a peaceful journey to discovery and clarity in your life.

What you need:

1 Thunder Agate

2 Green Tourmalines

4 Quartzes, tumbled or raw

1 Quartz Point

1 Cavansite

1 Turquoise

1 Moss Agate

1 Moonstone

Why these crystals harmonize together:

The Thunder Agate brings Earth energy to release unwanted toxins of life, from thoughts to daily actions, to bring one back to nature, a healthy lifestyle, and honoring oneself and nature. Green Tourmaline heals all wounds of the soul while Quartz clarifies the intent and purpose of your healing and provides insight into correcting your path. Turquoise brings protection and healing on etheric levels as the Moonstone addresses a safe journey. The Quartz Point calls in the power of the sky to enhance your body's functions, and Cavansite enlightens you to new directions and finding your soul's purpose. The Moss Agate stabilizes the path of your journey.

The Thunder Agate keeps your body grounded, which guides your earthly body to acknowledge what your higher self believes is the best course of action. You receive this information on a conscious and subconscious level with the Green Tourmaline's energy. The Quartz and the Cavansite give you the high frequencies to "hear" the information clearly and/or vividly through vi-

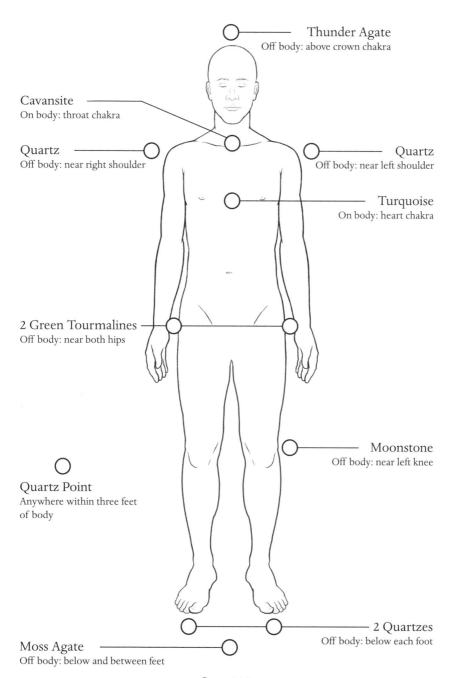

Thunder Agate
Off body: above crown chakra

Cavansite
On body: throat chakra

Quartz
Off body: near right shoulder

Quartz
Off body: near left shoulder

Turquoise
On body: heart chakra

2 Green Tourmalines
Off body: near both hips

Moonstone
Off body: near left knee

Quartz Point
Anywhere within three feet
of body

2 Quartzes
Off body: below each foot

Moss Agate
Off body: below and between feet

Layout 16

sons or feelings. The Quartz Point draws strong energy within and around your auric fields to protect the shared knowledge from your soul's energy (the core of your existence) and transmit the knowledge to the physical body.

Best essential oils for this session (optional):
Rosemary oil or tangerine oil. I dab the oil on the third eye chakra and on both wrists.

High-vibe mantra (repeat it three times):
Ohhhhhhhhha rhiiiiiiiiiii

How long should I lie with this crystal layout?
30–60 minutes is best.

Reminder:
You should always sit or lie with your crystal layout for at least 20 minutes to receive proper balancing and harmonizing. Longer sessions (up to 90 minutes) are positive for you as well. If you need to set an alarm for your session, please do. Place all cell phones or electronic devices in a nearby room or hallway; they should be at least eight feet away from you and your crystals. Cellular phones, computers, and power outlets create negative energies for meditation and healing.

Crystal Body Layout
1. Find a quiet, Zen place to lie down. You can add light music if you prefer. I like Native American tribal drum or flute music for this session.
2. Make yourself comfortable. Lie faceup.
3. See the diagram on page 169. This is where to place the crystals; this layout is placed on your physical body.
4. Set a specific intention; say it aloud or in your mind as you are ready to close your eyes and relax. Intention means what you desire and project with your thoughts. Here are two intentions; you can use one or both. **Intention one:** *"I am and I allow myself to completely relax. I am healing my body physically, emotionally, and mentally. I accept this healing and am al-*

ways protected by the light that surrounds me." **Intention two:** *"I give my-self permission."* Focus on your third eye chakra between your eyebrows. This allows you to open that chakra and clarifies any inner knowing you receive. Next, bring your focus to the crown chakra at the top of your head. This focus will allow you to feel and sense. Continue by invoking the universe, your guides, or your higher self: *"Please allow me to see, sense, or feel a clear message from an animal or nature guide; give me self-realization and understanding at this time in my life, year 20__. Gratitude; I am open to receive this positive information now."*

5. If you are a visual person, as you close your eyes and state your intentions, try to imagine a white or gold healing light moving over your entire body. Just relax, and if you fall asleep, know it is just fine to do so.

6. When you wake or open your eyes after the session is complete, focus on your feet and imagine them as roots going into the ground like a tree. This visualization will help you feel more alert and return to your physical body. Say in your mind or aloud, "I am perfectly fine and well, and my body is self-healing. I am balanced and feel great." Ask again what your purpose at this time in your life is. As you open your eyes and state you are balanced and well, you will notice both of your feet. This helps you come back into the present moment and ground. Take a few minutes before you get completely up, and slowly arise when ready. Please drink water to hydrate.

Layout #17: Self-Love, Trust, and Connection to Higher Self

The purpose of this crystal layout:

This crystal layout is for those who want to find peace with themselves, understand the deep connection to their inner being, and trust/feel that unconditional love banishes loneliness. This layout allows you to accept and truly understand that you deserve unconditional love from within your soul and source. The knowledge that you are surrounded with beautiful vibrations on Earth and beyond gives you a sense that you *are* love and that you can trust your intuitive senses.

What you need:

1 Lapis Lazuli

1 Kunzite

6 Carnelians

2 Angelites

Why these crystals harmonize together:

Lapis Lazuli helps you understand emotional issues or occurrences and access your subconscious while the Kunzite harmonizes with it to restructure your thoughts to promote understanding, inner knowing, and positive actions. The Carnelians activate the energy within, and the Angelites connect you to your higher, all-knowing soul.

Best essential oils for this session (optional):

Ylang-ylang or rose oil. I dab the oil on the third eye chakra and on both wrists. You can combine the two—both are amazing. I occasionally put ylang-ylang on my ankles and rose on my wrists.

High-vibe mantra (repeat it three times):

Sawaaaaaaaaaaleeeeeeeeommmmmm

How long should I lie with this crystal layout?

45–90 minutes is best.

Reminder:

You should always sit or lie with your crystal layout for at least 20 minutes to receive proper balancing and harmonizing. Longer sessions (up to 90 minutes) are positive for you as well. If you need to set an alarm for your session, please do. Place all cell phones or electronic devices in a nearby room or hallway; they should be at least eight feet away from you and your crystals. Cellular phones, computers, and power outlets create negative energies for meditation and healing.

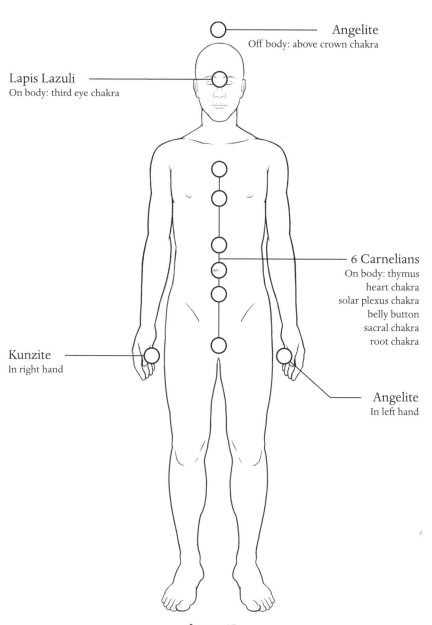

Angelite
Off body: above crown chakra

Lapis Lazuli
On body: third eye chakra

6 Carnelians
On body: thymus
heart chakra
solar plexus chakra
belly button
sacral chakra
root chakra

Kunzite
In right hand

Angelite
In left hand

Layout 17

Crystal Body Layout

1. Find a quiet, Zen place to lie down. You can add light music if you prefer. I love "Reiki Sleep Gold" and "Glimpse of Paradise" by Llewellyn. Both are great tracks for all relaxing meditations and crystal sessions.

2. Make yourself comfortable. Lie faceup.

3. See the diagram on page 173. This is where to place the crystals; this layout is placed on your physical body.

4. Set a specific intention; say it aloud or in your mind as you are ready to close your eyes and relax. Intention means what you desire and project with your thoughts. Here are two intentions; you can use one or both. **Intention one:** *"I am and I allow myself to completely relax. I am healing my body physically, emotionally, and mentally. I accept this healing and am always protected by the light that surrounds me."* **Intention two:** *"I give myself permission. My session today is to connect to my higher self, the all-knowing me. I will feel unconditional love and accept it happily and fully on all levels of my existence."*

5. If you are a visual person, as you close your eyes and state your intentions, try to imagine a white or gold healing light moving over your entire body. Just relax, and if you fall asleep, know it is just fine to do so.

6. When you wake or open your eyes after the session is complete, focus on your feet and imagine them as roots going into the ground like a tree. This visualization will help you feel more alert and return to your physical body. Say in your mind or aloud, "I am perfectly fine and well, and my body is self-healing. I am balanced and feel great." As you open your eyes and state you are balanced and well, you will notice both of your feet. This helps you come back into the present moment and ground. Take a few minutes before you get completely up, and slowly arise when ready. Please drink water to hydrate.

Layout #18:
Mother Earth Grounding:
Being Present with Gratitude

The purpose of this crystal layout:

Being present is about mindfulness, not mindlessness! If you have noticed, or your friends and family are suggesting, that you need to be less floaty, this is your grid. This layout will help you be more grounded, appreciate life and all it has to offer, and become present in the moment.

What you need:

> 1 Apache Tear
>
> 1 Aragonite
>
> 1 Green Aventurine
>
> 1 Moss Agate
>
> 1 Pietersite
>
> 3 Rose Quartzes

Why these crystals harmonize together:

The Apache Tear is a grounding stone and is also a stone of respect—respect for self, other people, and all that exists. The Aragonite is also a grounding stone that can bring visions to fulfillment. Many people have high expectations of themselves and get disappointed because of that mind chatter; Aragonite can adjust that chatter to be positive and realistic. Green Aventurine brings loving notions and compassion and urges considerate behaviors. Moss Agate, a ground earth stone, connects one to the planet. Pietersite also instills the earth connection, combining with Rose Quartz to extend love to all on Earth and beyond.

Best essential oils for this session (optional):

Sage or sandalwood oil. I dab the oil on the third eye chakra and on both wrists.

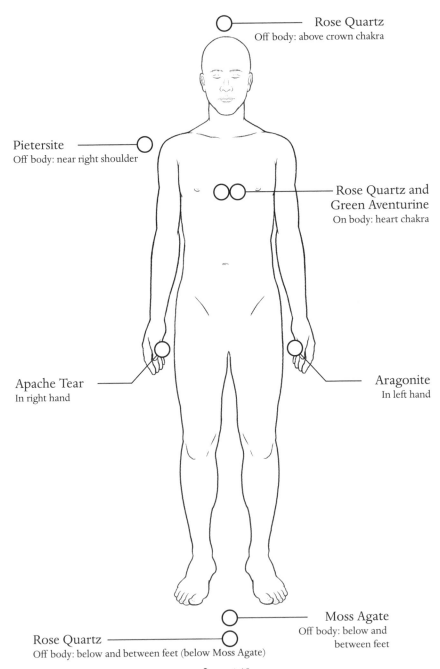

Rose Quartz
Off body: above crown chakra

Pietersite
Off body: near right shoulder

Rose Quartz and
Green Aventurine
On body: heart chakra

Apache Tear
In right hand

Aragonite
In left hand

Moss Agate
Off body: below and
between feet

Rose Quartz
Off body: below and between feet (below Moss Agate)

Layout 18

High-vibe mantra (repeat it three times):
Motherrrr Earth

How long should I lie with this crystal layout?
30–45 minutes is best.

Reminder:
You should always sit or lie with your crystal layout for at least 20 minutes to receive proper balancing and harmonizing. Longer sessions (up to 90 minutes) are positive for you as well. If you need to set an alarm for your session, please do. Place all cell phones or electronic devices in a nearby room or hallway; they should be at least eight feet away from you and your crystals. Cellular phones, computers, and power outlets create negative energies for meditation and healing.

Crystal Body Layout

1. Find a quiet, Zen place to lie down. You can add light music if you prefer. Llewellyn's "Reiki Gold 2" is perfect for this session; it's long enough and calming.

2. Make yourself comfortable. Lie faceup.

3. See the diagram on page 176. This is where to place the crystals; this layout is placed on your physical body.

4. Set a specific intention; say it aloud or in your mind as you are ready to close your eyes and relax. Intention means what you desire and project with your thoughts. **Intention:** *"I love Mother Earth. As I notice my body touching the ground, I become mindful and present. I identify the positive in my life, and I am grateful for it."*

5. If you are a visual person, as you close your eyes and state your intention, try to imagine a white or gold healing light moving over your entire body. Just relax, and if you fall asleep, know it is just fine to do so.

6. When you wake or open your eyes after the session is complete, focus on your feet and imagine them as roots going into the ground like a tree. This visualization will help you feel more alert and return to your physical body. Say in your mind or aloud, "I am perfectly fine and well, and my

body is self-healing. I am balanced and feel great." As you open your eyes and state you are balanced and well, you will notice both of your feet. This helps you come back into the present moment and ground. Take a few minutes before you get completely up, and slowly arise when ready. Please drink water to hydrate.

Layout #19: Body Rejuvenation

The purpose of this crystal layout:

Who doesn't love feeling younger (and possibly looking it too)? Our energy says a lot about us; if you are energized and have a great attitude, you'll have plenty of vitality. Perform this session once a month to keep a positive outlook.

What you need:

2 Fluorites

1 Herkimer Diamond

1 Lemurian Seed

2 Quartzes

6 Shungites

Why these crystals harmonize together:

Fluorite of any color creates healing vibrations for human bodies and their functions. The Herkimer Diamond helps you relax and see deeper into your body and being as a whole. The Lemurian Seed of ancient healing modalities enriches your body as the Quartz filters any negativity to keep the vibes clear and cleansed. The six Shungites deeply cleanse all of your auric layers and release any junk in your chakras. Shungite also adds healing frequencies to your energy centers.

Best essential oils for this session (optional):

Sweet orange or grapefruit oil. I dab the oil only on the feet; anywhere on the ankles or bottoms is ideal. Use a minimal amount and wash your hands and wrists. An uplifting smell too close to your nose can keep you from going deep into a meditative state to induce self-healing.

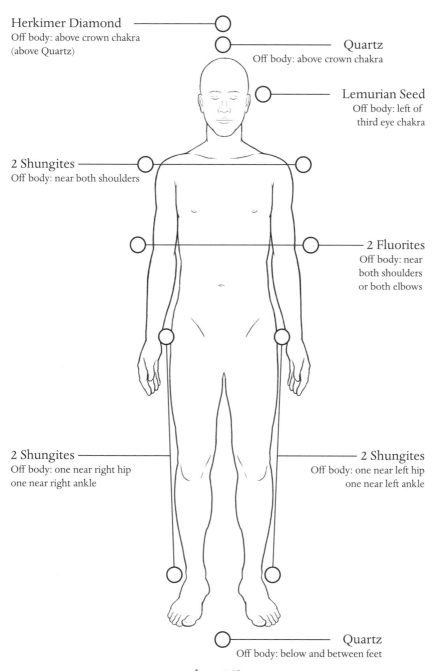

Herkimer Diamond
Off body: above crown chakra
(above Quartz)

Quartz
Off body: above crown chakra

Lemurian Seed
Off body: left of
third eye chakra

2 Shungites
Off body: near both shoulders

2 Fluorites
Off body: near
both shoulders
or both elbows

2 Shungites
Off body: one near right hip
one near right ankle

2 Shungites
Off body: one near left hip
one near left ankle

Quartz
Off body: below and between feet

Layout 19

High-vibe mantra (repeat it three times):

Eye Looove

How long should I lie with this crystal layout?

35–60 minutes is best.

Reminder:

You should always sit or lie with your crystal layout for at least 20 minutes to receive proper balancing and harmonizing. Longer sessions (up to 90 minutes) are positive for you as well. If you need to set an alarm for your session, please do. Place all cell phones or electronic devices in a nearby room or hallway; they should be at least eight feet away from you and your crystals. Cellular phones, computers, and power outlets create negative energies for meditation and healing.

Crystal Body Layout

1. Find a quiet, Zen place to lie down. You can add light music if you prefer. I enjoy crystal bowls music or any ambiance music with no vocals.

2. Make yourself comfortable. Lie faceup.

3. See the diagram on page 179. This is where to place the crystals; this layout is placed on your physical body.

4. Set a specific intention; say it aloud or in your mind as you are ready to close your eyes and relax. Intention means what you desire and project with your thoughts. **Intention:** *"My body is physically, emotionally, mentally, and spiritually well. Every cell and organ in my body is perfectly functioning and perfectly healthy and well. My mind is strong, my emotions are balanced, I am rational in thoughts, and my spirit is connected. I am and I allow all healing of my entire being to occur."*

5. If you are a visual person, as you close your eyes and state your intention, try to imagine a white or gold healing light moving over your entire body. Just relax, and if you fall asleep, know it is just fine to do so.

6. When you wake or open your eyes after the session is complete, focus on your feet and imagine them as roots going into the ground like a tree.

This visualization will help you feel more alert and return to your physical body. Say in your mind or aloud, "I am perfectly fine and well, and my body is self-healing. I am balanced and feel great." As you open your eyes and state you are balanced and well, you will notice both of your feet. This helps you come back into the present moment and ground. Take a few minutes before you get completely up, and slowly arise when ready. Please drink water to hydrate.

Layout #20:
Achieving Levels of Contentment

The purpose of this crystal layout:

We all have different likes and dislikes, especially about ourselves and our lives. Are you judgmental? Stuck in a rut? Avoiding fulfillment in favor of familiarity? Unappreciative of all that you possess? I got your number. Find your level of contentment, at least at this particular time in your life.

What you need:

> 1 Amazonite
>
> 1 Apatite
>
> 1 Black Tourmaline
>
> 1 Chrysoprase
>
> 1 Citrine
>
> 1 Chalcedony
>
> 1 Green Aventurine
>
> 1 Rutile Quartz
>
> 1 White Howlite

Why these crystals harmonize together:

Amazonite brings balance to the energy centers, and Apatite allows the emotions to be pure and honorable in all you strive for. Black Tourmaline helps you release fears and self-sabotage that hold you back from your dreams, Chrysoprase enlightens your mind to new ways of obtaining your desires, and Citrine keeps

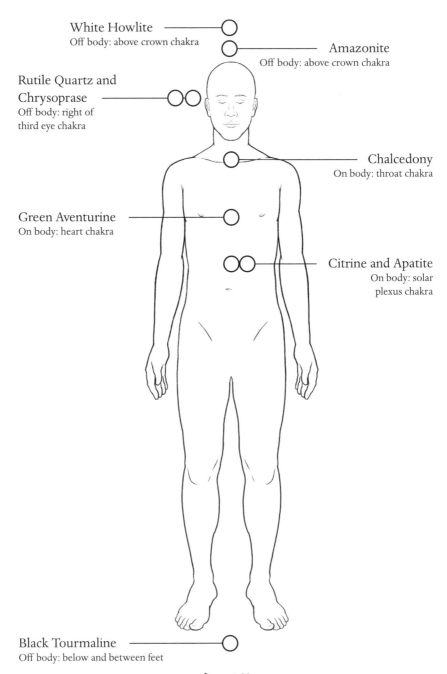

White Howlite
Off body: above crown chakra

Amazonite
Off body: above crown chakra

Rutile Quartz and
Chrysoprase
Off body: right of
third eye chakra

Chalcedony
On body: throat chakra

Green Aventurine
On body: heart chakra

Citrine and Apatite
On body: solar
plexus chakra

Black Tourmaline
Off body: below and between feet

Layout 20

your track clean and clear with happiness and thoughts of positivity. Chalcedony lets you hear the truth of your desires, and Green Aventurine makes you accept those truths in your heart. Rutile Quartz zips out negative old patterns that impede success, and White Howlite keeps you on the right track.

Best essential oils for this session (optional):

Rose or geranium oil. I dab the oil on the third eye chakra and on both wrists.

High-vibe mantra (repeat it three times):

Meeeiiii (Me-eye)

How long should I lie with this crystal layout?

40–60 minutes is best.

Reminder:

You should always sit or lie with your crystal layout for at least 20 minutes to receive proper balancing and harmonizing. Longer sessions (up to 90 minutes) are positive for you as well. If you need to set an alarm for your session, please do. Place all cell phones or electronic devices in a nearby room or hallway; they should be at least eight feet away from you and your crystals. Cellular phones, computers, and power outlets create negative energies for meditation and healing.

Crystal Body Layout

1. Find a quiet, Zen place to lie down. You can add light music if you prefer. My fav is "Reiki Gold" by Llewellyn. It's about one hour in length.

2. Make yourself comfortable. Lie faceup.

3. See the diagram on page 182. This is where to place the crystals; this layout is placed on your physical body.

4. Set a specific intention; say it aloud or in your mind as you are ready to close your eyes and relax. Intention means what you desire and project with your thoughts. **Intention:** *"I am giving myself permission to achieve my level of contentment, which is for me to reach* [state your goal here]. *I see and allow my goals to fully be completed and allow them to come to fruition in this Earth dimension in the month* [month] *and year of 20___."*

5. If you are a visual person, as you close your eyes and state your intention, try to imagine a white or gold healing light moving over your entire body. Just relax, and if you fall asleep, know it is just fine to do so.

6. When you wake or open your eyes after the session is complete, focus on your feet and imagine them as roots going into the ground like a tree. This visualization will help you feel more alert and return to your physical body. Say in your mind or aloud, "I am perfectly fine and well, and my body is self-healing. I am balanced and feel great." As you open your eyes and state you are balanced and well, you will notice both of your feet. This helps you come back into the present moment and ground. Take a few minutes before you get completely up, and slowly arise when ready. Please drink water to hydrate.

Creating who we want to be is easy with a crystal body layout. After your experiences with these layouts, you must be waves ahead. The personal transformation layout supersedes old, unwanted ways of life so that new, precious life begins.

Chapter 9

Layouts for Spiritual Enhancement

Are you ready for some fun? If you are thinking, "I don't know about this section," then step out of your comfort zone and do one! You will be more than encouraged by spirit to do another shortly after. Start out with asking for a spirit guide. If you feel up to it (and you will), connect with a passed loved one; you will do great. Then move on to Layout #22: Angel Connections. If you don't know any Angel names, I have one for you: ask Archangel Michael to come visit. He is a protector and has a strong presence. You may feel beautiful, unconditional love during Layout 22. The next session is downloading—it is utterly astounding to be able to accept such ancient knowledge. You will feel light-years ahead in many subjects, some you may have never heard of. Layout 25 is a session with star energy, and it is absolutely breathtaking. You can feel colors surround you as light fills your energy fields. Last but not least, Layout 26, the sacred number, brings prophecy to those who accept and are intrigued by insights of the future.

Layout #21:
Ask for Spirit Visitors and
Loved Ones Who Have Passed Over

The purpose of this crystal layout:

Loss is never a happy occasion, except when you can reconnect through a feeling or vision. Receiving signs from a passed loved one is a gift, and you can accept it. Asking for a visit is a big part of making a meaningful connection, but you must be relaxed to receive visitors. I ask you not to think too much before this layout, but purely enjoy it. It is important that you don't over expect—that can block the flow of high vibrations that allow the visitor to come. The idea is to get on the highest frequency within your body and aura layers with the help of the crystals to allow the high vibes of your guest to transmit to you. It is safe to do this; you are not summoning them or creating anything that is uncomfortable for them. If you call upon them by using the proper high vibration wording in the intention I provided and your true loving intent, you most likely will get some sort of contact. If you do not feel or sense anything during your session, you may connect or receive within the next few days, mainly with a sign. A sign can be something someone else randomly says to you that sounds much like something your passed loved one would say, or a bird or nature message, like finding a feather. A sign could be many things, from a dream of them visiting you, a flicker of a light, a license plate with their name, or finding something they liked.

What you need:

   1 Apache Tear

   1 Celestite

   1 Herkimer Diamond

   1 Epidote

   2 Selenites

   1 Snowflake Obsidian

Why these crystals harmonize together:

Apache Tears bring compassion to the source you are calling upon. Celestite keeps only the light energy of positivity in your aura and space while you are

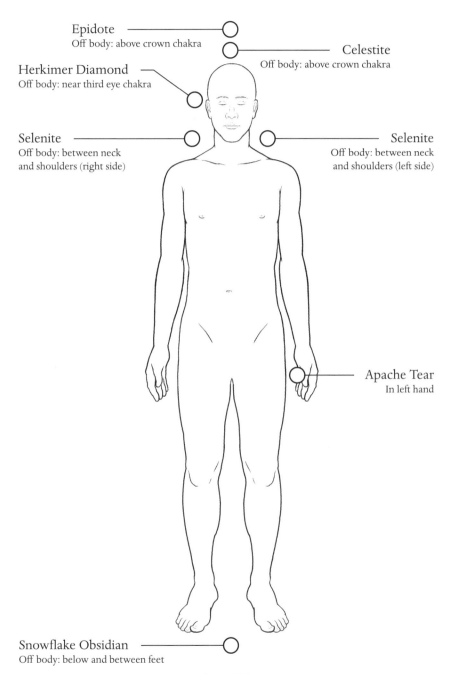

Epidote
Off body: above crown chakra

Celestite
Off body: above crown chakra

Herkimer Diamond
Off body: near third eye chakra

Selenite
Off body: between neck
and shoulders (right side)

Selenite
Off body: between neck
and shoulders (left side)

Apache Tear
In left hand

Snowflake Obsidian
Off body: below and between feet

Layout 21

having your session. The Herkimer is for potent visions and feelings as you wish to sense your loved one. Epidote creates favorable energy for the ones who have passed over to express themselves while Selenite clears the way for messages or visions and brings the energy of the past alive. Snowflake Obsidian inserts welcoming frequencies that clear all that is around your space in the session.

Best essential oils for this session (optional):

Bergamot or chamomile oil. I dab the oil between my pointer finger and thumb and on my wrists.

High-vibe mantra (repeat it three times):

Cooome

How long should I lie with this crystal layout?

45–60 minutes is best.

Reminder:

You should always sit or lie with your crystal layout for at least 20 minutes to receive proper balancing and harmonizing. Longer sessions (up to 90 minutes) are positive for you as well. If you need to set an alarm for your session, please do. Place all cell phones or electronic devices in a nearby room or hallway; they should be at least eight feet away from you and your crystals. Cellular phones, computers, and power outlets create negative energies for meditation and healing.

Crystal Body Layout

1. Find a quiet, Zen place to lie down. You can add light music if you prefer. My fav is "Reiki Gold" by Llewellyn. It's about one hour in length.
2. Make yourself comfortable. Lie faceup.
3. See the diagram on page 187. This is where to place the crystals; this layout is placed on your physical body.
4. Set a specific intention; say it aloud or in your mind as you are ready to close your eyes and relax. Intention means what you desire and project with your thoughts. **Intention:** *"I am asking for my spirit guide or loved one,*

named ____, to please connect with me during this meditation. I would love to see, hear, or sense your presence. I allow and gracefully accept any messages you have for me. I will relax my mind; this way, I can accept and allow this connection without force. Gratitude."

5. If you are a visual person, as you close your eyes and state your intention, try to imagine a white or gold healing light moving over your entire body. Just relax, and if you fall asleep, know it is just fine to do so.

6. When you wake or open your eyes after the session is complete, focus on your feet and imagine them as roots going into the ground like a tree. This visualization will help you feel more alert and return to your physical body. Say in your mind or aloud, "I am perfectly fine and well, and my body is self-healing. I am balanced and feel great." As you open your eyes and state you are balanced and well, you will notice both of your feet. This helps you come back into the present moment and ground. Take a few minutes before you get completely up, and slowly arise when ready. Please drink water to hydrate.

Layout #22: Angel Connections

The purpose of this crystal layout:

The more you meditate, the more you want to open up to receiving. That seems the case for many people, including myself! I love to connect to the high realms and Angels—there are so many to teach you or come visit. Here are just a few: Archangel Michael, Archangel Raphael, Archangel Uriel, Archangel Metatron, and Archangel Chamuel. You can get a book that speaks solely about Angels. Pick an Angel whose name intrigues you and ask them to teach or share with you. By the way, you can ask for more than one to visit you.

What you need:

1 Angelite

1 Aquamarine

1 Cavansite

1 Celestite

1 Herkimer Diamond

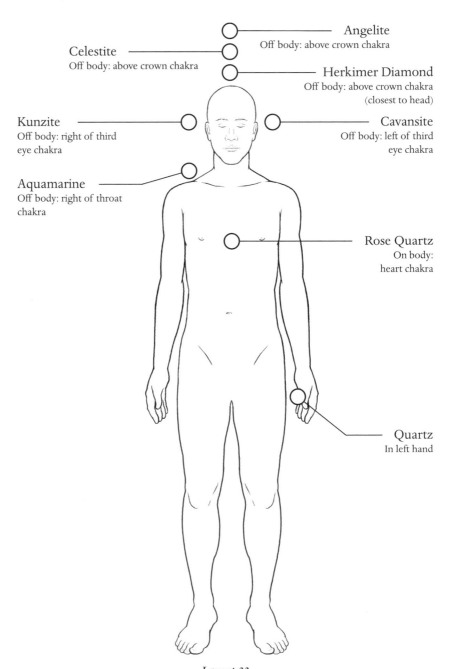

Angelite
Off body: above crown chakra

Celestite
Off body: above crown chakra

Herkimer Diamond
Off body: above crown chakra
(closest to head)

Kunzite
Off body: right of third
eye chakra

Cavansite
Off body: left of third
eye chakra

Aquamarine
Off body: right of throat
chakra

Rose Quartz
On body:
heart chakra

Quartz
In left hand

Layout 22

1 Kunzite

1 Quartz

1 Rose Quartz

Why these crystals harmonize together:

Angelite is your direct connection to the Angel's frequencies, and Aquamarine opens your throat and ears to hear and sense. Cavansite brings clairvoyant intuition, and Celestite allows high Angelic energy to move through the heart and upper chakras and flow beautifully within and around you. Herkimer Diamond amplifies frequencies and brings vivid visions. Kunzite resonates with Archangels and all Angels. Quartz cleanses the senses to receive connections, and Rose Quartz resonates with and matches the Angel's unconditional love.

Best essential oils for this session (optional):

Rose or geranium lavender oil. I dab the oil on both wrists.

High-vibe mantra (repeat it three times):

Eye-ahammm

How long should I lie with this crystal layout?

45–60 minutes is best.

Reminder:

You should always sit or lie with your crystal layout for at least 20 minutes to receive proper balancing and harmonizing. Longer sessions (up to 90 minutes) are positive for you as well. If you need to set an alarm for your session, please do. Place all cell phones or electronic devices in a nearby room or hallway; they should be at least eight feet away from you and your crystals. Cellular phones, computers, and power outlets create negative energies for meditation and healing.

Crystal Body Layout

1. Find a quiet, Zen place to lie down. You can add light music if you prefer. Llewellyn's "Keep Calm and Relax" on low volume is best so you can notice and sense for this layout session.

2. Make yourself comfortable. Lie faceup.

3. See the diagram on page 190. This is where to place the crystals; this layout is placed on your physical body.

4. Set a specific intention; say it aloud or in your mind as you are ready to close your eyes and relax. Intention means what you desire and project with your thoughts. **Intention:** *"Please may I ask the Angel named _____ to visit me as I meditate. I am and I allow your presence and accept any and all positive messages. Thank you."*

5. If you are a visual person, as you close your eyes and state your intention, try to imagine a white or gold healing light moving over your entire body. Just relax, and if you fall asleep, know it is just fine to do so.

6. When you wake or open your eyes after the session is complete, focus on your feet and imagine them as roots going into the ground like a tree. This visualization will help you feel more alert and return to your physical body. Say in your mind or aloud, "I am perfectly fine and well, and my body is self-healing. I am balanced and feel great." As you open your eyes and state you are balanced and well, you will notice both of your feet. This helps you come back into the present moment and ground. Take a few minutes before you get completely up, and slowly arise when ready. Please drink water to hydrate.

Layout #23: Downloading Higher Knowledge from Other Realms

The purpose of this crystal layout:

The concept of this layout may be foreign to some of you, but you have to try it! I am amazed at the connections you make from a crystal healing session. The crystals align with the frequencies of the light, or light beings that have been in existence for as long as we can comprehend (and then probably 100 times longer). On a side note, I believe there is no time, other than what we created with the clock, and that we are infinite. To be precise, I feel the energy of our souls is infinite, even if our skin and bones are not. That latter part we do know, since the oldest person alive today I believe is about 111. Anyway, back to now: let's get you connected to some higher knowledge. The crystals are like the cellular phone waves, and your body's energy is the receiver for the light beings calling from other realms/dimensions. I know, right? This is too cool! Years ago, crystal Quartzes were used to emit radio frequencies. That's super similar to what we are doing in this layout: we're connecting good high vibes to other good high vibes to receive incredible ancient or future information. Get those crystals out and get educated already!

What you need:

> 1 Herkimer Diamond
>
> 1 Lemurian Seed
>
> 3 Quartzes
>
> 1 Super 7

Why these crystals harmonize together:

The Herkimer Diamond boosts the power of the ancient ways that are programmed within the Lemurian Seed. Quartz, also an amplifier, clarifies that what you're downloading is pure. I like to think of it as protection comparable to antivirus software; Quartz only allows clarity and blocks the other spammy stuff. Lastly, the Super 7's energy creates a vortex of higher knowledge.

Best essential oils for this session (optional):

Myrrh and lavender oil. I dab the oils on both wrists.

High-vibe mantra (repeat it three times):

Gratitude

How long should I lie with this crystal layout?

60 minutes is best.

Reminder:

You should always sit or lie with your crystal layout for at least 20 minutes to receive proper balancing and harmonizing. Longer sessions (up to 90 minutes) are positive for you as well. If you need to set an alarm for your session, please do. Place all cell phones or electronic devices in a nearby room or hallway; they should be at least eight feet away from you and your crystals. Cellular

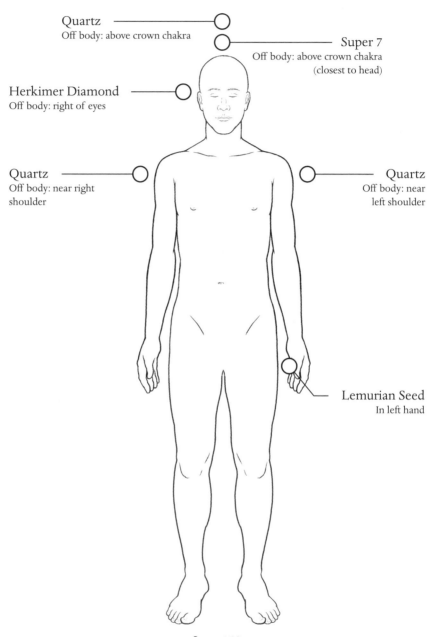

Quartz
Off body: above crown chakra

Super 7
Off body: above crown chakra
(closest to head)

Herkimer Diamond
Off body: right of eyes

Quartz
Off body: near right
shoulder

Quartz
Off body: near
left shoulder

Lemurian Seed
In left hand

Layout 23

phones, computers, and power outlets create negative energies for meditation and healing.

Crystal Body Layout

1. Find a quiet, Zen place to lie down. You can add light music if you prefer. Ambiance music on a low volume is preferred as you want to connect your intuitive senses to receive messages or downloads during this session.

2. Make yourself comfortable. Lie faceup.

3. See the diagram on page 194. This is where to place the crystals; this layout is placed on your physical body.

4. Set a specific intention; say it aloud or in your mind as you are ready to close your eyes and relax. Intention means what you desire and project with your thoughts. **Intention:** *"I am asking those of positive higher knowledge from the light only to please show me or download me with information that is for my greater good—I am gratefully ready to accept this information today in the month of* [month]*, year 20__, Earth dimension."*

5. If you are a visual person, as you close your eyes and state your intention, try to imagine a white or gold healing light moving over your entire body. Just relax, and if you fall asleep, know it is just fine to do so.

6. When you wake or open your eyes after the session is complete, focus on your feet and imagine them as roots going into the ground like a tree. This visualization will help you feel more alert and return to your physical body. Say in your mind or aloud, "I am perfectly fine and well, and my body is self-healing. I am balanced and feel great." As you open your eyes and state you are balanced and well, you will notice both of your feet. This helps you come back into the present moment and ground. Take a few minutes before you get completely up, and slowly arise when ready. Please drink water to hydrate.

Layout #24:
Advancement of the Human Soul Living on Earth

The purpose of this crystal layout:

This is a session that propels you to further advance your total being. Whether it be for physical, emotional, mental, or spiritual matters, you will move ahead. Your true soul, all of you that exists, will be ready to advance to your greatest potential. You will allow and accept the advancement happily.

What you need:

1 Auralite 23

1 Black Tourmaline

1 Charoite

1 Green Tourmaline

1 Nirvana

Why these crystals harmonize together:

Auralite 23 is pure greatness—I use it in powerful sessions like this one to get the energy vibe high and positive, cleansed and cleared; I then use Black Tourmaline for extra grounding to connect a client's greatness with this Earth dimension and to reveal their positive path. Charoite allows you to see who you are and what needs to change, adapt, or adjust on all levels, especially mentally. Green Tourmaline always brings one's purpose to the surface, and the Nirvana Crystal brings incredible compassion, self-love, and balance of what you need and desire to advance.

Best essential oils for this session (optional):

Geranium or rosemary oil. I dab the oil on the third eye chakra and on both wrists.

High-vibe mantra (repeat it three times):

Ahhh-heee

How long should I lie with this crystal layout?

45–60 minutes is best.

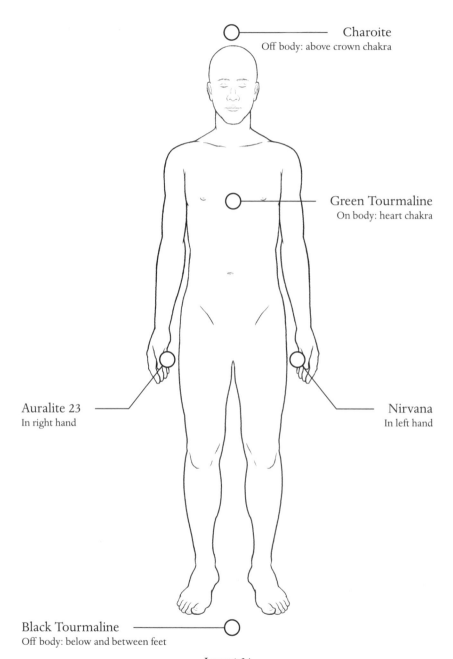

Charoite
Off body: above crown chakra

Green Tourmaline
On body: heart chakra

Auralite 23
In right hand

Nirvana
In left hand

Black Tourmaline
Off body: below and between feet

Layout 24

Reminder:

You should always sit or lie with your crystal layout for at least 20 minutes to receive proper balancing and harmonizing. Longer sessions (up to 90 minutes) are positive for you as well. If you need to set an alarm for your session, please do. Place all cell phones or electronic devices in a nearby room or hallway; they should be at least eight feet away from you and your crystals. Cellular phones, computers, and power outlets create negative energies for meditation and healing.

Crystal Body Layout

1. Find a quiet, Zen place to lie down. You can add light music if you prefer. Llewellyn's "Glimpse of Paradise" works in harmony with this session.

2. Make yourself comfortable. Lie faceup.

3. See the diagram on page 197. This is where to place the crystals; this layout is placed on your physical body.

4. Set a specific intention; say it aloud or in your mind as you are ready to close your eyes and relax. Intention means what you desire and project with your thoughts. **Intention:** *"My purpose in this meditation is to connect with my soul and my human presence—to work in harmony so I can reach my potential and goals in this lifetime on Earth dimension in the year of 20__."*

5. If you are a visual person, as you close your eyes and state your intention, try to imagine a white or gold healing light moving over your entire body. Just relax, and if you fall asleep, know it is just fine to do so.

6. When you wake or open your eyes after the session is complete, focus on your feet and imagine them as roots going into the ground like a tree. This visualization will help you feel more alert and return to your physical body. Say in your mind or aloud, "I am perfectly fine and well, and my body is self-healing. I am balanced and feel great." As you open your eyes and state you are balanced and well, you will notice both of your feet. This helps you come back into the present moment and ground. Take a few minutes before you get completely up, and slowly arise when ready. Please drink water to hydrate.

Layout #25:
Star Energy: Bring More Light to Your Eternal Being

The purpose of this crystal layout:

Accepting is the biggest conquest for most people, and they don't usually realize it at all. It's becoming normal for people to forget about the bright light within them, and they constantly dull their light with life's emotions. This session takes you to the space in your body that is a star, keeping that light on and allowing more light to come your way. Star energy is in everyone. Each person has and can tap into their eternal light—it is just a matter of never tuning it off or dimming it. It's time you turn it up a notch.

What you need:

1 Apophyllite

1 Black Tourmaline

1 Celestite

1 Moonstone

1 Pink Opal

1 Kunzite

1 Sunstone

1 Rose Quartz

Why these crystals harmonize together:

Apophyllite opens the gate to your soul and ignites energy that may be from other dimensions or portals. Black Tourmaline will keep you protected and grounded when the session is completed, while Celestite, along with the Moonstone, brings heavenly energy. The Pink Opal is a frequency changer for those above in higher realms to connect to and amp up. I added Kunzite as your receptor and Sunstone to keep your ego at bay during your star-loving soul opening. Lastly, add one lovely piece of Rose Quartz to keep unconditional love flowing from the heart chakra to the entire auric field.

Best essential oils for this session (optional):

Sage or jasmine oil. I dab the oil on both wrists.

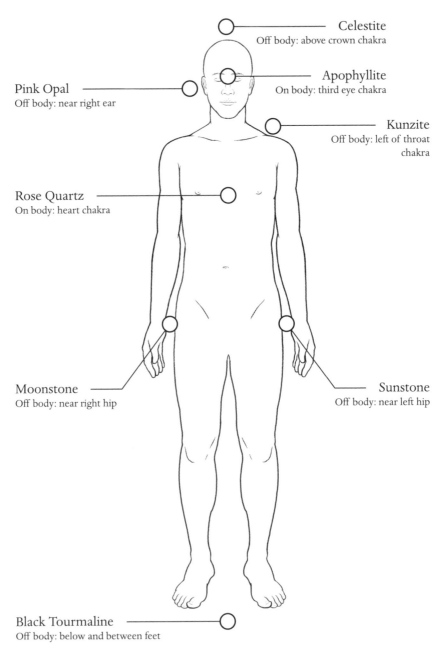

Celestite
Off body: above crown chakra

Apophyllite
On body: third eye chakra

Pink Opal
Off body: near right ear

Kunzite
Off body: left of throat
chakra

Rose Quartz
On body: heart chakra

Moonstone
Off body: near right hip

Sunstone
Off body: near left hip

Black Tourmaline
Off body: below and between feet

Layout 25

High-vibe mantra (repeat it three times):

Opeeeeeen

How long should I lie with this crystal layout?

45–60 minutes is best.

Reminder:

You should always sit or lie with your crystal layout for at least 20 minutes to receive proper balancing and harmonizing. Longer sessions (up to 90 minutes) are positive for you as well. If you need to set an alarm for your session, please do. Place all cell phones or electronic devices in a nearby room or hallway; they should be at least eight feet away from you and your crystals. Cellular phones, computers, and power outlets create negative energies for meditation and healing.

Crystal Body Layout

1. Find a quiet, Zen place to lie down. You can add light music if you prefer. My fav is "Reiki Gold" by Llewellyn. It's about one hour in length.

2. Make yourself comfortable. Lie faceup.

3. See the diagram on page 200. This is where to place the crystals; this layout is placed on your physical body.

4. Set a specific intention; say it aloud or in your mind as you are ready to close your eyes and relax. Intention means what you desire and project with your thoughts. **Intention:** *"My goal is to accept light energy which is to bring positive vibrations into my physical, emotional, mental, and spiritual bodies, connecting me with eternal light. My goal is to accept light of general goodness and equal energy exchanges with all that exists on Earth and beyond."*

5. If you are a visual person, as you close your eyes and state your intention, try to imagine a white or gold healing light moving over your entire body. Just relax, and if you fall asleep, know it is just fine to do so.

6. When you wake or open your eyes after the session is complete, focus on your feet and imagine them as roots going into the ground like a tree. This visualization will help you feel more alert and return to your physical body. Say in your mind or aloud, "I am perfectly fine and well, and my

body is self-healing. I am balanced and feel great." As you open your eyes and state you are balanced and well, you will notice both of your feet. This helps you come back into the present moment and ground. Take a few minutes before you get completely up, and slowly arise when ready. Please drink water to hydrate.

Layout #26:
Insights of the Future

The purpose of this crystal layout:

We all have a desire once in a while to know everything! It's not healthy, but it happens to the best of us. Getting accurate insight and guidance is really the key to utilizing our gifts. Nothing is written in stone; if it were, we wouldn't be able to manifest change in our lives, right? I say right. Either way, it is incredibly titillating to have an epic session with your crystals and receive some future information. This is one of my favorite sessions. I have one big tip for you: please do not watch television the day of or night before this crystal layout. Your subconscious holds a lot of information, so limit your exposure to subliminal messages (hint hint: TV ads) to ensure that your session will be pure with unembellished prophecies.

What you need:

1 Azurite

1 Auralite 23

1 Cavansite

1 Citrine

1 Herkimer Diamond

1 White Howlite

Why these crystals harmonize together:

Azurite opens up the third eye chakra, the entry to intuition. It allows visions and your senses to open, which enables you to receive information. Auralite 23 brings enlightenment while keeping you in a steady, balanced state; use it for insight and to balance your energy centers and aura to become a great conduit of messages. Cavansite allows clear hearing and amplifies your senses, es-

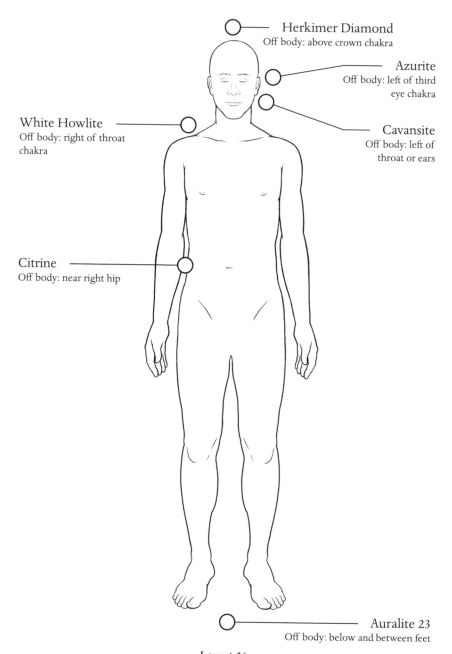

Herkimer Diamond
Off body: above crown chakra

Azurite
Off body: left of third
eye chakra

White Howlite
Off body: right of throat
chakra

Cavansite
Off body: left of
throat or ears

Citrine
Off body: near right hip

Auralite 23
Off body: below and between feet

Layout 26

pecially the ears and the throat chakra. Citrine is used to keep happy energy surrounding you and erase anything you release from everyday stressors. The beautiful Herkimer Diamond amplifies all of that energy, and White Howlite keeps the focus on receiving future messages.

Best essential oils for this session (optional):

Frankincense, rosemary, or lavender. I dab the oil on the third eye chakra and on both wrists or between my thumbs and pointer fingers. Be mindful if you have sensitivities or allergies. Some people cannot put pure essential oils on sensitive skin areas like the face. If this is the case for you, use the oils on the wrists, dilute the oils, or avoid them altogether.

High-vibe mantra (repeat it three times):

Sho-meee

How long should I lie with this crystal layout?

60 minutes is best.

Reminder:

You should always sit or lie with your crystal layout for at least 20 minutes to receive proper balancing and harmonizing. Longer sessions (up to 90 minutes) are positive for you as well. If you need to set an alarm for your session, please do. Place all cell phones or electronic devices in a nearby room or hallway; they should be at least eight feet away from you and your crystals. Cellular phones, computers, and power outlets create negative energies for meditation and healing.

Crystal Body Layout

1. Find a quiet, Zen place to lie down. You can add light music if you prefer. Pick any low volume music you love and that totally relaxes you. I choose no vocal ambiance music.
2. Make yourself comfortable. Lie faceup.
3. See the diagram on page 203. This is where to place the crystals; this layout is placed on your physical body.

4. Set a specific intention; say it aloud or in your mind as you are ready to close your eyes and relax. Intention means what you desire and project with your thoughts. Here are two intentions; you can use one or both. **Intention one:** *"Please may I ask one guide from the light only to show me visually or by feeling and sensing information of my future that I can acquire or change if need be this Earth dimension of the month [month] and year 20___."* **Intention two:** *"Please share information that will assist me and all those involved in positive ways. Gratitude."*

5. If you are a visual person, as you close your eyes and state your intentions, try to imagine a white or gold healing light moving over your entire body. Just relax, and if you fall asleep, know it is just fine to do so.

6. When you wake or open your eyes after the session is complete, focus on your feet and imagine them as roots going into the ground like a tree. This visualization will help you feel more alert and return to your physical body. Say in your mind or aloud, "I am perfectly fine and well, and my body is self-healing. I am balanced and feel great." As you open your eyes and state you are balanced and well, you will notice both of your feet. This helps you come back into the present moment and ground. Take a few minutes before you get completely up, and slowly arise when ready. Please drink water to hydrate.

———————

Hopefully you have tried one or more sessions by now; especially with all these layouts for spiritual enhancement, you should be beaming bright! These are all great to do whenever you need a lighter outlook on life. You will feel loved and secure. Connecting to spirit is a gift; all you have to do is say, "I accept and allow." Now set up another crystal grid!

Conclusion

Now that you have mastered all avenues with your crystals, gemstones, and minerals, you can offer crystal sessions and become your town's new crystal healer and master gridder! You should be proud that you learned a healthy healing modality and super fun hobby. You went through the amazing process of knowing each stone and its purpose, feeling, sensing, and understanding the seven chakras and four auric layers, and learning how to adjust your energy in a harmonizing crystal healing session. The best part of all this education is experiencing. If you aren't a crystal junkie after this book, I'd be surprised. I'm sure by now you have a nice selection of crystals from trying all of the crystal body layout sessions. Kudos, my friend! If you want to learn more, stay tuned for crystal retreats near you. If I run into you on my tour, you better have a crystal stash on you! Remember that no matter what is going on in your life, there is always a stone to help!

Appendix A

Reference to Crystal and Gemstone Use for Specific Ailments or Issues

Here is your quick and easy chart for all 66 crystals. You can find a crystal to harmonize with your chakras, ailments, or emotional, mental, and spiritual needs! Remember: "I got a stone for that!"

The first group of stones in the chart is for emotional wellness. Stones for spiritual, physical, and chakra wellness follow.

Emotional Wellness	Crystal/ Gemstone	Vibe Meter	Stone Color	Chakras
	Agate, Blue Lace #1	Mellow Soother	light blue and white	5th throat
	Agate, Various #4	Grounded Chill	various colors	2nd sacral, 1st base root
	Amethyst #7	Enlightened	pale to deep purple	7th crown, 6th third eye, 4th heart
	Angelite #8	Enlightened	soft blue with white exterior	7th crown, 6th third eye, 4th heart
	Aragonite #13	Yowzer and Grounded Chill	white, gray, reddish, yellow-green, gray-green, blue, purple	2nd sacral, 1st base root
	Carnelian #18	Mellow Soother	pale orange to deep-red orange	4th heart, 2nd sacral
Anxiety (Calming)	Cavansite #20	Yowzer and Enlightened	blue to bluish-green	7th crown, 6th third eye, 5th throat, 4th heart
	Celestite #20	Enlightened	blue-gray	7th crown, 6th third eye, 5th throat, 4th heart
	Chalcedony #21	Mellow Soother	purple or blue	5th throat
	Chrysoprase #23	Mellow Soother	green	5th throat, 4th heart, 3rd solar plexus
	Danburite #25	Mega Yowzer	colorless	7th crown, 6th third eye, 5th throat, 4th heart, 3rd solar plexus, 2nd sacral
	Kunzite #35	Yowzer	pink-violet	7th crown, 6th third eye, 5th throat, 4th heart, 3rd solar plexus

Emotional Wellness	Crystal/ Gemstone	Vibe Meter	Stone Color	Chakras
Anxiety (Calming) (continued)	Lepidolite #39	Mellow Soother	pink or lavender	6th third eye, 5th throat, 4th heart, 3rd solar plexus, 2nd sacral, 1st base root
	Moonstone #42	Mellow Soother and Enlightened	blue-white	7th crown, 6th third eye, 5th throat
Body Image	Agate, Various #4	Grounded Chill	various colors	2nd sacral, 1st base root
	Carnelian #18	Mellow Soother	pale orange to deep-red orange	4th heart, 2nd sacral
	Kyanite, Blue #36	Grounded Chill	indigo, black, blue, green, orange	All
Detox	Amethyst #7	Enlightened	pale to deep purple	7th crown, 6th third eye, 4th heart
	Azurite #16	Yowzer and Enlightened	deep blue	7th crown, 6th third eye, 5th throat
Grief/Loss	Apache Tears #9	Mellow Soother	black/brown	4th heart, 1st base root
	Obsidian, Snowflake #45	Yowzer and Enlightened	black with white spots	7th crown, 6th third eye, 5th throat, 4th heart, 3rd solar plexus, 2nd sacral
	Turquoise #65	Grounded Chill	blue	5th throat, 3rd solar plexus, 2nd sacral, 1st base root

Emotional Wellness	Crystal/ Gemstone	Vibe Meter	Stone Color	Chakras
Relationship /Love	Agate, Thunder #3	Yowzer	creamy white swirls	All
	Chrysoprase #23	Mellow Soother	green	5th throat, 4th heart, 3rd solar plexus
	Nirvana/Ice Crystal #43	Yowzer and Enlightened	clear, colorless	All
	Quartz, Rose/Pink #51	Mellow Soother	pink	7th crown, 6th third eye, 5th throat, 4th heart, 3rd solar plexus, 2nd sacral
	Rhodochro-site #54	Mellow Soother	pink, shades of pink	4th heart, 3rd solar plexus, 2nd sacral
	Sodalite #59	Mellow Soother	shades of blue to purple	7th crown, 6th third eye, 5th throat
	Tourmaline, Green #64	Yowzer and Enlightened	pale to deep green	All
Self-Love	Angelite #8	Enlightened	soft blue with white exterior	7th crown, 6th third eye, 4th heart
	Calcite #17	Yowzer	orange	5th throat, 4th heart, 2nd sacral
	Dioptase #26	Yowzer	emerald green to deep bluish green	7th crown, 6th third eye, 4th heart
	Kunzite #35	Yowzer	pink-violet	7th crown, 6th third eye, 5th throat, 4th heart, 3rd solar plexus
	Kyanite, Blue #36	Grounded Chill	indigo, black, blue, green, orange	All

Emotional Wellness	Crystal/ Gemstone	Vibe Meter	Stone Color	Chakras
Self-Love (continued)	Malachite #40	Mellow Soother	blue-green	4th heart
	Nirvana/Ice Crystal #43	Yowzer and Enlightened	clear, colorless	All
	Obsidian, Snowflake #45	Yowzer and Enlightened	black with white spots	7th crown, 6th third eye, 5th throat, 4th heart, 3rd solar plexus, 2nd sacral
	Pietersite #48	Grounded Chill	gold, brown, gray, blue-gray and black	3rd solar plexus, 2nd sacral, 1st base root
	Quartz, Rose/Pink #51	Mellow Soother	pink	7th crown, 6th third eye, 5th throat, 4th heart, 3rd solar plexus, 2nd sacral
	Tourmaline, Green #64	Yowzer and Enlightened	pale to deep green	All
	Turquoise #65	Grounded Chill	blue	5th throat, 3rd solar plexus, 2nd sacral, 1st base root
Self-Determination	Amazonite #5	Mellow Soother	blue-green or green	All
	Howlite, White #32	Grounded Chill	white and black	6th third eye, 1st base root
	Ruby Zoisite #55	Yowzer	green with red specks	5th throat, 4th heart, 3rd solar plexus, 2nd sacral

Emotional Wellness	Crystal/ Gemstone	Vibe Meter	Stone Color	Chakras
Balancing Moods and Releasing Anger; Bringing Happiness	Amazonite #5	Mellow Soother	blue-green or green	All
	Agate, Moss #2	Grounded Chill	green	2nd sacral, 1st base root
	Amber #6	Yowzer	yellow to reddish-brown	3rd solar plexus, 2nd sacral
	Aventurine, Green #15	Mellow Soother	green	4th heart
	Citrine #24	Mellow Soother	yellowish	7th crown, 6th third eye, 3rd solar plexus, 2nd sacral
	Dioptase #26	Yowzer	emerald green to deep bluish-green	7th crown, 6th third eye, 4th heart
	Obsidian, Black #44	Grounded Chill	black	1st base root
	Obsidian, Snowflake #45	Yowzer and Enlightened	black with white spots	7th crown, 6th third eye, 5th throat, 4th heart, 3rd solar plexus, 2nd sacral
	Opal, Pink #46	Enlightened	light to medium pink	7th crown, 6th third eye, 5th throat, 4th heart
	Pyrite #49	Yowzer	gold	4th heart, 3rd solar plexus, 2nd sacral
	Quartz, Smoky #53	Grounded Chill	varies, tan to chocolate brown	1st base root
	Rhodochro-site #54	Mellow Soother	pink, shades of pink	4th heart, 3rd solar plexus, 2nd sacral
	Tourmaline, Green #64	Yowzer and Enlightened	pale to deep green	All
	Unakite #66	Grounded Chill	green-red	1st base root

Emotional Wellness	Crystal/ Gemstone	Vibe Meter	Stone Color	Chakras
	Apache Tears #9	Mellow Soother	black/brown	4th heart, 1st base root
Rational Thinking	Charoite #22	Yowzer	purple	7th crown, 6th third eye, 4th heart, 3rd solar plexus, 2nd sacral
	Citrine #24	Mellow Soother	yellowish	7th crown, 6th third eye, 3rd solar plexus, 2nd sacral
Sobriety	Amethyst #7	Enlightened	pale to deep purple	7th crown, 6th third eye, 4th heart
Relaxation/ Sleep	Amethyst #7	Enlightened	pale to deep purple	7th crown, 6th third eye, 4th heart
	Lepidolite #39	Mellow Soother	pink or lavender	6th third eye, 5th throat, 4th heart, 3rd solar plexus, 2nd sacral, 1st base root
Focus and Clarity	Aquamarine #12	Mellow Soother	blue-green or blue	5th throat
	Charoite #22	Yowzer	purple	7th crown, 6th third eye, 4th heart, 3rd solar plexus, 2nd sacral
	Emerald #27	Mellow Soother	green	7th crown, 6th third eye, 4th heart, 3rd solar plexus, 2nd sacral

Emotional Wellness	Crystal/ Gemstone	Vibe Meter	Stone Color	Chakras
Focus and Clarity (continued)	Howlite, White #32	Grounded Chill	white and black	6th third eye, 1st base root
	Obsidian, Snowflake #45	Yowzer and Enlightened	black with white spots	7th crown, 6th third eye, 5th throat, 4th heart, 3rd solar plexus, 2nd sacral
	Quartz, Rutile #52	Yowzer and Enlightened	gold-yellow, reddish-brown, red or black	7th crown, 6th third eye, 5th throat, 4th heart, 3rd solar plexus, 2nd sacral
	Quartz, Smoky #53	Grounded Chill	varies, tan to chocolate brown	1st base root
	Tiger's Eye #62	Grounded Chill	yellow-brown to golden	7th crown, 6th third eye, 3rd solar plexus, 2nd sacral, 1st base root
Positive Energy and Actions	Amethyst #7	Enlightened	pale to deep purple	7th crown, 6th third eye, 4th heart
	Dioptase #26	Yowzer	emerald green to deep bluish-green	7th crown, 6th third eye, 4th heart
	Emerald #27	Mellow Soother	green	7th crown, 6th third eye, 4th heart, 3rd solar plexus, 2nd sacral
	Jasper, Red #34	Grounded Chill	wide variety	2nd sacral, 1st base root
	Malachite #40	Mellow Soother	blue-green	4th heart

Emotional Wellness	Crystal/ Gemstone	Vibe Meter	Stone Color	Chakras
	Opalite #47	Mellow Soother	white-yellow, cream	7th crown, 6th third eye, 4th heart
	Pyrite #49	Yowzer	gold	4th heart, 3rd solar plexus, 2nd sacral
Positive Energy and Actions (continued)	Quartz, Rose/Pink #51	Mellow Soother	pink	7th crown, 6th third eye, 5th throat, 4th heart, 3rd solar plexus, 2nd sacral
	Ruby Zoisite #55	Yowzer	green with red specks	5th throat, 4th heart, 3rd solar plexus, 2nd sacral
	Sunstone #60	Mellow Smoother	orange to red-brown mixed with white	7th crown, 3rd solar plexus, 2nd sacral
	Agate, Various #4	Grounded Chill	various colors	2nd sacral, 1st base root
	Apache Tears #9	Mellow Soother	black/brown	4th heart, 1st base root
	Auralite 23 #14	Yowzer	mixture of up to 23 mineral colors	All
Releasing Patterns	Dioptase #26	Yowzer	emerald green to deep bluish-green	7th crown, 6th third eye, 4th heart
	Garnet #30	Mellow Soother	red, green, black, orange-red	4th heart, 3rd solar plexus, 2nd sacral
	Jasper, Ocean #33	Grounded Chill	wide variety	3rd solar plexus, 2nd sacral, 1st base root

Emotional Wellness	Crystal/ Gemstone	Vibe Meter	Stone Color	Chakras
Releasing Patterns (continued)	Quartz, Rutile #52	Yowzer and Enlightened	gold-yellow, reddish-brown, red or black	7th crown, 6th third eye, 5th throat, 4th heart, 3rd solar plexus, 2nd sacral
	Selenite #57	Yowzer	white and clear	7th crown, 6th third eye, 5th throat, 4th heart, 3rd solar plexus, 2nd sacral
	Shungite #58	Mellow Soother	black	All
Communication	Angelite #8	Enlightened	soft blue with white exterior	7th crown, 6th third eye, 4th heart
	Agate, Blue Lace #1	Mellow Soother	light blue and white	5th throat
	Chalcedony #21	Mellow Soother	purple or blue	5th throat
	Lapis Lazuli #37	Enlightened	blue	7th crown, 6th third eye, 5th throat, 3rd solar plexus
Increased Creativity	Citrine #24	Mellow Soother	yellowish	7th crown, 6th third eye, 3rd solar plexus, 2nd sacral

Emotional Wellness	Crystal/ Gemstone	Vibe Meter	Stone Color	Chakras
	Pyrite #49	Yowzer	gold	4th heart, 3rd solar plexus, 2nd sacral
Weight	Ruby Zoisite #55	Yowzer	green with red specks	5th throat, 4th heart, 3rd solar plexus, 2nd sacral
	Quartz, Rutile #52	Yowzer and Enlightened	gold-yellow, reddish-brown, red or black	7th crown, 6th third eye, 5th throat, 4th heart, 3rd solar plexus, 2nd sacral

The next group of stones is for spiritual wellness.

Spiritual Wellness	Crystal/ Gemstone	Vibe Meter	Stone Color	Chakras
	Agate, Various #4	Yowzer	various colors	2nd sacral, 1st base root
Aura Balance	Auralite 23 #14	Yowzer	mixture of up to 23 mineral colors	All
	Rhodochro-site #54	Mellow Soother	pink, shades of pink	4th heart, 3rd solar plexus, 2nd sacral
	Apophyllite #11	Yowzer	clear or green	7th crown, 6th third eye, 4th heart
Astral Travel	Celestite #20	Enlightened	blue-gray	7th crown, 6th third eye, 5th throat, 4th heart
	Danburite #25	Mega Yowzer	colorless	7th crown, 6th third eye, 5th throat, 4th heart, 3rd solar plexus, 2nd sacral

Spiritual Wellness	Crystal/ Gemstone	Vibe Meter	Stone Color	Chakras
Astral Travel (continued)	Herkimer Diamond #31	Yowzer and Enlightened	clear to colorless	7th crown, 6th third eye, 5th throat, 4th heart, 3rd solar plexus, 2nd sacral
	Quartz, Rutile #52	Yowzer and Enlightened	gold-yellow, reddish-brown, red or black	7th crown, 6th third eye, 5th throat, 4th heart, 3rd solar plexus, 2nd sacral
	Selenite #57	Yowzer	white and clear	7th crown, 6th third eye, 5th throat, 4th heart, 3rd solar plexus, 2nd sacral
Dreams	Herkimer Diamond #31	Yowzer and Enlightened	clear to colorless	7th crown, 6th third eye, 5th throat, 4th heart, 3rd solar plexus, 2nd sacral
	Moonstone #42	Mellow Soother and Enlightened	blue-white	7th crown 6th third eye, 5th throat
	Selenite #57	Yowzer	white and clear	7th crown, 6th third eye, 5th throat, 4th heart, 3rd solar plexus, 2nd sacral
Connection with Angels	Angelite #8	Enlightened	soft blue with white exterior	7th crown, 6th third eye, 4th heart
	Apophyllite #11	Yowzer	clear or green	7th crown, 6th third eye, 4th heart
	Celestite #20	Enlightened	blue-gray	7th crown, 6th third eye, 5th throat, 4th heart

Spiritual Wellness	Crystal/ Gemstone	Vibe Meter	Stone Color	Chakras
Connection with Angels (continued)	Lemurian Seeds #38	Yowzer and Enlightened	clear to smoky	7th crown, 6th third eye
	Quartz, Clear #50	Enlightened	clear, colorless	7th crown, 6th third eye
	Kyanite, Blue #36	Grounded Chill	indigo, black, blue, green, orange	All
	Lapis Lazuli #37	Enlightened	blue	7th crown, 6th third eye, 5th throat, 3rd solar plexus
Past Life	Obsidian, Black #44	Grounded Chill	black	1st base root
	Rhodochrosite #54	Mellow Soother	pink, shades of pink	4th heart, 3rd solar plexus, 2nd sacral
	Obsidian, Snowflake #45	Yowzer and Enlightened	black with white spots	7th crown, 6th third eye, 5th throat, 4th heart, 3rd solar plexus, 2nd sacral
Spiritual Awakening	Apophyllite #11	Yowzer	clear or green	7th crown, 6th third eye, 4th heart
	Aragonite #13	Yowzer and Grounded Chill	white, gray, reddish, yellow-green, gray-green, blue, purple	2nd sacral, 1st base root
	Azurite #16	Yowzer and Enlightened	deep blue	7th crown, 6th third eye, 5th throat
	Cavansite #19	Yowzer and Enlightened	blue to bluish-green	7th crown, 6th third eye, 5th throat, 4th heart

Spiritual Wellness	Crystal/ Gemstone	Vibe Meter	Stone Color	Chakras
Spiritual Awakening (continued)	Herkimer Diamond #31	Yowzer and Enlightened	clear to colorless	7th crown, 6th third eye, 5th throat, 4th heart, 3rd solar plexus, 2nd sacral
	Lemurian Seeds #38	Yowzer and Enlightened	clear to smoky	7th crown, 6th third eye
	Moldavite #41	Yowzer and Enlightened	deep green	7th crown, 6th third eye, 4th heart, 2nd sacral
	Pietersite #48	Grounded Chill	gold, brown, gray, blue-gray and black	3rd solar plexus, 2nd sacral, 1st base root
	Opal, Pink #46	Enlightened	light to medium pink	7th crown, 6th third eye, 5th throat, 4th heart
	Quartz, Rose/Pink #51	Mellow Soother	pink	7th crown, 6th third eye, 5th throat, 4th heart, 3rd solar plexus, 2nd sacral
	Selenite #57	Yowzer	white and clear	7th crown, 6th third eye, 5th throat, 4th heart, 3rd solar plexus, 2nd sacral
Meditation	Agate, Various #4	Grounded Chill	various colors	2nd sacral, 1st base root
	Lapis Lazuli #37	Enlightened	blue	7th crown, 6th third eye, 5th throat, 3rd solar plexus
	Opalite #47	Mellow Soother	white-yellow, cream	7th crown, 6th third eye, 4th heart

Spiritual Wellness	Crystal/ Gemstone	Vibe Meter	Stone Color	Chakras
Meditation (continued)	Quartz, Rutile #52	Yowzer and Enlightened	gold-yellow, reddish-brown, red or black	7th crown, 6th third eye, 5th throat, 4th heart, 3rd solar plexus, 2nd sacral
	Tourmaline, Green #64	Yowzer and Enlightened	pale to deep green	All
Focus and Clarity	Angelite #8	Enlightened	soft blue with white exterior	7th crown, 6th third eye, 4th heart
	Howlite, White #32	Grounded Chill	white and black	6th third eye, 1st base root
	Quartz, Clear #50	Enlightened	clear, colorless	7th crown, 6th third eye
Telepathy	Apophyllite #11	Yowzer	clear or green	7th crown, 6th third eye, 4th heart
	Cavansite #19	Yowzer	blue to bluish-green	7th crown, 6th third eye, 5th throat, 4th heart
	Kyanite, Blue #36	Grounded Chill	indigo, black, blue, green, orange	All
	Lapis Lazuli #37	Enlightened	blue	7th crown, 6th third eye, 5th throat, 3rd solar plexus
Clairvoyance	Apophyllite #11	Yowzer	clear or green	7th crown, 6th third eye, 4th heart
	Aquamarine #12	Mellow Soother	blue-green or blue	5th throat
	Kunzite #35	Yowzer	pink-violet	7th crown, 6th third eye, 5th throat, 4th heart, 3rd solar plexus

Spiritual Wellness	Crystal/ Gemstone	Vibe Meter	Stone Color	Chakras
Clairvoyance (continued)	Kyanite, Blue #36	Grounded Chill	indigo, black, blue, green, orange	All
	Lemurian Seeds #38	Yowzer and Enlightened	clear to smoky	7th crown, 6th third eye
	Super 7 #61	Yowzer and Enlightened	combination of seven colored stones	All
Grounding/ Presence	Agate, Various #4	Grounded Chill	various colors	2nd sacral, 1st base root
	Agate, Thunder #3	Yowzer	creamy white swirls	All
	Apache Tears #9	Mellow Soother	black/brown	4th heart, 1st base root
	Obsidian, Black #44	Grounded Chill	black	1st base root
	Tourmaline, Black #63	Grounded Chill	opaque black	1st base root
	Agate, Moss #2	Grounded Chill	green	2nd sacral, 1st base root
	Quartz, Smoky #53	Grounded Chill	varies, tan to chocolate brown	1st base root
Psychic Abilities	Azurite #16	Yowzer and Enlightened	deep blue	7th crown, 6th third eye, 5th throat
	Cavansite #19	Yowzer and Enlightened	blue to bluish-green	7th crown, 6th third eye, 5th throat, 4th heart
	Lapis Lazuli #37	Enlightened	blue	7th crown, 6th third eye, 5th throat, 3rd solar plexus
	Lemurian Seeds #38	Yowzer and Enlightened	clear to smoky	7th crown, 6th third eye

Spiritual Wellness	Crystal/ Gemstone	Vibe Meter	Stone Color	Chakras
Psychic Abilities (continued)	Moonstone #42	Mellow Soother and Enlightened	blue-white	7th crown, 6th third eye, 5th throat
	Opal, Pink #46	Enlightened	light to medium pink	7th crown, 6th third eye, 5th throat, 4th heart
	Obsidian, Snowflake #45	Yowzer and Enlightened	black with white spots	7th crown, 6th third eye, 5th throat, 4th heart, 3rd solar plexus, 2nd sacral
	Sodalite #59	Mellow Soother	shades of blue to purple	7th crown, 6th third eye, 5th throat
	Sunstone #60	Mellow Soother	orange to red-brown mixed with white	7th crown, 3rd solar plexus, 2nd sacral
	Super 7 #61	Yowzer and Enlightened	combination of seven colored stones	All
Manifesting Abundance and Opportunities	Aventurine, Green #15	Mellow Soother	green	4th heart
	Citrine #24	Mellow Soother	yellowish	7th crown, 6th third eye, 3rd solar plexus, 2nd sacral
	Emerald #27	Mellow Soother	green	7th crown, 6th third eye, 4th heart, 3rd solar plexus, 2nd sacral
	Garnet #30	Mellow Soother	red, green, black, orange-red	4th heart, 3rd solar plexus, 2nd sacral

Spiritual Wellness	Crystal/ Gemstone	Vibe Meter	Stone Color	Chakras
Manifesting Abundance and Opportunities (continued)	Pietersite #48	Grounded Chill	gold, brown, gray, blue-gray and black	3rd solar plexus, 2nd sacral, 1st base root
	Sunstone #60	Mellow Soother	orange to red-brown mixed with white	7th crown, 3rd solar plexus, 2nd sacral
	Auralite 23 #14	Yowzer	mixture of up to 23 mineral colors	All
	Obsidian, Black #44	Grounded Chill	black	1st base root
	Tourmaline, Black #63	Grounded Chill	opaque black	1st base root
	Herkimer Diamond #31	Yowzer and Enlightened	clear to colorless	7th crown, 6th third eye, 5th throat, 4th heart, 3rd solar plexus, 2nd sacral
Cleansing and Clearing Aura or Space	Moldavite #41	Yowzer and Enlightened	deep green	7th crown, 6th third eye, 4th heart, 2nd sacral
	Rhodochrosite #54	Mellow Soother	pink, shades of pink	4th heart, 3rd solar plexus, 2nd sacral
	Salt #56	Mellow Soother	white	5th throat, 4th heart, 3rd solar plexus, 2nd sacral, 1st base root
	Selenite #57	Yowzer	white and clear	7th crown, 6th third eye, 5th throat, 4th heart, 3rd solar plexus, 2nd sacral

Spiritual Wellness	Crystal/ Gemstone	Vibe Meter	Stone Color	Chakras
Cleansing and Clearing Aura or Space (continued)	Shungite #58	Mellow Soother	black	All
	Sodalite #59	Mellow Soother	shades of blue to purple	7th crown, 6th third eye, 5th throat
Healing	Apache Tears #9	Mellow Soother	black/brown	4th heart, 1st base root
	Aventurine, Green #15	Mellow Soother	green	4th heart
	Carnelian #18	Mellow Soother	pale orange to deep-red orange	4th heart, 2nd sacral
	Celestite #20	Enlightened	blue-gray	7th crown, 6th third eye, 5th throat, 4th heart
	Fluorite #29	Mellow Soother	green, purple, white, yellow, red, pink, black	7th crown, 6th third eye, 5th throat, 4th heart, 3rd solar plexus, 2nd sacral
	Jasper, Red #34	Grounded Chill	wide variety	2nd sacral, 1st base root
	Lapis Lazuli #37	Enlightened	blue	7th crown, 6th third eye, 5th throat, 3rd solar plexus
	Lemurian Seeds #38	Yowzer and Enlightened	clear to smoky	7th crown, 6th third eye
	Lepidolite #39	Mellow Soother	pink or lavender	6th third eye, 5th throat, 4th heart, 3rd solar plexus, 2nd sacral, 1st base root
	Malachite #40	Mellow Soother	blue-green	4th heart
	Opal, Pink #46	Enlightened	light to medium pink	7th crown, 6th third eye, 5th throat, 4th heart

Spiritual Wellness	Crystal/ Gemstone	Vibe Meter	Stone Color	Chakras
	Pyrite #49	Yowzer	gold	4th heart, 3rd solar plexus, 2nd sacral
	Quartz, Clear #50	Enlightened	clear, colorless	7th crown, 6th third eye
	Rhodochro-site #54	Mellow Soother	pink, shades of pink	4th heart, 3rd solar plexus, 2nd sacral
	Ruby Zoisite #55	Yowzer	green with red specks	5th throat, 4th heart, 3rd solar plexus, 2nd sacral
Healing (continued)	Selenite #57	Yowzer	white and clear	7th crown, 6th third eye, 5th throat, 4th heart, 3rd solar plexus, 2nd sacral
	Obsidian, Snowflake #45	Yowzer and Enlightened	black with white spots	7th crown, 6th third eye, 5th throat, 4th heart, 3rd solar plexus, 2nd sacral
	Super 7 #61	Yowzer and Enlightened	combination of seven colored stones	All
	Tourmaline, Green #64	Yowzer and Enlightened	pale to deep green	All
	Turquoise #65	Grounded Chill	blue	5th throat, 3rd solar plexus, 2nd sacral, 1st base root
	Unakite #66	Grounded Chill	green-red	1st base root

Spiritual Wellness	Crystal/ Gemstone	Vibe Meter	Stone Color	Chakras
Protection	Apache Tears #9	Mellow Soother	black/brown	4th heart, 1st base root
	Obsidian, Black #44	Grounded Chill	black	1st base root
	Tourmaline, Black #63	Grounded Chill	opaque black	1st base root
	Lapis Lazuli #37	Enlightened	blue	7th crown, 6th third eye, 5th throat, 3rd solar plexus
	Moldavite #41	Yowzer and Enlightened	deep green	7th crown, 6th third eye, 4th heart, 2nd sacral
	Quartz, Smoky #53	Grounded Chill	varies, tan to chocolate brown	1st base root
	Tiger's Eye #62	Grounded Chill	yellow-brown to golden	7th crown, 6th third eye, 3rd solar plexus, 2nd sacral, 1st base root

The next group of stones is for physical wellness.

Physical Wellness	Crystal/ Gemstone	Vibe Meter	Stone Color	Chakras
Extremities	Aventurine, Green #15	Mellow Soother	green	4th heart
	Jasper, Red #34	Grounded Chill	wide variety	2nd sacral, 1st base root
	Pietersite #48	Grounded Chill	gold, brown, gray, blue-gray and black	3rd solar plexus, 2nd sacral, 1st base root
Vitality, Regeneration, Youthfulness, and General Health	Chrysoprase #23	Mellow Soother	green	5th throat, 4th heart, 3rd solar plexus

Physical Wellness	Crystal/ Gemstone	Vibe Meter	Stone Color	Chakras
Vitality, Regeneration, Youthfulness, and General Health (continued)	Herkimer Diamond #31	Yowzer and Enlightened	clear to colorless	7th crown, 6th third eye, 5th throat, 4th heart, 3rd solar plexus, 2nd sacral
	Jasper, Red #34	Grounded Chill	wide variety	2nd sacral, 1st base root
	Pietersite #48	Grounded Chill	gold, brown, gray, blue-gray and black	3rd solar plexus, 2nd sacral, 1st base root
	Pyrite #49	Yowzer	gold	4th heart, 3rd solar plexus, 2nd sacral
	Ruby Zoisite #55	Yowzer	green with red specks	5th throat, 4th heart, 3rd solar plexus, 2nd sacral
	Tiger's Eye #62	Grounded Chill	yellow-brown to golden	7th crown, 6th third eye, 3rd solar plexus, 2nd sacral, 1st base root
	Turquoise #65	Grounded Chill	blue	5th throat, 3rd solar plexus, 2nd sacral, 1st base root
	Shungite #58	Mellow Soother	black	All
	Super 7 #61	Yowzer and Enlightened	combination of seven colored stones	All
Autoimmune Disorders	Apache Tears #9	Mellow Soother	black/brown	4th heart, 1st base root
	Aquamarine #12	Mellow Soother	blue-green or blue	5th throat

Physical Wellness	Crystal/ Gemstone	Vibe Meter	Stone Color	Chakras
Autoimmune Disorders (continued)	Aragonite #13	Yowzer and Grounded Chill	white, gray, reddish, yellow-green, gray-green, blue, purple	2nd sacral, 1st base root
Allergies	Aquamarine #12	Mellow Soother	blue-green or blue	5th throat
Hypo-/ Hyperthy-roid	Amber #6	Yowzer	yellow to reddish-brown	3rd solar plexus, 2nd sacral
	Calcite #17	Yowzer	orange	5th throat, 4th heart, 2nd sacral
	Carnelian #18	Mellow Soother	pale orange to deep-red orange	4th heart, 2nd sacral
	Lepidolite #39	Mellow Soother	pink or lavender	6th third eye, 5th throat, 4th heart, 3rd solar plexus, 2nd sacral, 1st base root
	Malachite #40	Mellow Soother	blue-green	4th heart
	Turquoise #65	Grounded Chill	blue	5th throat, 3rd solar plexus, 2nd sacral, 1st base root
Skeleton and Joints (Arthritis)	Apatite #10	Grounded Chill	green, gold, or blue	5th throat, 3rd solar plexus, 2nd sacral, 1st base root
	Fluorite #29	Mellow Soother	green, purple, white, yellow, red, pink, black	7th crown, 6th third eye, 5th throat, 4th heart, 3rd solar plexus, 2nd sacral
	Malachite #40	Mellow Soother	blue-green	4th heart
	Quartz, Smoky #53	Grounded Chill	varies, tan to chocolate brown	1st base root

Physical Wellness	Crystal/ Gemstone	Vibe Meter	Stone Color	Chakras
Nervous System	Amazonite #5	Mellow Soother	blue-green or green	All
	Azurite #16	Yowzer and Enlightened	deep blue	7th crown, 6th third eye, 5th throat
	Charoite #22	Yowzer	purple	7th crown, 6th third eye, 4th heart, 3rd solar plexus, 2nd sacral
	Kunzite #35	Yowzer	pink-violet	7th crown, 6th third eye, 5th throat, 4th heart, 3rd solar plexus
	Kyanite, Blue #36	Grounded Chill	indigo, black, blue, green, orange	All
	Nirvana/Ice Crystal #43	Yowzer and Enlightened	clear, colorless	All
	Quartz, Clear #50	Enlightened	clear, colorless	7th crown, 6th third eye
	Rhodochrosite #54	Mellow Soother	pink, shades of pink	4th heart, 3rd solar plexus, 2nd sacral
	Unakite #66	Grounded Chill	green-red	1st base root
Circulation and Cardiovascular System (Heart)/ Respiratory System (Lungs)	Aventurine, Green #15	Mellow Soother	green	4th heart
	Carnelian #18	Mellow Soother	pale orange to deep-red orange	4th heart, 2nd sacral

Physical Wellness	Crystal/ Gemstone	Vibe Meter	Stone Color	Chakras
	Charoite #22	Yowzer	purple	7th crown, 6th third eye, 4th heart, 3rd solar plexus, 2nd sacral
	Emerald #27	Mellow Soother	green	7th crown, 6th third eye, 4th heart, 3rd solar plexus, 2nd sacral
	Fluorite #29	Mellow Soother	green, purple, white, yellow, red, pink, black	7th crown, 6th third eye, 5th throat, 4th heart, 3rd solar plexus, 2nd sacral
Circulation and Cardio-vascular System (Heart)/ Respiratory System (Lungs) (continued)	Jasper, Red #34	Grounded Chill	wide variety	2nd sacral, 1st base root
	Malachite #40	Mellow Soother	blue-green	4th heart
	Agate, Moss #2	Grounded Chill	green	2nd sacral, 1st base root
	Nirvana/Ice Crystal #43	Yowzer and Enlightened	clear, colorless	All
	Pietersite #48	Grounded Chill	gold, brown, gray, blue-gray and black	3rd solar plexus, 2nd sacral, 1st base root
	Quartz, Rose/Pink #51	Mellow Soother	pink	7th crown, 6th third eye, 5th throat, 4th heart, 3rd solar plexus, 2nd sacral
	Salt #56	Mellow Soother	white	5th throat, 4th heart, 3rd solar plexus, 2nd sacral, 1st base root

Physical Wellness	Crystal/ Gemstone	Vibe Meter	Stone Color	Chakras
Circulation and Cardio-vascular System (Heart)/ Respiratory System (Lungs) (continued)	Sodalite #59	Mellow Soother	shades of blue to purple	7th crown, 6th third eye, 5th throat
	Tourmaline, Green #64	Yowzer and Enlightened	pale to deep green	All
	Turquoise #65	Grounded Chill	blue	5th throat, 3rd solar plexus, 2nd sacral, 1st base root
	Unakite #66	Grounded Chill	green-red	1st base root
Muscular System	Amethyst #7	Enlightened	pale to deep purple	7th crown, 6th third eye, 4th heart
	Aragonite #13	Yowzer and Grounded Chill	white, gray, reddish, yellow-green, gray-green, blue, purple	2nd sacral, 1st base root
	Charoite #22	Yowzer	purple	7th crown, 6th third eye, 4th heart, 3rd solar plexus, 2nd sacral
	Dioptase #26	Yowzer	emerald green to deep bluish-green	7th crown, 6th third eye, 4th heart
	Moonstone #42	Mellow Soother and Enlightened	blue-white	7th crown, 6th third eye, 5th throat
Pain	Amethyst #7	Enlightened	pale to deep purple	7th crown, 6th third eye, 4th heart
	Aragonite #13	Yowzer and Grounded Chill	white, gray, reddish, yellow-green, gray-green, blue, purple	2nd sacral, 1st base root

Physical Wellness	Crystal/ Gemstone	Vibe Meter	Stone Color	Chakras
	Aventurine, Green #15	Mellow Soother	green	4th heart
Pain (continued)	Fluorite #29	Mellow Soother	green, purple, white, yellow, red, pink, black	7th crown, 6th third eye, 5th throat, 4th heart, 3rd solar plexus, 2nd sacral
Liver, Gall-bladder, Kidneys, Adrenal Glands, and Pancreas	Amber #6	Yowzer	yellow to reddish-brown	3rd solar plexus, 2nd sacral
	Garnet #30	Mellow Soother	red, green, black, orange-red	4th heart, 3rd solar plexus, 2nd sacral
Eyes, Ears, Nose, and Throat	Angelite #8	Enlightened	soft blue with white exterior	7th crown, 6th third eye, 4th heart
	Aquamarine #12	Mellow Soother	blue-green or blue	5th throat
	Agate, Blue Lace #1	Mellow Soother	light blue and white	5th throat
	Chalcedony #21	Mellow Soother	purple or blue	5th throat
ADHD	Amethyst #7	Enlightened	pale to deep purple	7th crown, 6th third eye, 4th heart
	Fluorite #29	Mellow Soother	green, purple, white, yellow, red, pink, black	7th crown, 6th third eye, 5th throat, 4th heart, 3rd solar plexus, 2nd sacral
	Ruby Zoisite #55	Yowzer	green with red specks	5th throat, 4th heart, 3rd solar plexus, 2nd sacral
	Howlite, White #32	Grounded Chill	white and black	6th third eye, 1st base root

Physical Wellness	Crystal/ Gemstone	Vibe Meter	Stone Color	Chakras
ADHD (continued)	Lepidolite #39	Mellow Soother	pink or lavender	6th third eye, 5th throat, 4th heart, 3rd solar plexus, 2nd sacral, 1st base root
	Quartz, Smoky #53	Grounded Chill	varies, tan to chocolate brown	1st base root
Sexual Organs	Calcite #17	Yowzer	orange	5th throat, 4th heart, 2nd sacral
	Jasper, Ocean #33	Grounded Chill	wide variety	3rd solar plexus, 2nd sacral, 1st base root
	Ruby Zoisite #55	Yowzer	green with red specks	5th throat, 4th heart, 3rd solar plexus, 2nd sacral
	Sunstone #60	Mellow Soother	orange to red-brown mixed with white	7th crown, 3rd solar plexus, 2nd sacral
Digestive System (Stomach/ Intestines)	Amber #6	Yowzer	yellow to reddish-brown	3rd solar plexus, 2nd sacral
	Aragonite #13	Yowzer and Grounded Chill	white, gray, reddish, yellow-green, gray-green, blue, purple	2nd sacral, 1st base root
	Citrine #24	Mellow Soother	yellowish	7th crown, 6th third eye, 3rd solar plexus, 2nd sacral
	Malachite #40	Mellow Soother	blue-green	4th heart
	Quartz, Rutile #52	Yowzer and Enlightened	gold-yellow, reddish-brown, red or black	7th crown, 6th third eye, 5th throat, 4th heart, 3rd solar plexus, 2nd sacral

Physical Wellness	Crystal/ Gemstone	Vibe Meter	Stone Color	Chakras
Digestive System (Stomach/ Intestines) (continued)	Sunstone #60	Mellow Soother	orange to red-brown mixed with white	7th crown, 3rd solar plexus, 2nd sacral
	Apatite #10	Grounded Chill	green, gold, or blue	5th throat, 3rd solar plexus, 2nd sacral, 1st base root
	Epidote #28	Yowzer	black, dark green, yellow-green	All
Aura Relief: Negative EMFs and Radioactive Vibrations	Herkimer Diamond #31	Yowzer and Enlightened	clear to colorless	7th crown, 6th third eye, 5th throat, 4th heart, 3rd solar plexus, 2nd sacral
	Nirvana/Ice Crystal #43	Yowzer and Enlightened	clear, colorless	All
	Quartz, Smoky #53	Grounded Chill	varies, tan to chocolate brown	1st base root
	Selenite #57	Yowzer	white and clear	7th crown, 6th third eye, 5th throat, 4th heart, 3rd solar plexus, 2nd sacral
	Shungite #58	Mellow Soother	black	All
Pituitary Gland and Hormonal Imbalance	Agate, Various #4	Grounded Chill	various colors	2nd sacral, 1st base root
	Aquamarine #12	Mellow Soother	blue-green or blue	5th throat
	Tiger's Eye #62	Grounded Chill	yellow-brown to golden	7th crown, 6th third eye, 3rd solar plexus, 2nd sacral, 1st base root

Physical Wellness	Crystal/ Gemstone	Vibe Meter	Stone Color	Chakras
Skin	Aventurine, Green #15	Mellow Soother	green	4th heart
	Fluorite #29	Mellow Soother	green, purple, white, yellow, red, pink, black	7th crown, 6th third eye, 5th throat, 4th heart, 3rd solar plexus, 2nd sacral
	Quartz, Rose/Pink #51	Mellow Soother	pink	7th crown, 6th third eye, 5th throat, 4th heart, 3rd solar plexus, 2nd sacral
	Shungite #58	Mellow Soother	black	All

The next group of stones is for chakra wellness.

Chakra Wellness	Crystal/ Gemstone	Vibe Meter	Stone Color	Chakras
1st Chakra, Root: Grounding/ Presence	Agate, Thunder #3	Yowzer	creamy white swirls	All
	Agate, Various #4	Grounded Chill	various colors	2nd sacral, 1st base root
	Apache Tears #9	Mellow Soother	black/brown	4th heart, 1st base root
	Auralite 23 #14	Yowzer	mixture of up to 23 mineral colors	All
	Obsidian, Black #44	Grounded Chill	black	1st base root
	Tourmaline, Black #63	Grounded Chill	opaque black	1st base root
	Charoite #22	Yowzer	purple	7th crown, 6th third eye, 4th heart, 3rd solar plexus, 2nd sacral

Chakra Wellness	Crystal/ Gemstone	Vibe Meter	Stone Color	Chakras
1st Chakra, Root: Grounding/ Presence (continued)	Citrine #24	Mellow Soother	yellowish	7th crown, 6th third eye, 3rd solar plexus, 2nd sacral
	Emerald #27	Mellow Soother	green	7th crown, 6th third eye, 4th heart, 3rd solar plexus, 2nd sacral
	Epidote #28	Yowzer	black, dark green, yellow-green	All
	Fluorite #29	Mellow Soother	green, purple, white, yellow, red, pink, black	7th crown, 6th third eye, 5th throat, 4th heart, 3rd solar plexus, 2nd sacral
	Garnet #30	Mellow Soother	red, green, black, orange-red	4th heart, 3rd solar plexus, 2nd sacral
	Jasper, Red #34	Grounded Chill	wide variety	2nd sacral, 1st base root
	Moldavite #41	Yowzer and Enlightened	deep green	7th crown, 6th third eye, 4th heart, 2nd sacral
	Agate, Moss #2	Grounded Chill	green	2nd sacral, 1st base root
	Nirvana/Ice Crystal #43	Yowzer and Enlightened	clear, colorless	All
	Obsidian, Snowflake #45	Yowzer and Enlightened	black with white spots	7th crown, 6th third eye, 5th throat, 4th heart, 3rd solar plexus, 2nd sacral

Chakra Wellness	Crystal/ Gemstone	Vibe Meter	Stone Color	Chakras
	Quartz, Clear #50	Enlightened	clear, colorless	7th crown, 6th third eye
	Ruby Zoisite #55	Yowzer	green with red specks	5th throat, 4th heart, 3rd solar plexus, 2nd sacral
	Quartz, Rutile #52	Yowzer and Enlightened	gold-yellow, reddish-brown, red or black	7th crown, 6th third eye, 5th throat, 4th heart, 3rd solar plexus, 2nd sacral
1st Chakra, Root: Grounding/ Presence (continued)	Shungite #58	Mellow Soother	black	All
	Quartz, Smoky #53	Grounded Chill	varies, tan to chocolate brown	1st base root
	Obsidian, Snowflake #45	Yowzer and Enlightened	black with white spots	7th crown, 6th third eye, 5th throat, 4th heart, 3rd solar plexus, 2nd sacral
	Super 7 #61	Yowzer and Enlightened	combination of seven colored stones	All
	Tiger's Eye #62	Grounded Chill	yellow-brown to golden	7th crown, 6th third eye, 3rd solar plexus, 2nd sacral, 1st base root
2nd Chakra, Sacral: Sexual Organs and Creativity	Agate, Various #4	Grounded Chill	various colors	2nd sacral, 1st base root
	Apache Tears #9	Mellow Soother	black/brown	4th heart, 1st base root
	Aragonite #13	Yowzer and Grounded Chill	white, gray, reddish, yellow-green, gray-green, blue, purple	2nd sacral, 1st base root

Chakra Wellness	Crystal/ Gemstone	Vibe Meter	Stone Color	Chakras
	Auralite 23 #14	Yowzer	mixture of up to 23 mineral colors	All
	Agate, Blue Lace #1	Mellow Soother	light blue and white	5th throat
	Calcite #17	Yowzer	orange	5th throat, 4th heart, 2nd sacral
	Carnelian #18	Mellow Soother	pale orange to deep-red orange	4th heart, 2nd sacral
	Chalcedony #21	Mellow Soother	purple or blue	5th throat
	Citrine #24	Mellow Soother	yellowish	7th crown, 6th third eye, 3rd solar plexus, 2nd sacral
2nd Chakra, Sacral: Sexual Organs and Creativity (continued)	Emerald #27	Mellow Soother	green	7th crown, 6th third eye, 4th heart, 3rd solar plexus, 2nd sacral
	Epidote #28	Yowzer	black, dark green, yellow-green	All
	Fluorite #29	Mellow Soother	green, purple, white, yellow, red, pink, black	7th crown, 6th third eye, 5th throat, 4th heart, 3rd solar plexus, 2nd sacral
	Garnet #30	Mellow Soother	red, green, black, orange-red	4th heart, 3rd solar plexus, 2nd sacral
	Jasper, Red #34	Grounded Chill	wide variety	2nd sacral, 1st base root
	Moldavite #41	Yowzer and Enlightened	deep green	7th crown, 6th third eye, 4th heart, 2nd sacral

Chakra Wellness	Crystal/ Gemstone	Vibe Meter	Stone Color	Chakras
2nd Chakra, Sacral: Sexual Organs and Creativity (continued)	Nirvana/Ice Crystal #43	Yowzer and Enlightened	clear, colorless	All
	Quartz, Clear #50	Enlightened	clear, colorless	7th crown, 6th third eye
	Quartz, Rutile #52	Yowzer and Enlightened	gold-yellow, reddish-brown, red or black	7th crown, 6th third eye, 5th throat, 4th heart, 3rd solar plexus, 2nd sacral
	Shungite #58	Mellow Soother	black	All
	Sunstone #60	Mellow Soother	orange to red-brown mixed with white	7th crown, 3rd solar plexus, 2nd sacral
	Super 7 #61	Yowzer and Enlightened	combination of seven colored stones	All
	Tiger's Eye #62	Grounded Chill	yellow-brown to golden	7th crown, 6th third eye, 3rd solar plexus, 2nd sacral, 1st base root
3rd Chakra, Solar Plexus: Emotions	Agate, Thunder #3	Yowzer	creamy white swirls	All
	Amber #6	Yowzer	yellow to reddish-brown	3rd solar plexus, 2nd sacral
	Apatite #10	Grounded Chill	green, gold, or blue	5th throat, 3rd solar plexus, 2nd sacral, 1st base root
	Auralite 23 #14	Yowzer	mixture of up to 23 mineral colors	All

Chakra Wellness	Crystal/ Gemstone	Vibe Meter	Stone Color	Chakras
3rd Chakra, Solar Plexus: Emotions (continued)	Charoite #22	Yowzer	purple	7th crown, 6th third eye, 4th heart, 3rd solar plexus, 2nd sacral
	Chrysoprase #23	Mellow Soother	green	5th throat, 4th heart, 3rd solar plexus
	Emerald #27	Mellow Soother	green	7th crown, 6th third eye, 4th heart, 3rd solar plexus, 2nd sacral
	Epidote #28	Yowzer	black, dark green, yellow-green	All
	Fluorite #29	Mellow Soother	green, purple, white, yellow, red, pink, black	7th crown, 6th third eye, 5th throat, 4th heart, 3rd solar plexus, 2nd sacral
	Garnet #30	Mellow Soother	red, green, black, orange-red	4th heart, 3rd solar plexus, 2nd sacral
	Malachite #40	Mellow Soother	blue-green	4th heart
	Moldavite #41	Yowzer and Enlightened	deep green	7th crown, 6th third eye, 4th heart, 2nd sacral
	Nirvana/Ice Crystal #43	Yowzer and Enlightened	clear, colorless	All
	Pietersite #48	Grounded Chill	gold, brown, gray, blue-gray and black	3rd solar plexus, 2nd sacral, 1st base root

Chakra Wellness	Crystal/ Gemstone	Vibe Meter	Stone Color	Chakras
	Pyrite #49	Yowzer	gold	4th heart, 3rd solar plexus, 2nd sacral
	Quartz, Clear #50	Enlightened	clear, colorless	7th crown, 6th third eye
	Rhodochro-site #54	Mellow Soother	pink, shades of pink	4th heart, 3rd solar plexus, 2nd sacral
	Quartz, Rutile #52	Yowzer and Enlightened	gold-yellow, reddish-brown, red or black	7th crown, 6th third eye, 5th throat, 4th heart, 3rd solar plexus, 2nd sacral
3rd Chakra, Solar Plexus: Emotions (continued)	Shungite #58	Mellow Soother	black	All
	Sunstone #60	Mellow Soother	orange to red-brown mixed with white	7th crown, 3rd solar plexus, 2nd sacral
	Super 7 #61	Yowzer and Enlightened	combination of seven colored stones	All
	Tiger's Eye #62	Grounded Chill	yellow-brown to golden	7th crown, 6th third eye, 3rd solar plexus, 2nd sacral, 1st base root
	Unakite #66	Grounded Chill	green-red	1st base root
4th Chakra, Heart: Love and Compas-sion for Self and Others	Agate, Various #4	Grounded Chill	various colors	2nd sacral, 1st base root

Chakra Wellness	Crystal/ Gemstone	Vibe Meter	Stone Color	Chakras
4th Chakra, Heart: Love and Compassion for Self and Others (continued)	Agate, Moss #2	Grounded Chill	green	2nd sacral, 1st base root
	Amazonite #5	Mellow Soother	blue-green or green	All
	Apatite #10	Grounded Chill	green, gold, or blue	5th throat, 3rd solar plexus, 2nd sacral, 1st base root
	Auralite 23 #14	Yowzer	mixture of up to 23 mineral colors	All
	Aventurine, Green #15	Mellow Soother	green	4th heart
	Chrysoprase #23	Mellow Soother	green	5th throat, 4th heart, 3rd solar plexus
	Danburite #25	Mega Yowzer	colorless	7th crown, 6th third eye, 5th throat, 4th heart, 3rd solar plexus, 2nd sacral
	Dioptase #26	Yowzer	emerald green to deep bluish-green	7th crown, 6th third eye, 4th heart
	Emerald #27	Mellow Soother	green	7th crown, 6th third eye, 4th heart, 3rd solar plexus, 2nd sacral
	Epidote #28	Yowzer	black, dark green, yellow-green	All
	Fluorite #29	Mellow Soother	green, purple, white, yellow, red, pink, black	7th crown, 6th third eye, 5th throat, 4th heart, 3rd solar plexus, 2nd sacral

Chakra Wellness	Crystal/ Gemstone	Vibe Meter	Stone Color	Chakras
	Kunzite #35	Yowzer	pink-violet	7th crown, 6th third eye, 5th throat, 4th heart, 3rd solar plexus
	Lepidolite #39	Mellow Soother	pink or lavender	6th third eye, 5th throat, 4th heart, 3rd solar plexus, 2nd sacral, 1st base root
	Malachite #40	Mellow Soother	blue-green	4th heart
4th Chakra, Heart: Love and Compassion for Self and Others (continued)	Moldavite #41	Yowzer and Enlightened	deep green	7th crown, 6th third eye, 4th heart, 2nd sacral
	Nirvana/Ice Crystal #43	Yowzer and Enlightened	clear, colorless	All
	Opal, Pink #46	Enlightened	light to medium pink	7th crown, 6th third eye, 5th throat, 4th heart
	Quartz, Clear #50	Enlightened	clear, colorless	7th crown, 6th third eye
	Quartz, Rose/Pink #51	Mellow Soother	pink	7th crown, 6th third eye, 5th throat, 4th heart, 3rd solar plexus, 2nd sacral
	Quartz, Rutile #52	Yowzer and Enlightened	gold-yellow, reddish-brown, red or black	7th crown, 6th third eye, 5th throat, 4th heart, 3rd solar plexus, 2nd sacral

Chakra Wellness	Crystal/ Gemstone	Vibe Meter	Stone Color	Chakras
	Rhodochro-site #54	Mellow Soother	pink, shades of pink	4th heart, 3rd solar plexus, 2nd sacral
4th Chakra, Heart: Love and Compassion for Self and Others (continued)	Ruby Zoisite #55	Yowzer and Enlightened	green with red specks	5th throat, 4th heart, 3rd solar plexus, 2nd sacral
	Shungite #58	Mellow Soother	black	All
	Super 7 #61	Yowzer and Enlightened	combination of seven colored stones	All
	Tourmaline, Green #64	Yowzer and Enlightened	pale to deep green	All
	Agate, Blue Lace #1	Mellow Soother	light blue and white	5th throat
	Agate, Various #4	Grounded Chill	various colors	2nd sacral, 1st base root
	Amazonite #5	Mellow Soother	blue-green or green	All
5th Chakra, Throat: Communication, Listening, Being Heard	Angelite #8	Enlightened	soft blue with white exterior	7th crown, 6th third eye, 4th heart
	Apatite #10	Grounded Chill	green, gold, or blue	5th throat, 3rd solar plexus, 2nd sacral, 1st base root
	Aquamarine #12	Mellow Soother	blue-green or blue	5th throat
	Auralite 23 #14	Yowzer	mixture of up to 23 mineral colors	All
	Cavansite #19	Yowzer and Enlightened	blue to bluish-green	7th crown, 6th third eye, 5th throat, 4th heart

Chakra Wellness	Crystal/ Gemstone	Vibe Meter	Stone Color	Chakras
	Celestite #20	Enlightened	blue-gray	7th crown, 6th third eye, 5th throat, 4th heart
	Chalcedony #21	Mellow Soother	purple or blue	5th throat
	Danburite #25	Mega Yowzer	colorless	7th crown, 6th third eye, 5th throat, 4th heart, 3rd solar plexus, 2nd sacral
	Emerald #27	Mellow Soother	green	7th crown, 6th third eye, 4th heart, 3rd solar plexus, 2nd sacral
5th Chakra, Throat: Communication, Listening, Being Heard (continued)	Epidote #28	Yowzer	black, dark green, yellow-green	All
	Fluorite #29	Mellow Soother	green, purple, white, yellow, red, pink, black	7th crown, 6th third eye, 5th throat, 4th heart, 3rd solar plexus, 2nd sacral
	Lapis Lazuli #37	Enlightened	blue	7th crown, 6th third eye, 5th throat, 3rd solar plexus
	Lemurian Seeds #38	Yowzer and Enlightened	clear to smoky	7th crown, 6th third eye
	Lepidolite #39	Mellow Soother	pink or lavender	6th third eye, 5th throat, 4th heart, 3rd solar plexus, 2nd sacral, 1st base root
	Moldavite #41	Yowzer and Enlightened	deep green	7th crown, 6th third eye, 4th heart, 2nd sacral

Chakra Wellness	Crystal/ Gemstone	Vibe Meter	Stone Color	Chakras
5th Chakra, Throat: Communication, Listening, Being Heard (continued)	Nirvana/Ice Crystal #43	Yowzer and Enlightened	clear, colorless	All
	Quartz, Clear #50	Enlightened	clear, colorless	7th crown, 6th third eye
	Quartz, Rutile #52	Yowzer and Enlightened	gold-yellow, reddish-brown, red or black	7th crown, 6th third eye, 5th throat, 4th heart, 3rd solar plexus, 2nd sacral
	Shungite #58	Mellow Soother	black	All
	Super 7 #61	Yowzer and Enlightened	combination of seven colored stones	All
	Turquoise #65	Grounded Chill	blue	5th throat, 3rd solar plexus, 2nd sacral, 1st base root
6th Chakra, Third Eye: All Senses and Intuition	Agate, Thunder #3	Yowzer	creamy white swirls	All
	Agate, Various #4	Grounded Chill	various colors	2nd sacral, 1st base root
	Amethyst #7	Enlightened	pale to deep purple	7th crown, 6th third eye, 4th heart
	Angelite #8	Enlightened	soft blue with white exterior	7th crown, 6th third eye, 4th heart
	Apatite #10	Grounded Chill	green, gold, or blue	5th throat, 3rd solar plexus, 2nd sacral, 1st base root

Chakra Wellness	Crystal/ Gemstone	Vibe Meter	Stone Color	Chakras
	Apophyllite #11	Yowzer	clear or green	7th crown, 6th third eye, 4th heart
	Auralite 23 #14	Yowzer	mixture of up to 23 mineral colors	All
	Azurite #16	Yowzer and Enlightened	deep blue	7th crown, 6th third eye, 5th throat
	Cavansite #19	Yowzer and Enlightened	blue to bluish-green	7th crown, 6th third eye, 5th throat, 4th heart
	Charoite #22	Yowzer	purple	7th crown, 6th third eye, 4th heart, 3rd solar plexus, 2nd sacral
6th Chakra, Third Eye: All Senses and Intuition (continued)	Danburite #25	Mega Yowzer	colorless	7th crown, 6th third eye, 5th throat, 4th heart, 3rd solar plexus, 2nd sacral
	Emerald #27	Mellow Soother	green	7th crown, 6th third eye, 4th heart, 3rd solar plexus, 2nd sacral
	Epidote #28	Yowzer	black, dark green, yellow-green	All
	Fluorite #29	Mellow Soother	green, purple, white, yellow, red, pink, black	7th crown, 6th third eye, 5th throat, 4th heart, 3rd solar plexus, 2nd sacral

Chakra Wellness	Crystal/ Gemstone	Vibe Meter	Stone Color	Chakras
6th Chakra, Third Eye: All Senses and Intuition (continued)	Herkimer Diamond #31	Yowzer and Enlightened	clear to colorless	7th crown, 6th third eye, 5th throat, 4th heart, 3rd solar plexus, 2nd sacral
	Kyanite, Blue #36	Grounded Chill	indigo, black, blue, green, orange	All
	Lapis Lazuli #37	Enlightened	blue	7th crown, 6th third eye, 5th throat, 3rd solar plexus
	Lemurian Seeds #38	Yowzer and Enlightened	clear to smoky	7th crown, 6th third eye
	Lepidolite #39	Mellow Soother	pink or lavender	6th third eye, 5th throat, 4th heart, 3rd solar plexus, 2nd sacral, 1st base root
	Moldavite #41	Yowzer and Enlightened	deep green	7th crown, 6th third eye, 4th heart, 2nd sacral
	Moonstone #42	Mellow Soother and Enlightened	blue-white	7th crown, 6th third eye, 5th throat
	Nirvana/Ice Crystal #43	Yowzer and Enlightened	clear, colorless	All
	Obsidian, Snowflake #45	Yowzer and Enlightened	black with white spots	7th crown, 6th third eye, 5th throat, 4th heart, 3rd solar plexus, 2nd sacral
	Opalite #47	Mellow Soother	white-yellow, cream	7th crown, 6th third eye, 4th heart

Chakra Wellness	Crystal/ Gemstone	Vibe Meter	Stone Color	Chakras
	Pietersite #48	Grounded Chill	gold, brown, gray, blue-gray and black	3rd solar plexus, 2nd sacral, 1st base root
	Quartz, Clear #50	Enlightened	clear, colorless	7th crown, 6th third eye
	Quartz, Rutile #52	Yowzer and Enlightened	gold-yellow, reddish-brown, red or black	7th crown, 6th third eye, 5th throat, 4th heart, 3rd solar plexus, 2nd sacral
6th Chakra, Third Eye: All Senses and Intuition (continued)	Ruby Zoisite #55	Yowzer	green with red specks	5th throat, 4th heart, 3rd solar plexus, 2nd sacral
	Selenite #57	Yowzer	white and clear	7th crown, 6th third eye, 5th throat, 4th heart, 3rd solar plexus, 2nd sacral
	Shungite #58	Mellow Soother	black	All
	Sodalite #59	Mellow Soother	shades of blue to purple	7th crown, 6th third eye, 5th throat
	Super 7 #61	Yowzer and Enlightened	combination of seven colored stones	All
7th Chakra, Crown: Connection to Your Source or Higher Self, Deities, Angels, or Spirits	Agate, Various #4	Grounded Chill	various colors	2nd sacral, 1st base root

Chakra Wellness	Crystal/ Gemstone	Vibe Meter	Stone Color	Chakras
	Amethyst #7	Enlightened	pale to deep purple	7th crown, 6th third eye, 4th heart
	Angelite #8	Enlightened	soft blue with white exterior	7th crown, 6th third eye, 4th heart
	Apache Tears #9	Mellow Soother	black/brown	4th heart, 1st base root
	Apophyllite #11	Yowzer	clear or green	7th crown, 6th third eye, 4th heart
	Auralite 23 #14	Yowzer	mixture of up to 23 mineral colors	All
7th Chakra, Crown: Connection to Your Source or Higher Self, Deities, Angels, or Spirits (continued)	Cavansite #19	Yowzer and Enlightened	blue to bluish-green	7th crown, 6th third eye, 5th throat, 4th heart
	Charoite #22	Yowzer	purple	7th crown, 6th third eye, 4th heart, 3rd solar plexus, 2nd sacral
	Danburite #25	Mega Yowzer	colorless	7th crown, 6th third eye, 5th throat, 4th heart, 3rd solar plexus, 2nd sacral
	Emerald #27	Mellow Soother	green	7th crown, 6th third eye, 4th heart, 3rd solar plexus, 2nd sacral
	Epidote #28	Yowzer	black, dark green, yellow-green	All

Chakra Wellness	Crystal/ Gemstone	Vibe Meter	Stone Color	Chakras
	Fluorite #29	Mellow Soother	green, purple, white, yellow, red, pink, black	7th crown, 6th third eye, 5th throat, 4th heart, 3rd solar plexus, 2nd sacral
	Herkimer Diamond #31	Yowzer and Enlightened	clear to colorless	7th crown, 6th third eye, 5th throat, 4th heart, 3rd solar plexus, 2nd sacral
7th Chakra, Crown: Connection to Your Source or Higher Self, Deities, Angels, or Spirits (continued)	Lemurian Seeds #38	Yowzer and Enlightened	clear to smoky	7th crown, 6th third eye
	Moldavite #41	Yowzer and Enlightened	deep green	7th crown, 6th third eye, 4th heart, 2nd sacral
	Moonstone #42	Mellow Soother and Enlightened	blue-white	7th crown, 6th third eye, 5th throat
	Nirvana/Ice Crystal #43	Yowzer and Enlightened	clear, colorless	All
	Opalite #47	Mellow Soother	white-yellow, cream	7th crown, 6th third eye, 4th heart
	Quartz, Rutile #52	Yowzer and Enlightened	gold-yellow, reddish-brown, red or black	7th crown, 6th third eye, 5th throat, 4th heart, 3rd solar plexus, 2nd sacral

Chakra Wellness	Crystal/ Gemstone	Vibe Meter	Stone Color	Chakras
7th Chakra, Crown: Connection to Your Source or Higher Self, Deities, Angels, or Spirits (continued)	Quartz, Clear #50	Enlightened	clear, colorless	7th crown, 6th third eye
	Selenite #57	Yowzer	white and clear	7th crown, 6th third eye, 5th throat, 4th heart, 3rd solar plexus, 2nd sacral
	Shungite #58	Mellow Soother	black	All
	Super 7 #61	Yowzer and Enlightened	combination of seven colored stones	All

Appendix B

Crystals for the
Home Grids and Other Uses

Since you are getting fabulous at your crystal body grids, it's time to master some home griddin'. I always like to add MORE. Here are some of my awesome bonus usages for crystals *other* than body layouts.

Crystals at Night

Sleeping with Crystals

As a crystal expert, I would vote against sleeping with crystals every night. When we use crystals intently, they "hear" us and work with our energy. If you keep one crystal or many by your bed all the time, you may be exhausting your mind. Some crystals make your mind and energy bodies active; this can be tiring to your physical and energy bodies if it is constant. I suggest switching your crystals and using them for certain purposes, such as deep sleep, astral travel, or healing. Try using specific crystals that harmonize together, and then I would suggest going a few nights without any crystals. It is a healthy break for your body and mind to naturally sync themselves.

Crystal-Charged Moon Water

Instead of sleeping with your crystals, you could have them enhance your moon-charged water. The moon brings great superpower energy that can enhance the molecules of your drinking water. It seriously can—test it out for yourself. On a full moon, take a glass (no plastic cups) and fill it with your drinking water. Sip it and remember how it tastes. Set the glass full of water outside in the moonlight for at least one hour or more, and then taste it again. You will notice a significant difference. This is moon-charged water. It is placing positive energy vibes inside your body, which can be healing and bring success to your projects.

You need to be conscious when placing crystals into moon-charged water; as you learned, there are a few crystals that are poisonous, such as Malachite and Azurite. If you don't feel comfortable placing stones in the water, you can place the crystals outside the glass cup. Please be mindful of not using crystal chips—you don't want to ingest any crystals. If you are loving this idea of crystal-infused water, there are completely safe borosilicate (free of lead), crystal-infused water bottles that are specifically for changing the energy of your water for your benefit.

The ability of crystals to enhance water was researched by Dr. Emoto, a famous scientist known for his experiments with charging molecules. He theorized that positive talking, words, and thoughts aimed at water and plants gave them positive charges. I know I love and feel great when people talk nicely to me; it changes my mood and vibe to be brighter and happier. Crystals and their energy makeup were included in the experiments and likewise enhanced the test subjects. The plants exposed to these positive energy sources grew stronger, healthier, and taller than the control group. He used plants because plants, like people, need water to survive and thrive. It is pretty amazing. Think of it—we are made of approximately 85 percent water. Water is hydrating, and now you can add to its benefits by adding crystals. Crystals are a natural elixir and are remedies for people, infusing positive vibes and enhancing molecules for the better.

Moonstone for Enhanced Dreams

Before you go to bed, get a glass (not a plastic cup). Fill the glass with water, then place one Moonstone in the glass. Place that glass under your bed or on your night table if it is within four feet of your body.

This Moonstone-infused water placed by your aura will enhance the dream state and bring you to an alternate life or incredible dream. Set your intention before you sleep to visually see a beautiful place. This works with many stones, especially Herkimer Diamonds, Super 7, or Auralite 23. Try them all separately and see which works best for you. Why water? Water works as a positive conduit for your aura and body. It also brings flow to your aura, your chi, and all of you! Don't forget to throw out the water once you're done as it may have gotten dust in it—but save those crystals!

Water and Crystals

You can crystal-charge your body! You are made up of approximately 85 percent water, and vibrations travel five times faster through water. Crystals and stones emit high vibrational frequencies; therefore, holding them while you are in the pool, bath, or shower will enhance the crystal properties and you!

Footbaths

I love doing crystal footbaths so much at home! I created three different combinations of 11 stones and crystals, one for releasing, one for advancement, and one for self-realization. The water can be hot, warm, or cold, but please don't put raw Malachite, Carbonite, or Selenite in the tub or footbaths—the latter two will disintegrate, and unpolished Malachite is poisonous. You can use other polished stones and crystals and add a handful of Himalayan or sea salt. The salt will dissipate in the water and make it extra nice and cleansing. Many unpolished crystals may not be best for bathing.

Footbath for Releasing:
Use four Lepidolites, five Smoky Quartzes, one Black Tourmaline, and one Danburite.

If you are not a seasoned healer, you may not know that most people release unwanted or negative energy from their feet. It's hard to describe; the best image I can provide is a gray, cloudy energy emitting from the body during a healing session. Releasing is good and healthy because it cleans out the negative emotions, thoughts, and stuck energy, or old patterns, so you can fill those spaces of your energy with new, positive vibrations. Visualize happy, smiley emoji faces going in where you let out the frowning emojis. You or anyone can release from anywhere in the energy body, but it is very likely that a lot will release from the feet as bad vibes come down the energy system when leaving the energy field.

Releasing baths shift your energy to remove any funk, especially that foot funk. In addition to the footbath, we can also do some crystal work while dry. To help the funk move along and out, you can place a pulling crystal, such as Black Tourmaline, Shungite, or Selenite, by your or your client's feet. The crystals can be off the body, but they should be below the feet. Selenite, Black Tourmaline, and Shungite work best to extract negative energy (remember not to put Selenite in water). If you have a Shungite healing pad, you can use that on both of your feet as well.

Footbath for Advancement:
Use six Amazonites, four Rose Quartzes, and one Herkimer Diamond.

Everyone needs to advance in their lives, right? I know I do. This specialized crystal footbath is for when you need to exude extraordinary energy to meet someone new, for a new job interview, or when working on a goal; it supersedes your regular good energy and supersizes it. This footbath balances all of your chakras with the Amazonite, bringing compassionate and loving energy and positivity, and, to top it all off, the Herkimer Diamond amplifies all that goodness with positive visions and thoughts of successful outcomes. My feet are in this combo right now while I'm writing this book.

Footbath for Self-Realization:
Use one Green Tourmaline, two Citrines, one Iolite, and seven Quartzes.

This one is for those that want insight on their lives. If you are afraid to look within, skip this one until you are ready. I can share that when I did this footbath, I relaxed and fell into a 45-minute nap. My dream/insight from this nap brought me to know that I was being irrational in a decision I had made earlier that day. It was a big epiphany! The best part was I changed that decision from okay to really incredible. I patted myself on the back and thanked all my crystal babies one by one: gratitude, seven Quartzes; gratitude, Iolite; much thanks to you, two Citrines; and mucho love to the master, Green Tourmaline. I love you all!

When you try any of these delightful footbaths, notice where you feel sensations in your body. That can tell you a lot about yourself. It is always beneficial to take notes.

Rub-A-Dub

I get a lot of clear messages from spirit guides when I am in water, whether I'm in a tub, shower, hot tub, or my pool. Water is a conduit and a great way to cleanse your body, mind, and crystals! Go in your tub tonight and notice what you feel or sense when you are relaxing with your crystal bath. Here is one way you can do it.

A few times at home, I filled my tub with approximately 100 Amethyst crystals and 50 Fluorites. I floated some chamomile and rose flowers in the water to soften my skin. This combo was for relaxing and healing my aches from working out. Man, I felt great; I stayed in the tub over two hours! The water got cold and I was pruned! Ha!

I was revived and felt incredible from the healing properties of all 150 crystal babies. However (and this is a *big* however), it took me 25 minutes to scoop all 150 crystals out of my tub and make sure none went in the drain. This act made me smarter. I thought to myself, "You know, you can put 20 crystals in the tub, and that will suffice!"

I learned the hard way; I guess I was just thinking crystal mania—woohoo! Make sure the crystals you place in the tub won't get stuck in your drain, especially if they are small ones. I now use a natural cloth pouch or cheesecloth to place the crystals, salts, and/or herbs into. I place the pouch with my crystal-herb combo in the tub water so there is no mess.

Pool-Bound

I have a flat foam float in my pool (say that three times fast—flat foam float!). I place about 16 crystals on top of it to, one, clean and cleanse my crystals and stones with the sunlight, and, two, charge my pool water. I can also make myself super charged and cleansed at the same time. You can feel the difference in your body from your charged crystals. I have a salt pool; this is a little bit better, in my opinion, than pure chlorine pools, especially for your skin.

I place all the water-safe crystals on my pool raft if my intention is to cleanse and charge them. Both sunlight and moonlight are awesome for this intention. If I am swimming or chillin' in my pool, I will set my intention of what I want to work on—to be happy, release, manifest, balance, or advance—and choose my crystals accordingly.

Everyone loves a cheat sheet, so here are my personal pool crystal concoctions. These are all tumbled or raw stones that are the size of a dime or bigger. I sit inside the water of my pool with the crystals on the mesh raft—this way, they are touching the water too. You can also place them in a bag to drop in your pool or set them on the steps or border of your pool. I personally prefer the crystals in the water because their energy feels stronger, but you do what works best for you. Here are some crystal combinations that I recommend:

Happiness and relaxion—Six or more Citrine and Amethyst.

Releasing—One Danburite, four Rutile Quartzes, one Smoky Quartz, and one Dioptase. This combination creates a nice releasing of the mind and body.

Manifesting—Citrine (at least six) and three Jade, Rainbow, or Crystal Quartzes of any shape or size. These manifest anything you desire; set your intention and relax in the water.

Balance—Nirvana Crystals, at least one pink and one white to balance. You could also use 11 Zebra Agates. This centers your thoughts and balances your aura and chakra frequencies.

Advancing—Any number or size of Celestite or Angelite, two Aquamarines, and one or more Herkimer Diamonds.

Interdimensional fun—One Moldavite, one Apophyllite, and one Kunzite. If you have more than one of each and a big pool, go for it!

Healing waters—Three Apatites, three or more Amethysts, two Carnelians, and five Shungites. This is more for physical healing.

Wanna get crazy? Okay, I am really serious when I say this, all joking aside. I will show you this if you promise to be responsible for your silly actions. Great. I heard you all say you promise. Thank you. Okay, remember how I said you can use certain crystal combos to make you feel up, down, and in-between when the crystals are synergizing? I would never suggest this unless you want to feel off-the-wall wacky, but, just for experimentation's sake and to prove to yourself that crystals really do affect you, dump all of your crystals in a mesh bag in your pool. Go into the pool for at least 30 minutes, and you should start feeling confused and nuts. I do suggest that you set up a nice balancing crystal grid afterwards to bring you back to your normal self, whatever that might be!

I don't suggest this if you have a community pool at your apartment. If you have a private hot tub, then right on. You can do the same—just place the crystals on the borders of the hot tub or put them in a mesh bag and drop them in the water!

Manifesting with Crystals Outdoors

Here is my infamous outdoor walking meditation. Bring a Quartz for clarity and a Rose Quartz for gratitude. Every Sunday, I put my walkin' shoes on, stones in my pocket, and ease on down that road.

I start from my doorstep. I say, "Today is a great day." I start walking at a brisk speed away from my home. If nobody's around, I say everything aloud—otherwise I say this all inside my head. I state everything I am thankful for: my business, my family, my clients, all of you reading this, all of my limbs and every part of my body, the sky, the air I breathe, the water I drink and food I eat. I give gratitude to the stars, the amazing Earth, all the Angels, and beyond. Once I get to my one-mile mark, I turn around and head back home.

On the way home, I start manifesting everything I desire with details. I say what it is, how I would like to receive it, and the energy exchanges that will take place for it to happen. I say when I would like this to occur. I manifest many things, not just one request. All the way home, I feel the energy surround me as I ask the universe for my desires and know I can have it all, as long as I believe I deserve it. I get home, and I feel the gratitude. I sense my passion for new comings and opportunities in my life. I know that I am loved. Plus, I got my butt moving for a two-mile walk.

Tincture

Early on in the book, I explained that if a crystal breaks or is broken, it doesn't mean something is bad, and you should keep those pieces because they are still good energy. This is something I concocted—it's brilliant and effective! The recipe for what I call "crystal junkie mist" is basically a combination of all your broken gem babies that can fit inside a three-ounce BPA-free or glass mister bottle.

Take up to a handful of your gem chips and scoot them inside the container you are using for your super special mist. For a three-ounce bottle, you will add ten drops of lavender pure essential oil, six drops of eucalyptus pure essential oil, and two and a half ounces of distilled water. Cap the sprayer tightly and shake the bottle. Now it's ready to mist and make you feel awesome and relaxed.

I have one more recipe for you. It is my secret recipe. I guess maybe not, anymore. This is my famous smoke-free clearing and cleansing spray. It's for people who don't like the smoke from burning sage in their home or space but who need a good cleansing of negative energy. I add more than just pure essential sage oil—I add a bundle of liquid bliss to my bottle of bad begone! Use a three-ounce spray bottle and pure essential oil only.

10 drops of sage oil

4 drops of eucalyptus oil

3 drops of lavender oil

3 drops of pine oil

3 drops of rosemary oil

Now add Quartz chips. You need only three mini pieces. Then add three pieces of Black Obsidian chips. I do this to harmonize the crystal energies for protection and clearing your home or office.

Lastly, add your two and a half ounces of distilled water, place the sprayer on tight, shake, and spray! This combination of essential oils can also be used as a bug begone, keeping mosquitoes and no-see-ums off the areas you spray. I suggest just misting your legs and arms. You want to be mindful that some people are allergic or sensitive to essential oils; never spray the oils on the face or in the eyes.

Holiday Crystal Centerpieces

Holiday centerpieces totally rock; I once made a long tablescape in the center of an eight-foot table in one of my client's homes. I added Red Jasper stones and Moss Agates between some pretty flowers. My client hired me so I could change the energy in the house due to a guest who could sometimes spoil the party. I not only smudged that house, but I rocked it out—Jolie-style!

We all have that one person who comes to the holiday party and either complains a lot or is never happy. You know what I'm talking about—*that* person. I ask you to send them light. The goal is for them to keep their bad energy to themselves or release it *before* they get to the holiday event and spew it among the rest of the company's holiday cheer. For this particular client's Negative Nelly, I set up a super Selenite and Citrine centerpiece display. Bang! Pow! Wham! Okay, I'm getting carried away; this person really wasn't that bad, but placing a bit of Selenite and Citrine in the centerpiece area where they were sitting sure kept the energy nicer. Remember that if the crystals are within four feet of the aura, they'll start working their high-vibe clearing magic!

One more! If you have a loved one or friend whom you invite to dinner, add a colorful flower arrangement with pieces of Lepidolite around it. You can also place Lepidolite inside the vase; the water will amplify its properties. Lepidolite is *Ze' Prozac* stone: it calms, balances mood swings, and helps bring positive behaviors. It's super nice for making that depressed person feel a bit more chipper at dinner! No one has to know—it's just a pretty centerpiece.

Grids for the Home

Call me the grid master. You will be too after I show you how to set up four purposeful home grids.

1. **PPP** is a grid to make your home feel super protected and positive.
2. **Loving Space** is a grid that helps your house sell.
3. **Space Cleanser** creates a vortex that clears negative EMFs to keep your home free of negative vibrations.
4. **Bad Begone** is a grid to protect your yard and home.

Grid 1: Powerful Protection and Positive Energy (PPP)

For this first grid, you will need these harmonizing stones: four Citrines, four Amethysts, and three Tiger's Eyes.

In a room that is approximately 12 by ten (an average bedroom size), place the Citrines in each corner. You can place them on a window sill or in a plant, they can be up high or on the floor—this does not matter. Next, place the Amethyst pieces in the same places. Lastly, place the three Tiger's Eye protectors anywhere in the proximity of the door or doors.

Grid 2: Loving Space

The second grid creates a loving space. You can use this to sell your home or create serenity. You will need Citrine, Selenite, salt lamps, and Rose Quartz.

Place Citrine near the front door and in each of the bathrooms to keep a happy and nice energy vibe. You can hide them or keep them in plain sight—that is up to you. Have your salt lamp turned on when people come to the showing to keep the vibes in the home clean and fresh. The light has to be switched on because salt needs the heat to work with the water vapor in the air to counteract the electromagnetic radiation of electronics, negativity, EMFs, allergens, dander, dust, and other basic pollutants that give a person a bad feeling. The lamp can be in an office, bedroom, or living room area—the more the merrier. Salt lamps are pretty and comforting to look at. You can place a few Selenite stones wherever you have electronics. I would hide the Selenite stones unless you have a beautiful Selenite lamp, which I would place near a television or computer room. Selenite works similarly to salt, keeping only positive vibes in its space. Lastly, select a few pieces of Rose Quartz and place them in the living room and or in the bedrooms near the door or bed; this will make the bedrooms feel loving.

Grid 3: Space Cleanser

The third grid is a space cleanser, creating a vortex of great vibes. You'll need one Selenite plate or stick, four harmonizing crystals such as Shungite or Selenite, three to five Shungites, one Black Tourmaline, and one Rainbow Quartz.

The energy vortex spiral clears negative EMFs to keep your home free of vibrations that make a space feel bad, yucky, and unwelcoming. The vortex vibes help vacuum those low vibrations out of the area. Bubye bad energy.

This grid is a tight grid, which means all the crystals are placed close together, making a pretty design. Lay a Selenite plate or stick down anywhere in the room of choice and place the four harmonizing crystals on top of it. The harmonizing crystals should be EMF protectors like Shungite and Selenite. Use three to five Shungites to protect the room from any electronics, then add one nice hunk of Black Tourmaline on the Selenite; Black Tourmaline absorbs any yuck that comes to the space. Place a shiny Rainbow Quartz in the middle of it all, and you'll have vortex action that cleans out the old and brings in new success!

Grid 4: Bad Begone

Have an undesirable neighbor? No problem; you can make a crystal yard grid! For this particular purpose, you can place stones for protection and to ward off negative energies from all sides of your yard and home. You will need a half pound of crushed Black Tourmaline or 20 small pieces and one pound of loose white sage.

Place the Black Tourmaline a few feet from your borderline and inside your property line or fenced area. If you're using crushed Black Tourmaline, sprinkle it along the border. If you're using the small pieces, place a stone every four to five feet. Between each stone, sprinkle some white sage flakes; as you do this, set the intent that only people of positive energy will cross the line of your property. If you set this intent, the vibration will also be set, as will the frequency of the stones and sage. Be happy as you do this task; after all, it's fun, and the crystals are going to absorb the negative vibes. It totally works! All you need are simple rocks to feel protected.

After reading the crystal recipes, I hope you found the perfect remedies for any situation. It is enjoyable to turn any obstacle or occurrence into a fun crystal adventure or experience. My thought process is to add crystals to everything so everyone can have happy vibes!

Appendix C

22 *Essential Oils to Enhance Your Crystal Layout Session*

Just to give a tiny bit of info as to why these oils are used for crystal healing and meditations, I added my 22 favorite essential oils here for you to learn more about. I only use therapeutic grade or organic oils. Please don't use faux chemical oils; they can give you headaches and lack the natural properties of pure grade essential oils. Essential oils can be pure, which means not diluted with any fillers or accompanying oils. The accompanying oils are called *carrier oils*. Carrier oils are fine since some people can be sensitive to applying a pure oil on their skin. If you are sensitive, you can purchase a pure essential oil and add your own carrier oil. Some great carrier oils to use are coconut oil, almond oil, and grapeseed oil. All essences of natural origin can be used as remedies and as enhancers. Essential oils enliven your sense of smell and heal your body. Oils can activate your body because, similarly to crystals and gems, each oil has properties that change your aura and connect to your body internally to heal and adjust. Some relieve anxiety, some wake your mind, some help with depression, and so on. Essential oils have legitimate and therapeutic use because they are essences distilled into molecules that our human skin can absorb instantly. If you place a dab of essential oil on the skin, it is absorbed within three seconds! I know people don't think of their skin as an organ—they imagine a heart or lung. Oddly enough, our skin is the biggest organ of the human body! Below is a list of essences that details what they can be used for and which chakras they can help balance. Coordinating the oils with your chakras can especially enhance your emotions. The list contains all the suggested essences that go with the accompanying crystal body layouts for optimal sessions. Essential oils are great for any meditation as well as an option for holistic healing.

Bergamot—Chakras: 4th, 3rd, 2nd. The fragrance of an orangey woodsy odyssey for happy thoughts and informative meditations. Bergamot gives a restful sleep; it can also release fear and tensions of everyday life. You may know it to be an ingredient in Earl Grey tea, a famous English black tea that is strong like black coffee. Earl Grey has added notes of bergamot for its amazing flavor. P.S. Don't drink Earl Grey tea before a crystal healing—it has a lot of caffeine and you won't relax!

Chamomile—Chakras: 5th, 4th, 3rd, 2nd. This lovely flower essence helps with relaxation, menstrual relief, and fevers. It is an anti-inflammatory agent that soothes and calms the skin, mind, and soul. Chamomile is a great bedtime tea to drink or, as an oil, to place in a soapstone burner as an aromatic, sending comfort through your home. I don't know why, but when I sniff dried chamomile, it smells like Pop-Tarts to me. Do any of you notice that? I like it.

Eucalyptus—Chakras: All seven. One of my favorites, it's great for colds, flu, sinus relief, insect bites, as an antibiotic and anti-inflammatory, and as repellant. Emotionally, it brings peace and clear feelings to the mind. I particularly love eucalyptus because it reminds me of Arizona and the seeded and silver dollar eucalyptus trees that are so large, fragrant, and beautiful I could sit under them all day.

Frankincense—Chakras: 7th, 6th. This favorite brings enlightenment and is great to put on your third eye for meditation and for prophetic visions. Frankincense opens you and connects spirits and the higher self, which is the all-knowing you. This ancient essential oil healer reduces stress and helps depression and exhaustion. It can actually reduce nightmares too! It is referenced in the Bible over 33 times and is used in anointments and protection ceremonies.

Geranium—Chakras: 6th, 5th, 4th, 3rd, 2nd. Another incredible flower that has a sweet scent and is strikingly beautiful. It has healing properties used for circulatory disorders and menopause. Geranium is great for happiness and protection. Geranium is also an anti-inflammatory. I love the red geraniums. They come in a variety, most commonly in white and red. They remind me of my sister; she loves them.

Grapefruit—Chakras: 6th, 1st. Grapefruit oil helps with detoxification, relieves headaches, and rejuvenates the mind. When using this oil or any fruity essential oil with high acidity, like orange and tangerine, know that it can be harsh on the skin and make the skin sun-sensitive.

Jasmine—Chakras: 6th, 5th, 4th. This flower is strong yet brings beauty and a peaceful mind. Jasmine is quite relaxing as its properties signify purity of the mind. I grow jasmine vines and have a few bushes in my backyard; they keep my yard filled with happy, beautiful vibes.

Juniper Berry—Chakras: 2nd, 1st. This is the berry from some of your holiday trees. A sharp, clean scent, great for house cleaning and energy cleansing of the aura, it also protects from negative thought forms in the energetic sense. Juniper berry is a potent antifungal.

Lavender—Chakras: All seven. *Ahhh…* this floral scent is true relaxation, relieves anxiety and headaches, and helps you sleep soundly and comfortably. A staple to all crystal healers. This flower is known worldwide for relaxation and most commonly used in all energetic healings. Lavender is great to mist anywhere, especially on your pillow for gently sleeping or napping. Spritzing your bathroom before a shower is nice to relax the mind and body. It's calming. Sometimes I spray my shower with a mix of eucalyptus oil, lavender oil, and distilled water. It steams and feels like a spa day!

Lemon—Chakras: 6th, 1st. An antibiotic and diuretic, lemon helps with waking up all your senses; it can bring alertness to your muscles and your mind. I would suggest sniffing this after a crystal healing or using it to make organic household cleaners.

Lemongrass—Chakras: 3rd, 2nd, 1st. A clean, fresh herb that can be used for many cleansing purposes. I put a few drops in my water diffuser to create a nonchemical aroma in my house. Use it for a household cleaner infused with distilled water or dab it on your wrists to tantalize your inner soul and true self.

Myrrh—Chakras: All seven. Super incredible. Myrrh helps with confusing thoughts or emotions, bringing a sense of clarity. It is also known to help release the angst of arthritis, asthma, eczema, colds, and coughs. When you meditate with myrrh, it brings a feeling of invincibility.

Patchouli—Chakras: All seven. A very important essence for healers to utilize when assisting in light work and cord cuttings. Patchouli helps release addictions and disorders. On a good note, patchouli helps in manifesting money and opens the mind for appropriate thought patterns.

Peppermint—Chakras: 6th, 3rd, 2nd. Bold and strong, peppermint has intense releasing abilities in healings and meditations. Peppermint is great for relieving nausea, sinuses, and headaches. It is perfect for better digestion. I have a mint plant on the side of my house. I just pinch a few leaves off to eat; it freshens my breath and tastes yummy. I enjoy seeing some in my tea or chopping a few to garnish my salad.

Pine—Chakras: 4th, 3rd, 2nd, 1st. This antifungal helps with asthma, sinus infections, and cleansing and clearing the home. It additionally clears your mental and emotional aura. Pine essential oil is a common ingredient in most clearing sprays or mists, and, yes, it does smell like holiday time!

Rose—Chakras: All seven. A beautiful rose brings genuine healing, love, strong protection, and happiness. Roses are the ultimate healing flower or essence to connect one's soul to Angelic realms and dimensions. They can also activate protection and good faith from one person to another. Rose oil was used by the Egyptians for keeping away negative spirits. My favorite scent in the whole world is fresh roses. As long as I can afford to have them, I will buy a dozen to create happiness in my home. Once they have wilted, I mulch them in my backyard. I give gratitude for their beauty and have them return to the earth.

Rosemary—Chakras: 7th, 6th, 5th, 4th, 3rd, 2nd. A great herb for cooking and also great for relieving hangovers. Rosemary helps with skin care, muscular pain, and overall release for emotional and psychical ailments, and brings a sense of love and fulfillment. I love this one when meditating with the crystal grid for finding my soul's purpose!

Sage—Chakras: All seven. The "elder" is how I refer to sage since it brings wise decisions and intelligent thoughts. Sage can lower blood pressure and is especially known for protection and clearing old and unwanted energies in the aura and living space. It cleanses and clears all entities on all dimensions—at least temporarily! As a crystal healer, you should cleanse your space where you hold your sessions before and after. Keep it clean!

Sandalwood—Chakras: 4th, 3rd, 2nd, 1st. The scent of sandalwood resembles men's perfume but is very, very light in intensity. Sandalwood brings grounding and solace, peace, and connection to Earth's element. It's perfect for when you don't want to be too floaty. I use it to enhance my Mother Earth meditations or appreciation of nature crystal sessions.

Sweet Orange—Chakras: 3rd, 2nd. An essence of pure cleansing for the household with antibiotic properties that remove impurities of the mind and eliminate toxins. Sweet Orange revitalizes the mind and brings readiness to move ahead in life; it also awakens you to new beginnings.

Tangerine—Chakras: 5th, 3rd, 2nd. Yum. Tangerine is an uplifting energizer with a relaxing sense of calmness. Tangerine is a perfect mix with lavender and is sweet and smooth when used as an aromatic for home or meditative uses.

Ylang-Ylang—Chakras: 4th, 3rd, 2nd. This one smells sugary sweet and is perfect to help with PMS. You can use it as a natural substitute to eating chocolate. Ha! Just smell ylang-ylang instead. It can help relieve headaches and assist in calming irritability. Ylang-ylang is used to relax the soul.

———

Essential oils are great enhancers for crystal healing sessions. In your crystal layout sessions, I gave one or two suggested oils that are specific to your healing layout purposes. If I named two oils, you can use one or the other. It is okay to mix the two listed; however, I wanted to give you an option of choosing in case you just have one available to you. If you are working on a client, you can ask them which scent, if any, they prefer. If they chose one or both, you can use one oil on their wrists and another on their ankles. Again, it is just an option to add to your crystal healing service. Remember when I explained mixing crystal energies? Some energies harmonize, and some do not. The same goes for the oils. You can combine them, but it is good to be aware of what they are perfect for. This way, you are able to use them accordingly and knowledgeably. Make sure if you are working on someone other than yourself to ask if they are sensitive or have allergies to any oils you might be using. Even if the oils are pure and organic, someone could still be sensitive or allergic to them.

It's good to use your senses and combine crystals and essential oils in a crystal healing. Together they can awaken, relax, open, and help a person heal.

Recommended Resources

If you are a newbie to all energy and crystal healing, I suggest you read *The Energy Exchange and How to Manifest with It.* I wrote this book for people to understand energy exchanges and the favorable energy within our human bodies. If you are interested in healing other people, you should definitely sign up for an energy healing workshop such as Reiki. Many metaphysical stores have classes on these subjects.

Obviously, I encourage you to sharpen your skills and know your crystals. I will be touring to teach the art of crystal healing for those who want to become a master gridder.

Resource List

DeMarco, Jolie. *The Energy Exchange and How to Manifest with It*. Boca Raton, FL: Self-published, 2010.

———. *Soul Talking and Relationships*. Boca Raton, FL: Self-published, 2010.

Emoto, Masaru. *The Healing Power of Water*. Carlsbad, CA: Hay House, 2008.

Gienger, Micheal. *Crystal Power, Crystal Healing*. London: Octopus Publishing Group, 1998.

Guilbault, Melody, and Julianne Guilbault. *Love Is in the Earth*. Wheat Ridge, CO: Earth-Love Publishing House, 1995.

Index

A

Abundance, 2, 4–6, 28, 33, 58, 65, 80, 125, 132, 133, 135, 136, 142, 225, 226

Advance, 6, 11, 12, 14, 21, 42, 68, 72, 81, 98, 103, 167, 196, 259, 260, 262

Agate, Thunder, 50, 51, 126, 156, 157, 168, 212, 224, 238, 242, 249

Agate, Various Colors, 51, 210, 211, 217, 219, 222, 224, 237, 238, 240, 244, 247, 249, 252

Agate, Blue Lace, 28, 29, 49, 56, 120, 122, 133, 212, 220, 237, 243, 249

Agate, Moss, 28, 49, 120, 122, 168, 175, 214, 224, 233, 239, 245, 264

Amazonite, 28, 30, 31, 52, 110, 181, 213, 214, 232, 245, 247, 260

Amber, 36, 52, 53, 133, 156, 157, 214, 231, 235, 236, 242

Amethyst, 4, 19, 29–31, 36, 53, 57, 75, 88, 113, 114, 117, 147, 156, 157, 210, 211, 215, 216, 234, 235, 249, 253, 261, 262, 265

Angelite, 29, 54, 172, 189, 191, 210, 212, 218, 220, 223, 235, 247, 249, 253, 262

Apache Tears, 54, 175, 186, 211, 215, 217, 224, 227, 229, 230, 238, 240, 253

Apatite, 54, 55, 181, 231, 237, 242, 245, 247, 249, 262

Apophyllite, 55, 56, 85, 147, 150, 199, 219–221, 223, 250, 253, 262

Aquamarine, 29, 36, 56, 162, 189, 191, 215, 223, 230, 231, 235, 237, 247, 262

Aragonite, 19, 34, 57, 113, 114, 175, 210, 221, 231, 234, 236, 240

Assessment, 4, 63, 95, 98–100, 103

Auralite 23, 13, 29, 32, 33, 36, 57, 58, 162, 196, 202, 217, 219, 226, 238, 241, 242, 245, 247, 250, 253, 259

Aventurine, Green, 28, 58, 63, 117, 133, 175, 181, 183, 214, 225, 227, 229, 232, 235, 238, 245

Azurite, 59, 113, 114, 139, 202, 211, 221, 224, 232, 250, 258

B

Bergamot, 133, 188, 270

C

Calcite, Yellow / Orange / Golden / Honey, 19, 32, 59, 212, 231, 236, 241

Carnelian, 60, 130, 172, 210, 211, 227, 231, 232, 241, 262

Cavansite, 29, 35, 60, 126, 168, 189, 191, 202, 210, 221, 223, 224, 247, 250, 253

Celestite, 29, 36, 61, 186, 189, 191, 199, 210, 219, 220, 227, 248, 262

Chalcedony, 29, 50, 61, 62, 181, 183, 210, 218, 235, 241, 248

Chamomile, 122, 188, 261, 270

Charoite, 62, 130, 162, 196, 215, 232–234, 238, 243, 250, 253

Chrysoprase, 62, 64, 181, 210, 212, 229, 243, 245

Citrine, 28, 29, 32, 33, 35, 57, 58, 63, 64, 75, 110, 117, 119, 133, 181, 202, 204, 214, 215, 218, 225, 236, 239, 241, 260, 262, 265, 266

Confidence, 15, 34, 70, 81, 87, 133

D

Danburite, 64, 153, 162, 210, 219, 245, 248, 250, 253, 259, 262

Dioptase, 65, 212, 214, 216, 217, 234, 245, 262

E

Emerald, 35, 65, 66, 117, 215, 216, 225, 233, 239, 241, 243, 245, 248, 250, 253

Epidote, 57, 66, 186, 188, 237, 239, 241, 243, 245, 248, 250, 253

Essences, 11, 166, 269, 270, 272, 273

Eucalyptus, 264, 270, 271

F

Fluorite, 29, 67, 117, 178, 227, 231, 233, 235, 238, 239, 241, 243, 245, 248, 250, 254, 261

Frankincense, 105, 150, 164, 204, 270

G

Garnet, 28, 36, 67, 68, 117, 217, 225, 235, 239, 241, 243

Geranium, 84, 133, 164, 183, 191, 196, 271

Grapefruit, 178, 271

H

Herkimer Diamond, 29, 35, 68, 90, 117, 119, 147, 153, 155, 178, 186, 188, 189, 191, 193, 202, 204, 220, 222, 226, 230, 237, 251, 254, 259, 260, 262

Howlite, White, 4, 19, 28, 29, 32, 33, 69, 70, 91, 120, 122, 133, 181, 183, 202, 204, 213, 216, 223, 235

J

Jasmine, 199, 271

Jasper, Ocean, 69, 70, 156, 157, 217, 236

Jasper, Red, 29, 34, 35, 70, 110, 112, 130, 216, 227, 229, 230, 233, 239, 241, 264

Juniper Berry, 38, 271

K

Kunzite, 35, 70, 71, 172, 191, 199, 210, 212, 223, 232, 246, 262
Kyanite, Blue, 28, 71, 110, 120, 122, 156, 157, 211, 212, 221, 223, 224, 232, 251

L

Lapis Lazuli, 71, 72, 87, 130, 156, 157, 172, 218, 221–224, 227, 229, 248, 251
Lavender, 38, 83, 84, 105, 112, 114, 119, 122, 130, 136, 147, 150, 191, 193, 204, 264, 271, 273
Lemon, 271
Lemongrass, 272
Lemurian Seeds, 72, 73, 178, 193, 221, 222, 224, 227, 248, 251, 254
Lepidolite, 28–32, 73, 74, 113, 114, 120, 122, 139, 211, 215, 227, 231, 236, 246, 248, 251, 259, 265
Let Go, 23, 30, 31, 45, 82, 99, 102, 103, 113, 116, 139, 144, 152, 162, 164

M

Malachite, 29, 59, 74, 213, 216, 227, 231, 233, 236, 243, 246, 258, 259
Mantra, 22, 38, 39, 41, 58, 83, 102, 103, 107, 112, 114, 119, 122, 128, 130, 133, 136, 139, 144, 147, 150, 155, 157, 164, 170, 172, 177, 180, 183, 188, 191, 193, 196, 201, 204
Moldavite, 4, 13, 29–32, 34, 40, 66, 68, 75, 76, 120, 122, 144, 222, 226, 229, 239, 241, 243, 246, 248, 251, 254, 262
Money, 28, 33, 44, 58, 63, 68, 125, 132, 133, 135, 142, 272
Moonstone, 76, 77, 136, 168, 199, 211, 220, 225, 234, 251, 254, 258
Mugwort, 38
Myrrh, 193, 272

N
Nirvana/Ice Crystal, 12, 36, 77, 196, 212, 213, 232, 233, 237, 239, 242, 243, 246, 249, 251, 254, 262

O
Obsidian, Black, 66, 78, 153, 162, 214, 221, 224, 226, 229, 238, 264
Obsidian, Snowflake, 78, 150, 186, 188, 211, 213, 214, 216, 221, 225, 228, 239, 240, 251
Oils, 2, 5, 6, 22, 23, 84, 101, 102, 104–106, 112, 114, 119, 122, 126, 130, 133, 136, 139, 144, 147, 150, 155, 157, 164, 170, 172, 175, 178, 183, 188, 191, 193, 196, 199, 204, 264, 269–274
Opal, Pink, 35, 79, 199, 214, 222, 225, 227, 246
Opalite, 79, 80, 110, 112, 217, 222, 251, 254

P
Patchouli, 272
Pendulum, 21, 63, 71, 95, 96, 98–101, 107, 116
Peppermint, 114, 272
Pietersite, 35, 80, 175, 213, 222, 226, 229, 230, 233, 243, 252
Pine, 38, 264, 272
Power Stones, 34, 72
Pyrite, 30, 31, 57, 80, 81, 87, 214, 217, 219, 228, 230, 244

Q
Quartz, Clear, 28, 29, 36, 68, 81, 88, 144, 162, 221, 223, 228, 232, 240, 242, 244, 246, 249, 252, 255
Quartz, Rose/Pink, 28–32, 34, 81, 113, 114, 129, 130, 175, 191, 199, 212, 213, 217, 222, 233, 238, 246, 260, 263, 266
Quartz, Rutile, 28, 29, 82, 120, 122, 153, 162, 181, 183, 216, 218–220, 223, 236, 240, 242, 244, 246, 249, 252, 254, 262
Quartz, Smoky, 29, 63, 82, 83, 88, 144, 147, 214, 216, 224, 229, 231, 236, 237, 240, 259, 262

R

Rhodochrosite, 28, 40, 83, 129, 130, 212, 214, 219, 221, 226, 228, 232, 244, 247

Rose, 50, 114, 130, 144, 172, 183, 191, 261, 272

Rosemary, 126, 139, 147, 170, 196, 204, 264, 273

Ruby Zoisite, 4, 28, 31, 32, 83, 84, 136, 213, 217, 219, 228, 230, 235, 236, 240, 247, 252

S

Sage, 37–39, 50, 103, 144, 155, 175, 199, 264, 267, 273

Salt, 37, 39, 41, 84, 85, 153, 226, 233, 259, 261, 266

Sandalwood, 157, 175, 273

Selenite, 11, 12, 28, 30, 37, 39, 41, 85, 86, 117, 144, 150, 153, 155, 186, 188, 218, 220, 222, 226, 228, 237, 252, 255, 259, 260, 265, 266

Shungite, 32, 33, 43, 44, 55, 86, 178, 218, 227, 230, 237, 238, 240, 242, 244, 247, 249, 252, 255, 260, 262, 266

Sodalite, 34, 35, 87, 212, 225, 227, 234, 252

Sunstone, 35, 87, 110, 136, 199, 217, 225, 226, 236, 237, 242, 244

Super 7, 29, 88, 193, 224, 225, 228, 230, 240, 242, 244, 247, 249, 252, 255, 259

Sweet Orange, 178, 273

T

Tangerine, 126, 170, 271, 273

Tiger's Eye, 30, 31, 35, 51, 88, 89, 153, 155, 216, 229, 230, 237, 240, 242, 244, 265

Tourmaline, Black, 19, 28, 29, 30, 32, 63, 64, 78, 89, 105, 117, 153, 162, 167, 181, 196, 199, 224, 226, 229, 238, 259, 260, 266, 267

Tourmaline, Green, 68, 90, 126, 168, 196, 212–214, 223, 228, 234, 247, 260

Turquoise, 36, 90, 91, 147, 168, 211, 213, 228, 230, 231, 234, 249

U
Unakite, 28, 34, 35, 91, 139, 162, 214, 228, 232, 234, 244

Y
Ylang-Ylang, 172, 273

To Write to the Author

If you wish to contact the author or would like more information about this book, please write to the author in care of Llewellyn Worldwide Ltd. and we will forward your request. Both the author and publisher appreciate hearing from you and learning of your enjoyment of this book and how it has helped you. Llewellyn Worldwide Ltd. cannot guarantee that every letter written to the author can be answered, but all will be forwarded. Please write to:

Jolie DeMarco
℅ Llewellyn Worldwide
2143 Wooddale Drive
Woodbury, MN 55125-2989

Please enclose a self-addressed stamped envelope for reply,
or $1.00 to cover costs. If outside the U.S.A., enclose
an international postal reply coupon.

Many of Llewellyn's authors have websites with additional information and resources. For more information, please visit our website at http://www.llewellyn.com.

Crystals

For Beginners

A Guide for Enhancing Your Health, Intuition
& Creativity Using Crystals and Stones

CORRINE KENNER

Crystals for Beginners
A Guide for Enhancing Your Health, Intuition & Creativity Using Crystals and Stones
CORRINE KENNER

Crystals for Beginners makes it easy to learn about crystals and how to use their positive energy in a variety of practical ways. This friendly introductory guide explores crystal magic, folklore, and wisdom. It features an alphabetical guide to crystals, along with advice on collecting, cleansing, and charging them. Handy reference charts help you quickly find information on birthstones, zodiac stones, precious metals, and more. You can empower, clarify, and illuminate your life with the help of these beautiful gems.

- Balance body, mind, and spirit
- Calm and center emotions
- Tap into inner wisdom
- Amplify and focus energy
- Experience richer dreams
- Develop intuition and creativity

978-0-7387-0755-6, 264 pp., 5 ³⁄₁₆ x 8   **$14.99**

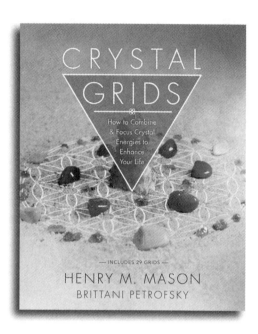

Crystal Grids
How to Combine & Focus Crystal Energies to Enhance Your Life
HENRY M. MASON AND BRITTANI PETROFSKY

Crystal grids are effective for transforming your life in a dazzling array of powerful and practical ways. Whether you desire to find love, attract wealth, bless your home, overcome anxiety, or clear negative energy, the crystal grids in this book will help you achieve your goals. With simple instructions and comprehensive insights, *Crystal Grids* shows you how to choose the best crystals for your purpose, select a grid shape that will enhance your intention, clear and position the stones, and activate the grid.

Discover how you can use crystal energy for improved health, wealth, relationships, and a better life. This book also includes twenty-nine expertly designed grids that you can use immediately to reinforce and magnify the power of your crystals.

978-0-7387-4688-3, 216 pp., 7½ x 9¼   **$17.99**

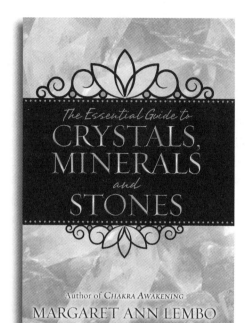

The Essential Guide to
CRYSTALS,
MINERALS
and
STONES

Author of CHAKRA AWAKENING
MARGARET ANN LEMBO

The Essential Guide to Crystals, Minerals and Stones
Margaret Ann Lembo

This ultimate go-to reference features 160 stones you can use to improve your life on all levels—mentally, physically, emotionally, and spiritually. Packed with practical information—from each stone's Mohs scale rating to its divinatory meaning—this unique guide has 190 beautiful full-color photos of specimens commonly found in metaphysical stores. Each page provides concise information: stone name, color, chakra, planet, element, zodiac sign, number, divinatory meaning, and mental, emotional, physical and spiritual uses. A series of positive affirmations is given for each stone, as well as guidance on how to use gemstones as oracles for personal development and spiritual awakening.

978-0-7387-3252-7, 456 pp., 6 x 9   **$24.99**